INSPIRED LIVING

by Kieth VonderOhe

D1533829

A·R·E
PRESS

November 1994

Previously titled *In Touch with the Light*

ISBN 87604-234-5

Cover Design by Richard Boyle

Acknowledgments

I wish to thank all those persons who allowed me to interview them and use excerpts from their lives for the stories in this book. It is their years of work with the ideas from the Edgar Cayce readings that made this work possible.

A special thanks goes to Dr. Mark Thurston and Elaine Hruska whose editorial work is reflected throughout these pages and to Eileen who was my special support and inspiration during the months it took me to write this manuscript.

The following stories are adaptations from previously published books:

Stories dated May 25, July 25, September 21, October 16, and December 3 are reprinted with permission from *Storytelling: Imagination and Faith* by William J. Bausch, copyright 1984 (paper, 240 pages, $7.95), published by Twenty-Third Publications, 185 Willow Street, Mystic, CT 06355-0180. Toll Free: 1-800-321-0411.

Stories dated February 28, April 2, June 10, June 22, August 12, and September 13 are reprinted from *Stories for Telling* by William R. White, copyright ©Augsburg Publishing House. Reprinted by permission of Augsburg Fortress.

Stories dated January 11, January 25, February 9, February 18, March 9, March 21, April 10, April 28, May 9, May 21, June 6, July 9, July 21, August 8, August 20, September 9, October 12, October 24, November 11, November 24, De-

Introduction

For many years people have looked to the Edgar Cayce readings for guidance and insight. The spiritual truths and encouraging words contained therein have enabled thousands of individuals to touch the Light of the Divine and inspired them to live the ideas found in the readings. The daily messages in this book come primarily from people who have applied the principles found in the readings and have experienced life-transforming results. Other stories come from a variety of religious sources, including Biblical, rabbinic, and Sufi traditions.

Edgar Cayce knew the value of studying the life stories of people, and he encouraged this pursuit. Because we are not merely engaged in abstract ideas but are learning about actual life experiences, we are inspired as we see how other people confronted the challenges of life. We are given new hope and insight as we see how they faced struggles, joys, disappointments, and moments of growth. From the triumphs of these people, we pick up possibilities that can help us approach life with new hope.

Along with a story, each daily selection offers a thought based on a passage from the Edgar Cayce readings. Because the original language of the readings sometimes consists of unusual sentence structures and word choices—features which can prevent the easy understanding necessary for devotional reading—modifications were made to remove these obstacles. Words which might be confusing to people unfamiliar with the readings were changed; for example, the word "entity" has become "soul." Most of the old expressions for "you," such as "ye" and "thee," have been updated to modern forms. A few sentences have been rearranged to conform to more conventional sentence structure. These changes have not altered the meanings of the passages but have made the selected excerpts more easily understood.

Because the selections have been dated only by month

and day, you can use this book as a daily inspirational guide year after year. On one day you may draw inspiration from the story or allow it to lead you into a meditation experience. On another day you may receive insight from the principle found in the Edgar Cayce readings excerpt. For other daily selections you may be able to use the application exercise in a difficult situation.

Regardless of how the selection becomes meaningful on a particular day, you can find real value in setting aside a few minutes each day to read just one selection. This approach offers a new thought each day upon which your mind can build. Remember that transforming events often don't happen in a big way but instead—as Cayce put it—"step by step and here a little, there a little." It's the daily application of a principle that is important. When you look back weeks or months later, you'll probably realize how much change has occurred because of the way you used each day.

The central purpose of *In Touch with the Light* is to provide hope and renewal for life. You—the seeker—will discover how best to utilize this book in order to find your own new spirit for life.

As you use what you know, the light comes.

Based on Edgar Cayce reading 262-7

Dedication

This book is dedicated to all those who shared their life stories so others may be inspired to use their days in new ways.

INSPIRED LIVING

JANUARY 1

In Living We Understand

Apply what you know. For we grow in grace, in knowledge, in the understanding of spiritual laws as we apply gentleness, kindness, patience, long-suffering to those we meet day by day.   Based on Edgar Cayce reading 1469-1

Headaches had bothered Patrick for several months. Finally, after a few visits to doctors the diagnosis came back—glaucoma. Normal treatments did not seem to work well so Patrick went to a psychic healer. The healing worked. Within a few weeks, his eyes were almost normal again.

Curiosity now led Patrick to read more about psychic phenomena and explore many types of experiences, including the spiritualist church. However, being in engineering school, he was wondering what to do with all this information.

After several years of searching on his own, he finally got involved in a weekly discussion group. He enjoyed meeting with the people but found himself constantly asking, "What is it about this group that is so helpful to people?" It took Patrick a while to find an answer, but he finally realized that this group was made up of ordinary people in ordinary professions who were applying the spiritual disciplines they talked about in their daily lives. It was the daily application of kindness, patience, and gentleness that made the difference.

Patrick realized that the answer to his question and his searching lay in applying in his own life the truths being discussed and in letting his life change in the process.

APPLICATION: Begin to express each of these fruits of the Spirit—gentleness, kindness, patience, and long-suffering. Watch what happens to your life as you do this.

The Real Child

Seek, don't blame creative energies—find within yourself the desire to do what you may do or say to others.

Based on Edgar Cayce reading 5284-1

Betty's work with mentally handicapped children was going well. She had been a volunteer for only six months, but already she had learned a lot. The paid staff appreciated her sensitivity and willingness to do almost anything to help.

What Betty didn't tell the staff or other volunteers was that she disliked being on one particular unit. This unit housed children who were very deformed physically as well as mentally handicapped. It almost made her sick to be in that unit and she felt she was not open to giving the kind of love those children needed.

One night she had a dream. She was surrounded by children, beautiful children. The faces, their eyes, their arms and legs, their whole bodies were beautiful. She reached out to touch them and talk with them. As she leaned over to give one child a kiss, she recognized him as one of the boys in that hospital unit. She looked around and saw that all the children were children on that unit.

She realized she was seeing these children as God saw them.

The next day she had to work that unit again. She walked in smiling, went over to the young boy, and smiled at him, seeing the real child for the first time.

APPLICATION: Often the physical features and behaviors we see are not the real person. Think of someone you have problems with and imagine the real person inside of that individual.

An Ideal to Live By

The person who is without an ideal is a wanderer, and if the ideal is set in material things, it will soon play out and fade.
Based on Edgar Cayce reading 323-1

Do you have an ideal for your life?

Jennifer was having trouble setting one. She finally realized she didn't completely understand what an ideal was, so she decided to talk to Maggie who had used this approach for years. Maggie summarized an ideal in the following way:

An ideal is:
- a yardstick by which your judgments are made;
- a standard by which you choose a course of action;
- an objective to strive for that you can never completely achieve;
- something you intend to act upon in your life.

Maggie explained further that an ideal is practical for everyday life. In other words, ideals are a middle ground between two extremes. They aren't so spiritual that they ignore down-to-earth issues, nor are they so materialistic (such as just making more money) that they fail to challenge us to further spiritual growth.

This explanation helped Jennifer. She now knew that somewhere in her searching she must find high standards to build her life upon that challenged her to live to her fullest and best.

APPLICATION: Spend time writing down the ideal you believe is the standard upon which you are currently basing your decisions and actions.

Laughter—A Key to Understanding Others

Humor may ever become the saving grace. For humor—to be able to see the fun, the ridiculous in the most sacred experience to many—is an attribute of this individual.

Based on Edgar Cayce reading 2775-1

Rick had read the Edgar Cayce readings before he began his teaching career. He liked the values he found in them and introduced them to his students, many of whom were very receptive. But in other students he found resistance, misbehavior, and stubbornness. This conflict created at times quite a bit of tension in the classroom.

Having learned that humor could be a helpful tool in times of tension like the ones he was facing, Rick tried it. He learned to tell light stories. He would compare what the students wanted and believed with what he wanted and believed, but would do it in such a way that they could see the humorous aspects of his belief and laugh at them. Then he would show them some of the humor in their beliefs so they too could laugh at themselves.

Although he and his students didn't always agree, they were able to keep their relationship on a positive note because of their ability to laugh with each other.

APPLICATION: The next time you are taking yourself too seriously, find some humor in your position and laugh at yourself a little.

Twenty Years Later

Do what you know to do to be right! Then leave it alone! God gives the increase. Worry and anxiety will only produce disorder in your own mind. Based on Edgar Cayce reading 601-11

Years ago Norma was looking for a worthwhile book as a gift for her parents' wedding anniversary. *There Is a River* had just been published and some of her colleagues at work suggested she buy that for a gift. She had not yet read it so she bought two copies—one for her parents and one for herself. She devoured it and then read more Edgar Cayce material. She also bought another copy of the book and sent it to her brother and his wife. She didn't get any response from her family so she assumed they were not at all interested.

More than twenty years later *The Sleeping Prophet* was published. She quickly received a phone call from her brother. They had read this new book and recognized the Cayce name from the book she had given them years earlier. Now they were suddenly very interested. They started a discussion group in their home and invited her to visit and speak to them. She did and shared her experiences of the last twenty years.

Norma learned something about how ideas speak to people. The ideas in the book spoke to her immediately, but it took her brother twenty years before it was meaningful to him, and her parents never did find it meaningful.

APPLICATION: Do what you know you can and then let God act, instead of worrying or being frustrated.

A Spoonful of Sugar

For as you think in your heart, so will your life be.
Based on Edgar Cayce reading 2829-1

Marlene was watching "Mary Poppins" on TV and singing along, since she had seen the movie so often she had learned by heart the words to the songs. When the title character sang, "A spoonful of sugar helps the medicine go down," Marlene realized she wasn't singing about sugar but about the attitude one has toward a situation.

This started her thinking about house work. She doesn't like doing the routine chores such as dusting and vacuuming. However, she knows she has to do them if she wants her house to look nice. So when she does house work, she finds something to occupy her mind while her body works automatically.

She turns on the radio, or she puts on one of her favorite opera tapes, and begins. She lets her mind follow the music or think about anything it wants to, but she doesn't think about doing house work. In less than three hours she has the house cleaned and her attitude is still positive and upbeat.

APPLICATION: The next time you have to do something you don't really want to do, focus your attitude on something that will help you do the job in a positive frame of mind.

The Influence of Prayer

*If those who are desirous of being of help will pray about it,
they will receive direction.*

Based on Edgar Cayce reading 1789-2

Working together as co-teachers for ten young people, ages 5-14, all children of alcoholic parents, is not easy. Anne and Joy have different temperaments and ideas about what works; however, they have agreed to spend a few minutes praying together before each session.

Once, when they prayed to be channels, to be open to the needs of the children, they had four or five angry youngsters that day and knew that their planned program would not meet the children's needs. So they quickly decided to cut out a paper flame and pass it around. They talked about what makes anger flare up and what to do with it. That evening several youth were helped to find ways of dealing with their anger.

Another evening everything went wrong. Every child began to act up. Anne and Joy's plans for the program were not working and neither received any insights on how to readjust the scheduled program.

Later, upon discussing the evening, they realized they had been in a hurry and had forgotten to spend those few minutes in prayer with one another before the session.

Now, regardless of how pressured they feel, Anne and Joy always make sure to have a prayer time together.

APPLICATION: Begin the habit of praying regularly before some situation.

Removing All Doubt

Meet yourself—your faults, your virtues—in such a manner as to make the experience a growth of your soul.

Based on Edgar Cayce reading 1745-1

The disciples sat astounded, mouths wide open in fear and amazement. When they had set sail, they had left Jesus praying on the shore. Now as they stared across the water, a figure was coming toward them. It was either Jesus or a ghost that looked like Him. Through the wind and rain they could not be sure.

Finally Peter spoke, "Master, if it is You, bid me walk to You on the waves."

The familiar voice responded, "Come, Peter."

Peter, a little hesitant at first, put his foot outside the boat. When he saw he wasn't sinking, he gained courage. He put out the other foot and walked several steps. Then a strong gust of wind blew, and Peter became aware again of the storm. He paused and began to sink.

"Master, save me!" he cried out.

Jesus reached out His hand, grabbed Peter's firmly, and together they walked back and stepped into the boat.

After they sat down, Jesus said, "You have much faith, my friend. Let us work on removing the doubt that still remains."

APPLICATION: The next time the storm of life whips around you, move forward with faith toward the Figure waiting on the waves.

Seeing the Christ in Others

Let the spirit of neighborly love guide you with loving indifference to those things that would mar or hinder you in any manner.
Based on Edgar Cayce reading 603-2

Pauline had endured just about enough of Betsy's critical and judgmental behavior. She found Betsy's voice, her clothes, and her manipulative way of working with people offensive. She knew that the two of them would probably have a big argument in the not too distant future.

Then in Pauline's discussion group one night the members spoke about loving indifference and how to use that approach sometimes when relating to people. For a while Pauline tried it with Betsy. She continued to listen to her and work with her, but this time she just let Betsy's critical remarks go by without commenting on them or reacting to them. Some of her anger and resentment began to diminish.

A few weeks later the group talked about seeing the light of Christ in everyone. Pauline knew this would be difficult, but she decided to try it. As she began each day to see the light of Christ in Betsy, her perception changed. She became aware of Betsy's insecurity and realized that her critical and controlling behavior stemmed from this insecurity.

Pauline then began to respond to Betsy in light of that new insight by helping to build Betsy's self-confidence and self-esteem. Betsy's negativity gradually diminished. Their work relationship changed and their friendship developed.

APPLICATION: Think of a fault in someone whom you see or work with almost daily. Decide how you can express loving indifference toward that fault and relate to the rest of that person positively.

Meditation Is Giving

Purify your mind if you would meditate. How? Depends upon what is your concept of purification. Does it mean a setting aside of yourself, a washing with water, or what?

Based on Edgar Cayce reading 281-41

For the past five days Tom had felt blocked during meditation. He had followed the standard procedure for meditation—finding a relaxed position, attuning himself by focusing on an affirmation, sitting silently for about twenty minutes, and closing with prayer for others. However, he had felt nothing but barriers all around him and couldn't attune himself.

Then he thought further about meditation. What was it to him? After a few minutes he realized that meditation involved a feeling of giving—giving of self to a Higher Self. He needed to find a new way to give.

The next time he meditated, he decided to begin with prayer. He prayed for other people. He set himself aside and became concerned for the next 5-10 minutes with the needs of his family, his friends, people he didn't know, and the world in general. Following this period of prayer, he felt open. He now could focus on an affirmation and be still. After those prayers he felt he was in touch with God, loving and giving again.

APPLICATION: For the next few days try praying for others at the beginning of meditation in order to put yourself out of the way.

Each Must Search

For indeed each individual, each soul is in the process of evolution toward the First Cause (God).

Based on Edgar Cayce reading 2079-1

A great Jewish rabbi was known for his understanding and insight into the scriptures. One day a young man approached him with this question: "Rabbi, why in the scriptures do we say, '*God of* Abraham, *God of* Isaac, and *God of* Jacob' instead of simply, '*God of* Abraham, Isaac, and Jacob'?"

The wise rabbi replied, "We say 'God of Abraham, God of Isaac, and God of Jacob' because Isaac and Jacob did not depend on Abraham's searching and relationship with God. Isaac and Jacob searched individually for their own relationship to God and how God was calling each of them to serve in a special way."

The Edgar Cayce readings encourage each individual to search for a transforming relationship to God. People cannot rely solely on the church, their parents, or other external sources to build a relationship to God for them. Each is called to travel his or her own spiritual journey in order to find the power, strength, and fullness of purpose of life that comes through attunement with the Creative Forces of the universe.

APPLICATION: Do something that expresses your individual way of relating to God.

Expecting Gratitude

Good as a virtue must be its own reward. Do not act for self-exaltation.   Based on Edgar Cayce reading 349-13

Do you find yourself expecting people to be grateful for what you do for them?

Anna and her husband were traveling around the world with friends. Their friends could afford the basic trip but did not have the finances for some of the extras, so Anna and her husband would assist them on occasion. She felt good about this arrangement until a conversation they had one day. Their friends commented that Anna and her husband probably owed them this because of some debt from a past life.

At first Anna was a bit offended but didn't say anything. Then she began thinking about what her unconscious attitude might be about all the assistance she and her husband were giving. She wondered if maybe she was expecting her friends to be more grateful and express that gratitude in some way.

She still doesn't know what was actually occurring, but she does know that she learned an important lesson about letting good acts be their own reward.

APPLICATION: The next time you expect someone to thank you for doing something, remind yourself that good acts are their own reward.

An Intuitive Choice

There are conditions in which the intuitive forces are to be relied upon wholly by turning within.

Based on Edgar Cayce reading 137-128

Trudy needed to hire a consultant for her business. Three recommendations had been given to her, and she had the resumes in front of her. Two of them had experience in the area she wanted, while the third had some in a related field but not in the specific area she was concerned about at the moment. However, all three were worth considering seriously.

She studied the three resumes for about a half hour. There were positive and negative aspects to all of them, and she couldn't make up her mind. Finally her intuition told her to pick the third one. She wasn't sure if she could trust this feeling so she tried another technique she always found helpful.

Placing the resume of the third person in front of her, she said to herself, "I have chosen this person. Is this the right choice?" Then she closed her eyes and meditated a few minutes to see what she would feel. After a few minutes the feelings were obvious. This *was* the right choice. Much to the surprise of her colleagues she picked this man.

A few weeks later plans at her business were modified, and she needed a consultant with skills in a different area than were considered earlier. Now the man whom she had recently hired fit this description exactly.

APPLICATION: When your intuition speaks strongly to you, follow it and see what happens.

How to Be a Success

Why do you want to be a success? For fame and fortune or that you may be a helpful influence? If your motives are for the universal forces—that God may be the greater glory in the lives of others through your own efforts, then success.

Based on Edgar Cayce reading 1494-1

After teaching computer classes in a high school for several years, Madalyn was being considered for department head. She really wanted the job.

Another teacher, Carl, had only been teaching in the school a couple of years. It was obvious to everyone that he was ambitious and also wanted the job as department head. Although a computer whiz, he was not a very good teacher. He didn't require his students to attend class and frequently would have parties in the classroom. The rest of the staff knew this, but the administration didn't.

When Carl was chosen to be department head, Madalyn was upset. She debated about whether or not to go to the administrative heads and tell them about his poor teaching skills. However, she finally decided to help him become a good department head.

She changed her attitude and worked with him. This helped the rest of the staff change their attitude as well. Carl began teaching better and became a successful department head for the few years he was in the school system. Madalyn never got to be department head but doesn't regret that loss at all.

APPLICATION: Help someone else be a success and know that in this activity you, too, are being a success.

Using Your Power

Use the power — not to self-indulgence but to make the world a better place because you have lived in it.

Based on Edgar Cayce reading 5392-1

When Edgar Cayce was first discovering his unusual gifts, he decided to try an experiment. He was in his second-floor photography studio talking with a friend when he saw a man walk by on the sidewalk below. He bet his friend that he could make this man come up to the studio in the next five minutes. The friend laughed and agreed to the bet.

Edgar concentrated very hard for a few minutes. Then they heard a knock on the door. Edgar opened the door, and the man who had been walking by stood there looking confused. When Edgar asked him what he wanted, the man said he didn't have the slightest idea why he was there.

Although it seemed like a harmless incident, it caused Edgar to think about how he was going to use the power he had been given. He could use it on self-indulgent pranks and to take advantage of people, or he could use it to help people who really needed his help.

He resolved to always use his gift to help people and to make the world a better place in which to live.

APPLICATION: We all have power. Use your power today to make the world a little better because of your presence.

A Life-Saving Dream

This dream is of the superconscious forces presenting to the soul those conditions in a symbolic form that are a warning for the soul.
Based on Edgar Cayce reading 137-32

Allen has listened to the advice in his dreams for years. He is convinced that once a dream saved his life.

About ten years ago he had been having angina pains, so he went to his doctor who said he had to have a heart catheterization.

A few days before this test he had a dream. In the dream he saw a Model A Ford with its hood up. Two mechanics in ill-fitting clothes were looking inside. Their faces resembled the two doctors who were scheduled to do the heart procedure.

Allen's interpretation was that he was the Model A car since he was born the same year it came out and his first name began with the letter "A". The mechanics were the doctors. The ill-fitting clothes meant they were not suited to do what they were supposed to do on him.

He canceled the test and began to do aerobic exercises, visualization, and meditation. Today he is stable and no longer has pains. At a recent check-up Allen's current doctor told him that today heart catheterizations aren't even done for people with his condition. It isn't necessary.

APPLICATION: Dreams can give messages about a variety of situations. Begin to watch your dreams for warnings about how to handle a situation.

Letter from Jesus

For Jesus is that friend who would ever guide, direct, and accompany you in trials and temptations, in your joys as well as in your sorrows.   Based on Edgar Cayce reading 1173-10

There is a reverie called "Letter from Jesus" that Carol used when leading spiritual growth workshops. It has helped many people in moments when they felt discouraged and overwhelmed by life. This adaptation is here for you to use when needed:

Get comfortable in a chair, close your eyes, relax.

Imagine you are walking down a quiet road in the Holy Land. The trees arch up on both sides of the road; the sun shines through the branches. Peace fills the air.

You look down the road and see Jesus coming toward you. As He approaches, He is smiling, happy to see you. Together you walk to the Sea of Galilee, sit down on a rock on the shore, and let your feet dangle in the cool water. You begin to talk, and He listens lovingly and intently. You talk about your hopes, desires, fears, discouragements, and moments of despair.

After you have finished sharing what is in your heart, you both get up. It is time to go. Before He goes, He promises to write you a letter. Then you both turn and go down the road in opposite directions.

Now open your eyes, pick up a piece of paper, and write the letter from Jesus to you.

APPLICATION: The next time you feel discouraged and disheartened, take yourself through this reverie and write yourself a letter from Jesus.

The Sacred in Everyday Life

Life is a manifestation of that sacred power you call God. As you use your life, it is your opportunity ever to be a manifestation of that power you would worship in your Maker.

Based on Edgar Cayce reading 3028-1

Do you feel that everything you do is sacred?

Jack had just finished another painting. He stood back and looked upon it in a new way. It wasn't a masterpiece, but it wasn't only just a painting either. It was an expression of his God-given gift. It was, therefore, a sacred work.

Recently Jack had read in the Edgar Cayce readings that everything he did could be viewed as sacred; that is, every activity had a deep spiritual dimension to it. For him this meant that life is like worshiping God every minute since everything has a spiritual relationship to God.

He also discovered that, as he took this new idea into his everyday life, his attitude toward his other talents, his job, his body, and other people changed. Now every task completed at work had a new meaning. Every effort he took to keep his body healthy and in good shape became more than a mere physical exercise. Every interaction with another person he viewed as an interaction between two spiritual beings who were learning and growing.

Everything, then, became an expression of the spiritual dimension of the universe.

APPLICATION: Stop several times in the next few days and look upon what you are doing as a "sacred" activity.

Win—Win

In the manner the approach is made, so will the result be. If it's by stealth, expect the same to be practiced on self. If it is by the right principles, expect to be met with the same.
Based on Edgar Cayce reading 257-106

The issue was rapidly coming to a head. If it were not dealt with openly and some decision made, both her department and Carl's department would feel greater tension between them. The best way for both sides to win was for the executive staff to come to a consensus about how to proceed. Louise had to figure out how to accomplish that.

Before the next staff meeting, she and Carl met together to decide how to present the issue. At the meeting Louise explained her position first. The two departments were working together to promote their concerns on the same product. Louise did not have a problem with helping Carl's department, but she did not like the procedure that had been instituted before she had arrived. She had heard some negative comments about Carl's promotion from customers and was afraid these comments might reflect the feelings of many more people. If this were true, sales were being hurt.

Carl then explained his viewpoint. Following the presentations, the staff discussed the issue. They presented ideas for Louise and Carl to discuss before the next staff meeting.

In between meetings she and Carl met and were able to present a compromise which the staff accepted by consensus at the next meeting. Louise felt both departments had won and no hard feelings existed between her and Carl.

APPLICATION: The next time your group has to make a decision, encourage the group to reach a consensus so that all sides will feel they have won.

Love Means Letting Go

Remember the new commandment, "Love one another." Not in a possessive manner. Oh that all would learn that LOVE is all-embracing and not merely possession!

Based on Edgar Cayce reading 1816-1

The decision was going to be a tricky one. Solomon had never before faced two such women. Up until recently they had been friends. They even lived in the same house and had had their babies only days apart. Now they were in front of him arguing over a child.

As he understood the story, one woman's child had died during the night. Now both claimed the living child. It was up to him to decide who was the real mother.

If there ever were a time he wanted wisdom, it was now. How does one discern a real mother's love? Is there more to love than just wanting to rear a baby?

Finally he had an idea. It was a risky one, and an infant might die if he were not correct in his judgment.

He summoned the guard. "Cut the infant in half and give half to each woman."

The crowd in the judgment hall gasped. The women looked stunned for a few seconds. Then one nodded her assent. The other paused a second and then shouted, "No! Give the baby to her. It is hers."

Solomon took the infant from the guard and handed it to the woman who had just suggested giving it away.

There was more to a mother's love than wanting to rear a child. Love was also a willingness to let go in order to give a loved one a life of its own.

APPLICATION: Look at a situation in your life in which a sign of love would mean letting go. Let go.

Becoming an Empty Vessel

As you would be a channel, as there is the willingness and the desire to be used by those forces or influences sought, there will be given that which will be of aid to others.

Based on Edgar Cayce reading 262-53

It was time for Irene to get her ego out of the way. As a counselor, she had discovered that one of the most important ideas in her work is to empty herself. She needs to set herself aside so that she can listen to the person and be clear to receive God's guidance in a situation. She finds this important when counseling all sorts of people and particularly when relating to teenagers.

Work with fifteen-year-old Mary had reached a stalemate two weeks ago and now Irene knew why. She was not listening closely enough and had to set herself aside now so she could be open to Mary's feelings. She had to be aware of what Mary was ready to hear and what would not be helpful for her to hear. In this case that was difficult. Irene was tempted to rush in with strong parental advice and show that she knew what she was talking about.

However, she chose the path of emptying herself. During her next session with Mary, Irene was able to hear what Mary had been trying to tell her. She was able to treat her like an adult by giving her some options from which to choose. Mary made her choice and returned for more help.

APPLICATION: Pray, "God, make me a channel to help others." Then look for one way to empty yourself and be a channel of God's love.

Reincarnation and Compassion

*If you count your suffering, your disappointments, your
heartaches as judgments upon yourself, you are unwise. For
whom the Lord loves, the Lord chastens and purges, that you
may bring forth fruit in due season.*

Based on Edgar Cayce reading 262-107

Dorothy was discussing reincarnation with three other
people she had just recently met. They were talking about
how this belief had influenced their lives and their views of
the world.

One woman was asked how she viewed people who are
handicapped, have severe illnesses, or are poor. The response came quickly and casually, "It's their karma. They
obviously deserve it."

This unfeeling comment upset Dorothy. She shared her
belief that these people could not be so casually dismissed.
Others needed to feel compassion, which does not necessarily mean offering a quick helping hand because that's the
easiest thing to do. However, it does mean reaching out with
the kind of help that is really needed.

Viewing life through the lens of reincarnation, Dorothy
continued, has made her realize that people are living in
these ways because someone needs to learn something.
Maybe it's the specific individual who needs to learn, or
maybe it's other people who need to learn how to feel compassion and to help in wise and constructive ways.

APPLICATION: Find a disadvantaged or handicapped person. Do one thing in a wise, compassionate way to assist
that person.

Pain from the Past

Though the soul sinks into the grimes of hate, God is there to quicken you—and use the very things about you as the growth into light in the darkened places.

Based on Edgar Cayce reading 288-36

Sandra didn't even want to be in the same room with Margaret. She had never come so close to hating anyone as she did Margaret, and she didn't know why. Margaret wasn't a bad person, but there was just something about her that Sandra detested.

For months Sandra prayed about this relationship. She meditated on love, surrounded Margaret with light, and tried to let go of her negative feelings. However, nothing worked.

During one evening meditation in the midst of surrounding Margaret with light, she suddenly had a past-life recall about her. The pain of that memory was so intense that Sandra began to cry. She cried until she fell into an exhausted sleep.

When she awoke the next morning, she wasn't aware that anything had changed. But three days later when Margaret called, Sandra found herself inviting her over to her home for a discussion. After hanging up the phone, Sandra realized that she had never invited Margaret into her home before. She knew then that the pain of the memory had been the final letting go of resentment that she had carried for several lifetimes. Now their relationship could begin on a new foundation.

APPLICATION: Think of someone you dislike intensely. Seek God's guidance for healing that relationship.

Losing Your Shirt

Each soul finds as it analyzes its relationships to the economic situations—life and its problems are not mere chance but the opportunity to meet self and to magnify the love which is the experience of those who seek to know God's will.

Based on Edgar Cayce reading 1102-5

After what had happened this past week, Jane was very thankful that she believed in reincarnation.

She had gotten involved in a business deal that really looked good at first. Prices were holding up, and it looked as if she were going to make a nice profit. Then suddenly overnight something happened. Prices fell, and she ended up losing several thousand dollars.

As she reflected on this incident, she looked at her recently acquired interest in metaphysics and reincarnation. One of the ideas that intrigued her was that you don't get in more trouble than you deserve. If something does happen, get through the karma and get rid of it. While it's happening, don't concentrate so much on the negative side of getting what you deserve, but try to respond in ways that are building what you want to have happen in the future.

While she was watching her money slip away, this wasn't easy. She wanted to blame other people. She wanted to file lawsuits. However, she realized she had no one to blame but herself and a sudden price change that no one had expected. She managed to control the vindictive impulses, learn what she could from the incident, and maintain positive attitudes about her experience and her future.

APPLICATION: Being on a spiritual journey does not guarantee that you will avoid all hardships. The next time one comes your way learn what you can and keep an attitude that is focused on a better future.

Finding the Way Together

Only by aiding others may the soul advance in its development toward following that purpose for which it came into the earth. Based on Edgar Cayce reading 423-3

During the month before the High Holy Days, people prepare their souls for the day of judgment. One rabbi used to tell stories to his congregation in order to move them to turn to God. Once he told this story:

"A man was lost in the forest. After many days of wandering, he came across another man who was also lost in the forest. The second man, not knowing the situation of the first man, asked how to get out of the woods. The first man responded, 'I do not know how to get out of the woods. However, I can point to paths that will lead further into the forest. After that, we can work together to find the way out.'"

The rabbi concluded by saying, "So, my congregation, let us look together for the way."

APPLICATION: Do you have a group of people with whom you are growing or sharing? If not, take a step to find one.

A Prayer of Forgiveness

If God had condemned, what opportunity would there be for us to find our way back to God? So we must do to others as we would have our brothers and sisters, the Christ, our God do to us. Indeed apply first, last, and always, "Forgive, O God, as I forgive. Find fault in me as I find fault in others."

Based on Edgar Cayce reading 5758-1

Following an experience in a hospital that left her deaf in one ear, Angela filed a lawsuit against the institution and the emergency room staff who had treated her.

Before the case came to trial, she tried the forty-day forgiveness prayer, which had been developed by people who followed the thoughts on forgiveness found in the Edgar Cayce readings. It worked like this: She was to say the prayer once a day for forty days. If she skipped one day, even if it were day thirty-nine, she was to start over until she did it for forty consecutive days.

So she began to say the following prayer daily, using the name of the emergency room doctor who had first treated her in that hospital:

"Dr. Clark, I am praying to you. Thank you for doing to me all that you have done. Forgive me, Dr. Clark, for doing to you all that I have done.

"Angela, I am praying to you. Thank you for doing to me all that you have done. Forgive me, Angela, for doing to you all that I have done. Thank You, Father."

After saying this prayer for forty days, Angela dropped the lawsuit. She realized that in spite of her pain, she had learned a great lesson from Dr. Clark. He had taught her to rely on her own intuition and not place her faith blindly in anyone, not even a doctor.

APPLICATION: Think of one person you have not been able to forgive. Try this forty-day forgiveness prayer.

Strength Along the Path

There is the attempt on the part of self to lead and to direct and to carry on in the better way possible, seeking at every turn, at every experience to use all of those influences that are necessary to keep the mental attitude in the proper direction or keep self in the proper frame of mind.

Based on Edgar Cayce reading 303-6

Katherine finally felt as if she were on the right path. She had joined a study group and had begun her spiritual journey. However, the next five years of her life got rougher instead of easier. Her marriage fell apart and during the divorce she went through a time of tough self-examination. She had to deal with anger, learning that it was an acceptable emotion. She discovered that being on a spiritual journey did not mean becoming a doormat.

During a spiritual growth conference she had a chance to talk to one of the speakers. She asked him why her life got rougher when she started this journey of growth. He asked her if maybe it wasn't the other way around. Maybe a part of her knew that life was going to get rough and brought the spiritual journey into her life at that time to give her the strength, courage, and support to get through.

Katherine couldn't answer that question. However, she admitted that the strength and courage to face those last few years had come from being on that journey and having support from the members of her study group.

APPLICATION: Look back at some of the unusual experiences in life that led you to where you are today. Point out the guidance of your Higher Self in those experiences.

Controlling the Tongue

Those who have no temper are of little value, but those who do not control their temper are worse than if they had none at all.   Based on Edgar Cayce reading 524-1

Carolyn was glad her misunderstanding with Marjorie was finally over. It was another indication to her of why she liked to include her work colleagues on any decision making.

In her business she and her co-workers sometimes consulted with one another. At times when they didn't, workers had to then find out later *who* made a particular decision and *why* it was made. Usually during the process of checking, people would get defensive because they thought they were being criticized instead of just being asked for information.

That's what had happened with Marjorie. Carolyn doesn't know if her words came out wrong or her timing was off, but Marjorie got upset quickly and responded sarcastically. Carolyn could feel a really great comeback on the tip of her tongue. However, she stopped for a few seconds and asked herself silently, "What purpose would be served for me to say this now?" She knew that friction could be stopped if one of the two didn't fuel the fire. So this time she decided not to perpetuate the argument in a nonproductive way and remained silent.

Later they resolved their differences in a more cordial atmosphere.

APPLICATION: The next time you get angry and feel like saying something inflammatory, stop and ask if expressing your anger will serve a good purpose at this point or if you should wait and speak later.

Imagining Past Lives

Let your imagination run wild and you will find you can make it just as interesting a life experience as you desire to make it. They may be called extravagant stories, may be called mysteries of the mind. But you can make it worthwhile.
Based on Edgar Cayce reading 5251-1

Carol discovered the relationship between her imagination and her past lives almost by accident. A friend had intuited that Carol's lifetime in Egypt had been significant for her, but the friend could not give specifics. Carol sensed this was correct but could not tune in to any specific information .

One day as she was thinking about this, she began to imagine herself as a former king of Egypt in a magnificent palace surrounded with lots of servants. After a few minutes this idea didn't seem to have any life to it so she shifted her mind to something else.

Two days later she found herself again thinking about Egypt. She suddenly saw herself as a writer and teacher. She let this thought develop and over the next twenty minutes created a detailed picture of a woman's life in ancient Egypt.

This image felt right to Carol. The thoughts came so easily; the feelings seemed real. In her present life she has done some writing and taken several literature classes in college.

She doesn't know if all the details created in her imagination were accurate, but she does believe the basics are correct. She thinks she has found a way to get in touch with some of her past lives. If her imagination produces images easily and her feelings respond, then this technique can help her touch other significant parts of her past.

APPLICATION: The next time your imagination leads you to a period in history, follow it for a while. See if you create anything that is important to your life now.

Where the Power Comes From

All of you may live at a oneness with the Creative Forces and thus fulfill the purposes for which your soul enters into an experience—that is, to be a material manifestation of what you hold as your concept of your relationship with the Creator.
Based on Edgar Cayce reading 361-9

The movie *Chariots of Fire* tells the story of Eric Liddell, a Scotsman born in China of a missionary family. After living there for several years, the family eventually returned to Scotland. It was his dream and his family's that he get a theological degree and return to China as a missionary. But he was also a good athlete—a fast runner. Others recognized this gift and encouraged him to train for the Olympics.

When he was running exhibitions and in training, he would close the day with a religious message to the people who had come to see the race. He would compare life to running a race and tell people, "I have no formula for winning the race. I can only point the way. Everyone runs in his or her own way. So where does the power come from to see the race to its end? From within."

As he started to spend more time in training, his sister began to worry that he had lost his sense of direction. He told her, "God made me for a purpose, China. But God also made me fast. When I run, I feel God's pleasure. To give it up is to hold God in contempt. It's not just fun. To run is to honor God."

APPLICATION: Look at everything you do today as being an activity that is honoring God. Be aware of how you feel.

Constructive Anger

Anger is correct, provided it is governed, directed to a constructive purpose.

Based on Edgar Cayce reading 361-4

After the big argument with John, one of her co-workers, Sally wanted help in dealing with her anger. She had said a lot of things she later regretted and felt the way she had handled her anger was not at all constructive.

Yet she knew that in her job expressions of anger had the potential to be positive and constructive. For example, if she were clear about the purpose of expressing her anger, then situations could be clarified and corrected.

She also knew that negativity could be created if she suppressed her anger. She would then begin to express those repressed feelings in indirect ways or begin to feel tension build up inside her.

Finally she asked her boss for some suggestions. He taught her one helpful way to express her anger without letting the emotions of the moment lead her to say and do things she might regret later. His technique was to be aware of the anger but not to respond immediately. Instead wait a while—sometimes an hour, sometimes a day. Then go to see the person or call the person on the phone and talk about the situation. He felt he could still clearly express his anger, but he also had a little more distance from the situation so the exchange could be more productive.

APPLICATION: At the next appropriate time, try waiting a while to express your anger. Then talk honestly to the person with whom you are angry.

What Am I Supposed to Be Doing?

Each soul enters with a purpose. And it is not merely to gain fame or fortune, nor to be thought well of in a material plane only, but it is a real spiritual and mental experience also.

Based on Edgar Cayce reading 2573-1

Andrea's prayer group had discussed an issue that concerned her. According to some of the people in that group, everyone could be given guidance and direction for his or her life. If people asked the question, "What should I be doing with my life?" they would find an answer.

Andrea had wondered for several months if she were supposed to be a part of this group. After the discussion today, she decided she would try her own approach to getting an answer.

She was an astrologer. The next time the question came to her mind, she would look at the time on her watch. Based on that, she would then construct an astrological chart to find the answer.

Having decided that, she put the discussion out of her mind and went about her daily work. That night in bed the question came to her. She sat up and looked at the clock. It was 11:26 p.m. She smiled. This was her birth time. The answer was obvious. She was born into this life in order to work with this prayer group.

APPLICATION: If you are sincere about wanting an answer, ask yourself, "What am I supposed to be doing in my life?" Then be open to some signs around you that can guide you to the answer.

Meeting People Where They Are

Be patient, be quiet, and see the glory of the Lord in what you do in your efforts day by day.

Based on Edgar Cayce reading 518-2

David became acquainted with the Edgar Cayce readings while in college. He was also deeply involved in and committed to his church. He served on the committee that planned worship services, he taught the junior high class, and he was a member of an ecumenical committee that planned special services with other churches in the community.

He discovered that he was able to use concepts from the Cayce readings, such as cooperation, fellowship, and patience. The worship committee appreciated the unique insights he brought to these familiar terms and liked his ideas for more involvement of people in special worship services.

David's junior high students enjoyed his approach to the Bible— seeing Biblical characters as symbols for situations they might encounter in life and then discussing how they might handle a similar situation.

By staying away from concepts like reincarnation which were unfamiliar to people, David had no trouble incorporating these other Cayce insights into his church work.

APPLICATION: Where in your life do you want to introduce a new concept to people? First meet people where they are so they don't feel threatened by your ideas.

Future-Oriented Reincarnation

As a soul builds in the present experience, creating an expression of divine love toward others, then where that building is left off—the next experience is begun.

Based on Edgar Cayce reading 294-189

Charles discovered that interest in reincarnation is predominantly past-oriented. People wanted to know about previous lifetimes and what happened to them in those lifetimes. This may have some value if people can use the information to influence present decisions.

However, Charles has learned to look at reincarnation in a new light. He now uses it in a future-oriented way. He believes that where he stops his development in this lifetime is where he will pick it up in the next.

This means that Charles can begin to work now for a purpose bigger than what he can accomplish in one lifetime. He can pick some ennobling ideal that will be challenging and of benefit to many people. It may take him several lifetimes to accomplish it, but he knows he will have those lifetimes available to him to continue that work.

For Charles, reincarnation has a future orientation that can inspire him to set big goals and begin to work toward them.

APPLICATION: Begin to develop a purpose for your life that may take several lifetimes to achieve.

The Preparation Is Over

Know that in whatever position a soul finds itself, it is that the greater opportunity may be had for fulfilling the purpose for which each soul enters an earthly experience.

Based on Edgar Cayce reading 1582-2

He wasn't really a coward. True, he had left Egypt rather hastily instead of facing a murder charge, but that was understandable. After all, when he had seen this burning bush, he hadn't run. He had walked toward it, and even stayed when the voice began to speak to him.

However, now Moses wasn't sure he wanted to go any further on this journey. God had told him about the suffering of the Hebrew people in Egypt. Then God had said, "You, Moses, I have chosen to go to Egypt to free my people."

Moses wanted nothing to do with that. He knew the current pharaoh. He had grown up with him. This guy would not tolerate anyone demanding that slaves be set free.

Of course, Moses' debate did not focus on that point. Instead, he asked how the people would know that God had really sent him. Then he talked about his lack of skill as a public speaker. However, he soon could sense that he was losing the debate.

As his arguments were aired, he began to feel inside that God was right. It was time to go back and do what he could. He didn't know quite how to do it, but he sensed that his life up to this moment had been God's way of preparing him for this task. God would be there to lead him through it.

APPLICATION: When you are called upon to do something for which you feel unprepared, look at your life as preparation for this task and think about God's promise to be with those who look to God's strength.

The Presence

The more often in prayer for others, the closer you draw to Him.   Based on Edgar Cayce reading 2574-1

Veronica was on the last leg of a disastrous overseas tour. Almost nothing had gone right. The food had been terrible. The transportation into certain areas of the country had been delayed so the members had lost hotel reservations. Rain had fallen for two straight days in one remote part of the country and left them all soaked with no place to change clothes for several hours. The tour leader had been challenged by several group members and his authority undermined by these people and the other happenings.

The final straw had occurred. They had arrived late again, and their luggage had gone on ahead. Now it was stored on the boat where no one could get to it. They hadn't been able to change clothes or brush their teeth for three days, and the boat trip was going to last overnight.

On the boat the group had to separate in order to find sleeping mats. Now, surrounded by people speaking a language she couldn't understand, Veronica reached the breaking point and began to cry. As she cried, she thought about how the tour leader must feel with so many things having gone wrong. She began to pray for him. In the midst of her prayer she was filled with the presence of Christ in a way she had never experienced before. She felt a comfort, peace, and strength that sustained her the entire night and made all the inconveniences recede into the background.

APPLICATION: When you are tempted to think only of yourself, pray for someone else.

Recognizing One's Gifts

For as has been said, the smile raised hope in the one to whom it was given, that hope made possible activity, that activity made possible a haven for some discouraged soul.

Based on Edgar Cayce reading 262-60

Paula's first impression of the psychic reading she had received in 1969 was not entirely to her liking. The psychic had mentioned that one of Paula's gifts was her smile. However, Paula really didn't think that comment was particularly insightful nor was it something a psychic should highlight in a reading.

However, as Paula interacted with others after that reading, more and more people began to notice her smile. When she saw how others responded to the warmth and openness they felt coming from her smile, she began to see how it *was* a manifestation of the love of Christ in her life.

This led her to think about how even the smallest things in other people's lives can be considered talents and gifts that can be used to manifest the love of Christ. As a result, she has been more observant, more receptive to receiving those gifts from other people and better able to help others recognize talents and gifts they didn't believe they had.

Twenty years later she was engaged in a conversation. Suddenly changing the subject, the man she was talking with mentioned how much he enjoyed her smile. Her gift was still being used.

APPLICATION: Ask a trusted friend to name one of your gifts that he or she appreciates. Celebrate that gift in some way.

Initiation to a New Job

Cultivate the ability to see the ridiculous and to retain the ability to laugh, even when clouds of doubt arise or when every form of disturbance arises.

Based on Edgar Cayce reading 2984-1

Ted couldn't believe what was about to happen to him. Tomorrow was going to be his first day on the job, and his boss was leaving tonight for three weeks on the road.

Since the job was new, no one else would be able to tell him what he was supposed to be doing. To make matters worse, Ted didn't know anyone in the organization and because the job had just been created, he didn't know how he or this position were going to be received. However, if any major decision had to be made quickly in the next few weeks and his boss couldn't be reached, Ted would be the one to make the decision. Needless to say, Ted didn't sleep well that night.

When he arrived the next day, he discovered that his office wasn't available yet. The secretary told him to use his boss's office for the next two weeks, and she would be his secretary when he needed her.

Ted walked in and sat down at the desk. There in front of him was a note from his boss. It said, "If you really need help, open the bottom right-hand desk drawer." Ted didn't wait; he reached down immediately. What he saw made him laugh and helped ease his anxiety.

Inside the desk drawer were a crystal ball and rosary beads.

APPLICATION: Humor is a great gift in tense situations. The next time the world seems a little too serious, find something at which to laugh.

We Are Not Yet Perfect

Not that you are perfect but that you would grow.
Based on Edgar Cayce reading 1800-28

Robert wanted to work on ideals. Since he taught art, he wanted to apply some that he could use in the classroom. So he decided to express the ideal of caring.

He felt he was doing well with this until an incident with Connie. Connie was a bit of a rebel. She had talent, but she was rejecting his attempts to help her put some structure on that talent. He finally got frustrated and gave her a low grade for the course. She got upset and complained to him and to the department head. The three of them had several discussions together.

After one heated exchange, he began to see that his ego was now deeply involved in this issue, and he was beginning to care more about that than about Connie. When he put his self-centeredness aside, then he could be more objective and arrive at a compromise.

Examining his ideal, Robert felt he had failed miserably. However, a friend helped him realize that good ideals will not always yield perfect results. Robert was learning how to be in relationship with people and with the universe, but he was not yet perfect. What was important was to maintain his ideal because he would be held more accountable for that than for every deed he did while he was learning.

APPLICATION: The next time you feel you have failed, recall your ideal. If you were trying to live out your ideal in that situation, don't judge yourself too harshly but be willing to learn from the experience.

FEBRUARY 9

Be Yourself

Keep in the way that you know to do, for God requires nothing other than that you be true to what you know in your heart to do. Based on Edgar Cayce reading 262-58

On his deathbed a famous rabbi was heard to whisper these words: "In the world to come I will not be asked, 'Why were you not Moses? Why were you not Abraham?' I will be asked, 'Why were you not yourself?'"

When David read this story, he began to think about his own life. He asked himself if he were being who he was meant to be. He had a good job which he enjoyed, but he knew he was capable of doing more.

When a branch office of his company opened a few weeks later, he looked at the jobs that were available. He could take a job similar to the one he had now, but it would mean a big cut in salary. His wife would have to go back to work. However, this job also offered him training for a better job in two or three years.

After several days of thinking about it and discussing it with his wife, he decided to apply. He knew he could handle the promotion he would get in three years. It would be challenging, but he could already feel that this challenge would help him grow and bring out new abilities in him.

APPLICATION: Spend two minutes thinking about this question: "How can I better be myself?" Then do at least one thing that came to your mind.

Beyond All Expectations

Count your hardships, your troubles, even your disappointments as stepping-stones to know God's way better.

Based on Edgar Cayce reading 262-83

Job hunting had become a hectic part of Richard's senior year in college. For the last several months he had been filling out applications, mailing off resumes, and even interviewing for positions. The interviews had gone well, but he was not excited about any of the jobs so far.

Then he received word of a job near St. Louis. He had visited that city before and loved it. He would work with a large staff and have excellent opportunity for promotion. The job sounded perfect and his interview went extremely well. However, a week later the firm called and told him another candidate was chosen for the job.

Richard was still feeling the disappointment of this rejection when he went for another interview. The position was in a small town with only two other employees in the business. He got lost on the back roads getting there so he was somewhat frustrated when he finally arrived.

However, the moment he walked in the building and said hello, he felt at home. By the end of the interview he really wanted this job. In spite of the fact that the location and the size of the firm were the opposite of what he had originally hoped to find, he knew this was the right place.

He got the job and stayed six years before moving on.

APPLICATION: Be open to getting what you don't expect. It may be the right opportunity for the moment.

Recharging

From the experience does the soul find that ability to turn within self and whatever the trial may be, in Him comes hope, comes the way. Based on Edgar Cayce reading 2136-1

Marilyn and Jim began reading the Edgar Cayce readings several years ago. They found the ideas stimulating and discovered that being on a spiritual journey together strengthened their relationship with each other. Wanting to give others what they were getting, they started a discussion group in their area.

They were surprised at the makeup of the group. All the people who attended were much younger than Marilyn and Jim. All were either divorced or having marriage or other emotional problems. These young people began looking to them for guidance, wisdom, and support in facing life.

While Marilyn and Jim were glad to help and felt the group was supporting people, they found the situation draining. Instead of being equals and learning from other members, they found themselves leaders and counselors. Many times one or two members would stay long after the others had left.

After such discussions, Marilyn felt completely exhausted, but was able to renew herself because of her meditation routine. Making that connection with the Higher Power gave her new strength to continue to reach out to the rest of the group.

APPLICATION: If you are feeling overwhelmed by some situations in your life, begin daily meditation to find strength from a Higher Source.

You Will Be Taken Care Of

You, too, often doubt, often fear. Yet God is surely with you.
Based on Edgar Cayce reading 5749-6

Karen's husband went in for another cancer operation when she was four months pregnant. They had been praying for years that the cancer would not reoccur and that they would not have to fight that battle again. However, his last test had been suspicious, and now those suspicions had been confirmed.

During this hospital stay, Karen continued to pray, but the words felt like nothing but words. She did not feel they were doing any good or being heard by a God who cared. She had lost the close contact with God she had felt for the past few years.

Then one night at home alone she experienced a special transcendent moment. For several minutes she was surrounded by a love and supporting strength that she had never felt before. The peace and comfort engulfed her and said, "You are not alone. Whatever happens, you will be taken care of."

That moment carried her through all the other operations her husband faced until his death.

APPLICATION: The next time you face a crisis in your life remember that this love and comforting strength is there for you as well.

Beginning at Sixty-Five

*Have you finished the work God gave you to do, have you
sought to know the work? Have you walked and talked with
God often? It is your privilege. Will you?*

Based on Edgar Cayce reading 3051-7

Sheila knew something was about to happen but didn't
know what. She was getting ready to retire and to look for
something to do when the following events occurred.

First, she had a dream in which she looked into her purse
and found a picture of the Pope in her calendar book. Then
she found herself in the presence of the Pope. When he saw
her picture, he blessed her. She woke up ecstatic, knowing
this dream had something to do with spiritual growth.

A few days later she heard a radio program discussing
ESP and psychic phenomena. She told her husband about it
and they discussed it many times for several days. The topic
intrigued her so much that she looked for more material to
study. She found some books based on the Edgar Cayce
readings and began to read them.

As she read, she felt she was finding what had been missing all her life. Now that she was retiring, she was open and
receptive to the new possibilities the universe was giving
her. Her retirement became the beginning of new growth.

APPLICATION: Open yourself to the new possibilities that
the universe has to offer you. Age is not a factor.

The Moment of Sight

Divine love may bring the knowledge, the understanding, the wisdom for the activities to bring the self in accord with Creative Forces.   Based on Edgar Cayce reading 1215-4

It happened so suddenly that Saul never did know what really occurred. One minute he was riding to Damascus to kill "God's enemies"; the next moment he lay blinded on the road listening to a voice accusing him of betraying his Lord.

Now for three days he had sat in this house reflecting on his life. He was tired and could think no more. He had failed his God and was ready to die. Yet God would not let him. He felt something trying to break through, but. . .

The knock on the door disturbed him. Saul, not knowing why, called for the visitor to be brought to him. An elderly cobbler, trembling with the thought of his mission, stood before Saul. Slowly the man reached out to touch Saul's eyes and, in the name of Jesus, gave him his sight again.

Saul looked at the poor cobbler, the instrument of divine forgiveness. In that monemt Saul died and Paul was resurrected. In that moment wisdom broke through. Divine love flooded Paul's heart and God lived again in the soul of this man.

APPLICATION: Show loving forgiveness to someone with whom you have had difficulties.

The Answer Is Never the Same

Individuals are manifestations of their unique portion of that Creative Force.   Based on Edgar Cayce reading 816-10

Larry was getting frustrated. He had spent several hours looking for the answer to his question in the Cayce readings. Yet he felt as if he weren't any further ahead than he was five hours ago.

The problem was that he was finding so many diverse answers. Each reading that dealt with his question gave a slightly different angle on the problem. There were common elements in some answers, but few of them were exactly the same.

He shut the book he was reading and sat back to think. What he had in front of him were readings given to individuals who came asking for help or guidance. Each individual had a unique history that had brought him or her to that meeting with Edgar Cayce. So what applied to one person did not apply in the same way to the next person. The recommendation had to vary from person to person.

That insight made Larry sit up and think. He was a unique individual, too. So why should the answer to his question be the same as for anyone else. He didn't have Edgar Cayce to give him his unique answer so he would have to find it for himself. He had guidelines in the readings, but he would have to pick out the ones that felt right for him and try them to see if they worked.

APPLICATION: Name a problem you are trying to solve in your life. Go where you can get suggestions for solving your problem, but remember the answer must be uniquely yours.

The Dream

In the dream we see there are conditions presented to the mind of the individual that is an emblematical condition of what is to happen in fact. Based on Edgar Cayce reading 294-53

Although she had heard about these kinds of dreams, Eileen had never had one like this before. It gave her great hope and confidence that her grandson, Billy, would be all right.

Billy had been born with a club foot. The family had begun working with it almost immediately, but at the moment the results were not noticeable. She had prayed about it many times.

Then she had a dream in which a deceased friend of hers — a man whom she had considered very spiritual — had come to visit her while she was babysitting Billy. The man picked up the baby and gently laid him on the floor. Then he picked up a Bible, opened it, and placed Billy's leg in it. He then closed the book and stood on it, rocking slowly back and forth. When he was finished, he gave the child back to her and said that he was now healed.

She didn't tell this dream to anyone for a while, but she did call her son more frequently to check on Billy's condition. Within a few weeks visible improvements were noticed and after a few months the foot had completely healed.

APPLICATION: The next time you dream about something happening to someone you know, write it down and see if it happens.

Start the Ball Rolling

What makes for the change? Will!
Based on Edgar Caycer reading 262-81

Bob and Marsha had talked about moving for a number of years. However, nothing seemed to be happening. The house had been on the market for several months and not one person had looked at it seriously.

At a party one night Marsha noticed Bob standing by himself. So she walked over to see if he was feeling all right.

He looked at her and said, "I can leave this."

Marsha thought he meant he was ready to go home.

He explained, "I can leave this community and this life style."

On the way home they talked. They told each other that if the house and their investment properties sold, they would move.

Bob told his real estate agent he would take less on the properties in order to sell them. Within three weeks all properties had sold at the asking price, and within two weeks the house was sold for cash at the asking price.

Later on they looked at the speed with which all that happened. They realized that once they had made a definite decision everything happened. What had been missing earlier was a decision to act.

APPLICATION: If you have a goal you have talked about but don't seem to be getting closer to, ask yourself if you have really decided to focus your life on that goal. If so, do one thing today necessary toward achieving that goal.

Keeping with God's Will

Know that each soul is a free-willed individual and chooses the way and application. It is either a co-worker with God in creation or in attune with that which is at variance with God.
Based on Edgar Cayce reading 2549-1

The disciples of one famous rabbi were studying the Talmud one day when they came to a curious passage. One student asked, "Rabbi, this passage tells us that our Father Abraham kept all the laws. How is this possible since the law had not yet been given?"

The rabbi replied, "All that is necessary is for a person to love God. If you find yourself ready to do something and you believe this act might lessen your love for God, you know it is not right to do it, but sinful. On the other hand, if you are about to do something and believe it will increase your love for God, then it is right and in keeping with God's will. This is the way that Abraham lived. Thus he lived keeping all the laws."

APPLICATION: Pause sometime and ask yourself if what you are doing is showing an increase or a decrease in your love for God. Act according to your answer to this question.

It Doesn't Fit

In various experiences the names of individuals indicated the purpose to which the soul had been called.

Based on Edgar Cayce reading 457-10

When Martha was pregnant, she knew she was going to have a boy. She liked the name William. Two of her cousins had that name, and she wanted to name her son William.

However, her husband didn't like that name. He said it didn't flow smoothly with their family name. They talked about it for several weeks, then he told her to take the name into her dreams and see what would happen.

That night Martha dreamed about seeing a young child's outfit hanging in the closet. The color was nice but the proportions were wrong. It was too big on top and too short on the bottom.

When she woke up, she told her husband about the outfit that didn't fit. He said, "You mean it doesn't suit him?"

She paused and then said, "All right. What name do you have in mind?"

He said, "How about Jason William." She agreed, and Jason William was born six months later.

APPLICATION: Most names have meanings. Find out what your name means or from what words or ideas your name is derived. See if it seems to suggest anything to you about your purpose in life.

A House Is Not a Home

The home is the nearest pattern in earth (where there is unity of purpose in the companionship) of our relationship to our Maker. For it is ever creative in purpose.

Based on Edgar Cayce reading 3577-1

For Ralph a house is not necessarily a home, and Ralph carries this attitude into his real estate business. A house can be just a building where people live to protect them from the heat in summer, cold in winter, and rain all year through.

A home is much more. Ralph remembers from his childhood how his home was a foundation for everything he did. It was security when the world treated him badly. It was a place to learn about life. It was where love was expressed and dreams were dreamed. It was where goals and ideals were nurtured and given a chance to grow.

Ralph also has cherished memories of family and friends. He remembers times with his brothers and sisters, and looks back on their childhood games and spats as an important part of growing up. He still can picture neighborhood friends coming in at the last minute for supper.

Knowing that people need the right environment for a house to become a home, he sees that part of his job as a real estate agent is to help people find that correct environment for their family.

He is not in the business of selling houses. Ralph is in the business of helping people create a home.

APPLICATION: Look at your memories and discover something that means "home" to you. Use that discovery to create a feeling of home where you are now.

Understanding Why

*Know in whom you have believed, and in what you have be-
lieved, and who is that author of your belief.*

Based on Edgar Cayce reading 1776-1

Being in college was challenging, but it did give Bob the
chance to discover what he really believed.

He had grown up with the Edgar Cayce readings and
with people who accepted reincarnation as a part of life.
Here at college it was not that way, and he had to defend his
beliefs.

Bob had just finished a lively discussion with Carl about
the nature of God. When Carl had admitted that justice was
a primary characteristic of God, Bob had used that as an
entry to talk about reincarnation. He reasoned that a just
God would have to give people equal opportunities for
growth. If people had only one lifetime, then those who
lived for a day hardly had the same chance as those who
lived 90 years. People born in poverty did not have the same
opportunity as those born to wealth. However, if over a
period of lifetimes everyone experienced a variety of life
spans and life conditions, that brought a sense of justice to
the situation.

Even though Carl had been resistant to the idea at first,
Bob could sense now that Carl understood his argument
and respected his position.

Bob was beginning to feel grown up by being able to clarify what he believed in and why. That felt good.

APPLICATION: The next time you have the opportunity, express clearly and confidently those ideas in which you believe.

It Can't Be Avoided

Life is earnest, life is true—that which each soul experiences is a part of that necessary if it will be used as such and not looked upon as a drudge or as a hindrance.

Based on Edgar Cayce reading 1463-2

Steve and Carolyn had been unsure about one particular principle from the Edgar Cayce readings—the idea that each soul has to go through some experiences. They had been reading in contemporary metaphysics about how the mind can control everything. They liked that positive attitude and had begun to try to think positively about themselves and their future. This Cayce idea seemed to contradict that positivism.

However, later they understood it. After a year of positive thinking and growth in their business, a series of investments went bad. Their rosy financial picture wilted almost overnight. Barely able to make house payments, they lived frugally for months until a new job brought in more income.

During those months they spent hours thinking about their positive attitudes and about the Cayce principle. They looked at their experience to see what they were learning from it. They tried to act in ways that did not blame others.

As a result, they came through the experience without feeling as if their world view was destroyed. They would continue to look positively to the future, but they realized that they would probably have to face other unpleasant experiences anyway. They would learn from them and move on.

APPLICATION: The next time unpleasant experiences come your way, learn from them but continue to look positively to your future.

Forgiveness Is a Circle

As I forgive may I be forgiven. Like only begets like. This is an irrefutable law, whether in spirit, in mind, or in body.
Based on Edgar Cayce reading 281-2

Jesus told this story: A king once had a servant who owed him several thousand dollars. On the day the debt was due the man came before the king, fell on his knees, and pleaded his case. He did not have the money. Would the king forgive his debt and not throw him into jail? The king showed mercy and let the man go.

The servant went joyfully into the streets where he met a man who owed him a hundred dollars. He demanded the money and, when the man couldn't pay, had him thrown in jail.

Word of this exchange got back to the king who had the servant brought before him.

The king said, "I forgave your debt of several thousand dollars and you could not forgive a debt of one hundred dollars. It appears to me you have a lesson to learn."

The king sent the servant to jail.

To this Jesus added, "Forgiveness is a circle. Break the circle, and the consequences are felt by many."

APPLICATION: Remember a time in your life when you were forgiven. Keep the circle unbroken by forgiving someone who needs your forgiveness.

No Need to Get Soaked

If the soul will strive first for a spiritual analysis of its purposes and desires and then with patience run the race, the soul may work toward application of the abilities which are latent within.   Based on Edgar Cayce reading 2117-1

Sylvia had been involved with metaphysical material for about six months now, and she loved it. She was reading books on meditation, dream interpretation, spiritual growth, and astrology. She devoured books within a few days of buying them and couldn't get enough. Then she had the following dream.

She walked outside. The sky was a little overcast so she took her umbrella. Soon it began to sprinkle. Then it rained a little harder. Finally she found herself walking in a downpour, but for some reason she did not use her umbrella.

When she woke up, she thought about this dream and realized it had to do with her recent interest in metaphysical topics. She felt it was telling her that she was getting too much, too quickly. Since she had an umbrella, she could use it and not get soaked. So Sylvia decided to cut back on her reading and let the material flow in slower. This way she could absorb it gradually rather than trying to take it in all at once.

APPLICATION: Too much of a good thing too fast may not be beneficial, even on a spiritual journey. Take time to let the soul absorb the new ideas and new insights without overloading yourself.

How Do You Pray

Let your prayer be, "Not my way, Lord. Have Your own way with me that I may ever be a channel of blessings to those I contact day by day."　Based on Edgar Cayce reading 3084-1

It was Bill who had brought Arthur to the organization. Since then they had worked together for many years to educate people about its spiritual philosophy. Both had seen many lives transformed because of the message they carried.

Today they were walking together to lunch. Bill had just discovered he had a serious illness and probably would be dead within a year.

As they walked, Bill asked, "Arthur, how would you pray for me, now?"

Arthur thought carefully. Then he said that he wouldn't pray specifically for a miracle healing for Bill, but would continue to pray for God's presence with him. Above all, Arthur would continue to pray for the work of the organization. It was this work that needed to continue long after both of them had passed on.

Bill looked at Arthur and heard the love and commitment they both shared for each other and for their work.

He quietly said, "You're right, Arthur. You're right."

APPLICATION: Prayers are powerful tools. When praying, be sure you are praying for the right things.

Hanging On to the Ideal

Individuals may at times fall short. If this happens in trying to do that which they believe is sincere, the effort is viewed in the light of the understanding they had.

Based on Edgar Cayce reading 2982-1

Laura had tried to put her ideals into practice and had apparently failed. She had chosen the word *service* to describe her spiritual ideal for the year; therefore, she had volunteered to be chairperson of the bazaar that each year raised several thousands of dollars for a local charity.

She expected few problems because everyone supported this cause and was surprised at the obstacles she encountered. A few people refused to donate items because the previous year someone had hurt their feelings. Some refused to work with other people because of petty jealousies. As a result, Laura couldn't get the cooperation necessary to make the bazaar as successful as in the past.

As she thought about this frustrating experience, she realized that even with high ideals she wouldn't always be able to accomplish what she wanted. That's when she began to understand the difference between spiritual ideals and other goals. Her material goal had been to raise more money than in previous years, but she had failed to accomplish that goal. Her spiritual ideal was service to the charity; in that she was a success.

She also realized it was the ideal behind her actions that had always left its mark on her life. From now on she would judge her experience and what she had learned by how well she remained faithful to that ideal.

APPLICATION: Do one thing today because of a good ideal and do not judge success or failure by the immediate results.

No More "Poor Me"

Keep your heart in attunement and every condition will open in the right time, place, and manner. Keep your self aright— all will come well.   Based on Edgar Cayce reading 39-4

Daniel had gone through the "poor me" routine before. This time he wasn't going to let that depressive attitude take over and spoil his life for the next several weeks.   He was disappointed; he had to admit that. He had worked hard on this real estate deal for about six months and had shown the property to several potential buyers. One person had almost bought it but had backed out at the last moment.

Then yesterday Carl, a new employee at the agency, had taken a client out to the site while Daniel was returning from it with another client. Carl's client came back two hours later and put down a deposit. He wanted to close as quickly as possible.

Daniel had done the best he could and someone else still got the deal.   However, he had learned by now that some sales he would get and some he wouldn't. He reasoned that since Carl got the sale in a legitimate way, this one was supposed to be Carl's.

Daniel already had his eye on another big property that his agency was acquiring. He wasn't going to wallow in self-pity.   He was ready to focus his attention on that one.

APPLICATION: You can do your best and still not have everything go your way. The next time this happens, affirm that you will have your day in the future.

The Puppy's Gift

Are there not trees of oak, of ash, of pine? Each is needed for meeting this or that experience. Have you chosen any one of these to meet all needs in your life? Then, all will fill their place. Don't find fault with any, but rather show how good a pine, ash or oak or vine you are.

Based on Edgar Cayce reading 254-87

One day the animals in the barn were talking among themselves while the new puppy came around to get acquainted.

The horse said, "The master loves me best because I can move heavy loads for him." Looking at the puppy he said, "I doubt a puppy your size could be of any value like that."

In the next stall the cow spoke up, "I am most honored because I give milk that makes butter and cheese. You," he said to the puppy, "give nothing of value to the farmer."

The sheep talked about her wool, the hen about her eggs, and all agreed the puppy could do nothing.

The puppy crept off to a dark corner to cry. An old dog found him and said, "It's true you will never do what those animals do. But instead of crying about what you can't do, use the ability the Creator gave you to do what you can."

That night when the farmer returned after a hard day in the field, the puppy ran to him, licked his feet, and jumped excitedly. The master fell to the ground and spent several minutes laughing and playing with the puppy.

Holding the puppy close, the master said, "No matter how tired I am when I get home, you always make me feel better. You fill me with laughter and joy."

APPLICATION: Pick one place in your life where you think you don't contribute anything. Look again. Name something you do contribute and affirm your gift.

Dreams and Children

The dreams come for the soul's edification, for through them the issues of life may be understood and the soul more able to apply them in the life.   Based on Edgar Cayce reading 538-15

Mark and Susan didn't learn about the importance of dreams until shortly after their marriage. They decided at that time to expose their children to dream insights at a much younger age.

From the time their children could sit at the table, they heard their parents talking about the dreams they had had the night before. As the children grew up, Susan and Mark gently probed them to share their dreams. The children were hesitant at first. Many times they would refuse or just mention part of a dream. Gradually, however, they began to share more.

This exchange became especially important when their second daughter had a series of nightmares. As she became more comfortable speaking about the images in her dreams, she began to see that many of them had several meanings, not all of which were frightening; in fact, some proved to be helpful. As she grew in her understanding, she became less afraid of her dreams and could see the positive aspects of these images.

Now the entire family openly shares dreams at breakfast. This helps all of them to learn about themselves and builds a feeling of closeness and care among the family members.

APPLICATION: Find a few minutes each day to work with your dreams.

The Meaning of Crucifixion

Be guided by that ennobling influence as is in Jesus' way. Keep yourself in the way that follows His application of these principles, and there will be brought the greater good for others and for yourself. Based on Edgar Cayce reading 391-1

Have you ever wondered how Jesus' crucifixion could be a pattern for your life?

Ellen had been tossing and turning, unable to sleep well for the past three nights. She was thinking about something she had read: that Jesus is the pattern for your life. However, there was something else bothering her and she didn't know exactly what.

Suddenly she thought of Angela. At last she had the answer. She had not spoken to Angela for three months. Some comments Angela had made earlier had hurt her, and now her pride was standing in the way of a reconciliation.

She also realized that Jesus being the pattern for her life now meant that she had to follow the path of crucifixion. She had to crucify the pride within herself that was keeping her from being more attuned to God and more loving to others. She didn't have to die on a cross—only that part of her which caused the separation between her and Angela had to die.

For Ellen, seeing Jesus as the pattern meant experiencing crucifixion in a part of her so that a new resurrected relationship with Angela could grow.

APPLICATION: Name something in your life that is hindering your relationship with others. Take one step today in removing that hindrance.

Perfect Timing

When you are prepared for a thing, the opportunity to use it presents itself. Based on Edgar Cayce reading 3544-1

Laura was working in the Pacific islands but getting ready to retire. She was wondering what she was going to do with her life after retirement. When she began to have eye trouble, she flew to Hawaii for treatment. She missed her return flight and had to wait five hours for the next one. During that time she began talking with a couple in the airport. The lady mentioned Edgar Cayce, told Laura to find out more about him, and said Laura's eyes would be fine.

Laura forgot all about that conversation. However, several months later she was getting her eyes treated again. While she was waiting for eye surgery, she found a book which mentioned Edgar Cayce. It also discussed everything she had ever felt about spiritual growth, but she had always been so busy she never had time for her interest in this area.

While her eyes were healing, she joined the Cayce organization and began reading its literature. She was attracted to its philosophy and thus began her transformative spiritual journey.

Now she had time for her growth and for this organization, and numerous opportunities were opening up for her.

APPLICATION: Waiting for the right time is an important part of life. Choose one thing you want to do in life. Be patient, but also be alert for the opportunity to do it.

Choosing a Constructive Way

Life and its problems are not mere chance but indicate the love, the mercy of a loving Spirit who gives each soul the opportunity to meet self and to magnify that love, that mercy which is the experience of those who seek to know God's will.
Based on Edgar Cayce reading 1102-5

Karen used to be frustrated by problems in her life. She could never understand why they arose when they did. Then she read these words: Any problem or situation you encounter you have for the most part brought upon yourself and you are facing that problem at a time when you can find the proper tools to meet it and learn from it. To Karen this said that life's problems came to her when she was ready to come to grips with them in a constructive way.

To meet a problem in a constructive way, Karen knew that she had to be in touch with herself. When she was vulnerable to certain attitudes because of how she felt, she might respond in a nonconstructive way. At those times she stayed away from certain difficult situations for a while.

She remembered her argument with Nancy. After several weeks of disagreeing with Nancy over just about everything, she wanted to find out what was going on. However, around that same time a family incident occurred which upset her, and she knew those feelings would affect her talk with Nancy. So she avoided Nancy for a month until the other matter was resolved, knowing that eventually she would have to confront that relationship. However, in the moment of vulnerability caused by the family problem, dealing with Nancy constructively meant staying away from her until other negative feelings were overcome.

APPLICATION: Make plans to meet in a constructive way a recurring problem situation in your life.

Giant Killing

In God and in God's ways with you, may you find the answer to all of your promises, to all of your problems, to all of your fears, to all of your doubts.

Based on Edgar Cayce reading 1632-2

The guy looked huge—much bigger than he had from the Israelite camp a few hundred yards away. And David felt very uncomfortable in all this armor. He didn't regret volunteering to kill this giant, but he did realize that this heavy shield, sword, and helmet were only going to get in his way.

He stopped and turned around. He knew people were thinking he had lost his courage and was backing out. He could hear the laughter from the Philistine camp.

He calmly took off the armor. Then he picked up a few stones and turned to walk toward Goliath again, carrying only his slingshot and dressed only in his shepherd's garb. The laughter stopped. He could imagine the confused thoughts running through their minds now.

As he approached the giant, he said a prayer to his God, placing his trust in God's ability to calm his nerves, give him courage, and guide his stone. The mockery of Goliath at this point only made him more certain that the giant would make himself vulnerable at the right moment.

He loaded the stone in the slingshot, waited until the giant lowered his shield to raise his sword, and then let the stone fly. In a few seconds the giant lay dead at David's feet.

David had known that the power of God was strong enough for this task. Now the Israelites knew as well.

APPLICATION: The next time you face the "giants" in your life, find a way to take the power of God with you instead of a lot of unnecessary armor.

Hungering for Growth

The way of the Lord is that which brings relief to the sufferer, that which enables those who are hungry—in body, in mind—to be fed upon the bread of life through your efforts.
Based on Edgar Cayce reading 518-2

One of Debbie's goals on her spiritual journey was to be supportive to others. She never imagined how writing a few letters would be a step toward fulfilling that goal.

Her letter writing began when she heard about people who were working on spiritual growth but had no support. Sometimes these individuals didn't know where to look for like-minded seekers; others lived in small towns where there weren't any other people interested in such matters.

Through a series of coincidences and a mutual acquaintance, one woman in a remote town in the mountains heard about Debbie and began to write to her. This woman had no one to whom she could talk. She had no one to share with when she read an exciting new book about spiritual development or when she felt stuck in her growth efforts.

At first Debbie wasn't sure what to write back. But remembering her goal—to support others—she took a chance and simply wrote a little note in response. In her letter she commented on one of the ideas the woman had mentioned. Debbie was surprised when the woman wrote back saying how much that response meant.

Soon the two of them were exchanging letters every week. After a few months, Debbie finally saw she was achieving one of her goals. She was supporting someone who otherwise would be alone on her spiritual journey.

APPLICATION: Do one thing to support someone else's journey of spiritual growth.

The Cat Was the Key

God is love! The influence that motivates the life of each soul is love! Based on Edgar Cayce reading 1579-1

Though in the third week of their meditation class, Barb, the teacher, was still not able to help Jim. He was a quiet man who had difficulty talking with people, and Barb felt an aura of unhappiness and loneliness around him that she could not seem to penetrate or help him move beyond.

Her favorite way to get people into meditation was to have them focus on someone they loved. Then they would concentrate on the feeling of love and go with that.

However, with Jim, she was frustrated. He couldn't seem to move beyond his loneliness to choose anyone he loved enough to capture that feeling.

Finally one day he came into class with the story of a cat he had owned as a teenager. He had really loved that cat. Barb thought this was a bit unusual, but she agreed to let him work with that. She helped him picture the cat, then feel the love for the cat, and finally just to feel love.

It worked. Within a few weeks he was able to move from the cat to feelings of love for people in his life. This helped him get more in touch with his emotions and open up to express them to people and to others in the class. He also found himself having some intense meditation experiences.

APPLICATION: Where have you experienced love in your life? Use that memory as a starting point as you try focusing on love during your meditation periods.

An Ideal Day

Write your spiritual, mental, and physical ideals. Then, as you analyze yourself and apply, lay them aside. In three months check yourself and how you're doing. It will be worthwhile.   Based on Edgar Cayce reading 3032-2

Nick had struggled hard to define his ideal and wasn't having any luck. He had written down words under "physical," "mental" and "spiritual" categories as someone had recommended. However, they weren't meaningful for him.

Then, he had the idea of fantasizing a picture of an ideal day. He would write down his images and in the description see his physical, mental, and spiritual ideals at work. He described a day seven years in the future so he wouldn't be influenced by his current plans. He spent several weeks adding to this picture, making it very specific. He even named the kind of car he would be driving and the attitudes about life he would have. Then he put the paper away.

One day seven years later, he woke up and happened to look at his bookshelf. There he saw the book in which he had put the paper describing his "ideal day." He pulled it out and read it. Tears began running down his cheeks because so many of those specific images had come to pass.

For Nick this was a perfect example that mind is the builder. It could direct energies he was not even conscious of and bring into reality the ideal he held in his unconscious.

He resolved to make his ideal as conscious as possible so that his unconscious could work toward positive growth.

APPLICATION: Take time to write down your ideal day for the future. Then put the paper away so you are not consciously seeing it every day. Take a look at it every three months or so and see where you are toward fulfilling it.

Judging Without Wisdom

Be not too quick in your judgments of others. In your mind put yourself in their place before you pass judgment.
Based on Edgar Cayce reading 1510-1

While traveling from the village one afternoon, David broke the Sabbath unintentionally. His carriage broke down. Although he ran back to the village, he did not get home before the beginning of the Sabbath. A young rabbi imposed a long and severe penance on the man. David tried to carry it out, but his body could not endure it and he became ill.

David went to visit Rabbi Isaac, an elderly rabbi known for his great wisdom. When he told his story, Rabbi Isaac said, "Carry a pound of candles to the House of Prayer to be lit on the Sabbath. That will be your penance. And ask your rabbi, Rabbi Jacob, to come see me."

Rabbi Jacob went to visit Rabbi Isaac. On his way the wheel of his carriage broke. He ran, but try as he might he could not get to the village until after dark.

When he arrived, he saw that Rabbi Isaac had already begun the blessing over the wine which begins the Sabbath.

Rabbi Isaac paused and said, "Good Sabbath, my friend. You had not before this moment known the sorrow of the sinner, your heart had never before beat with the despair of sin—thus it was easy for you to hand out such a harsh penance."

Rabbi Jacob stayed for the meal and for many days thereafter in order to learn more from wise Rabbi Isaac.

APPLICATION: Think of an instance where you have judged someone recently. Pause now and try to view the situation from that person's perspective.

Making the Right Selections

Be sure the ideal is proper. Follow that irrespective of outside influences. Know that self is right and then go straight ahead.
Based on Edgar Cayce reading 1739-6

Esther had taken over the manager's position of the bookstore a few weeks ago and now had some decisions to make. The policies on book purchases were being reviewed. The guidelines set in these policies would determine criteria for choosing the books the store would sell, and she wanted to be sure the guidelines reflected the ideal of the total organization of which the bookstore was only a part.

She remembered something she had read in the Edgar Cayce readings. Books should always be helpful and hopeful. One should never choose a book to impress someone.

As she thought about these words, she realized the emphasis was on quality and the book's ability to give people good guidance. This meant refusing some books that might be best sellers or that were just sensationalistic.

She felt she was on the right track when she was asked to set up a book table at a conference on mental health and creativity. All the attendees were professionals in the health field. She received numerous compliments on the quality of her books. One person said he had not even seen this kind of selection at a recent conference in New York City.

Esther may have lost a few good sellers with her strict criteria, but she knew that the books she had were helpful.

APPLICATION: Living up to ideals sometimes means not doing something even though it might be successful by one set of standards. Name a place in your life where this tension exists.

Falling Off a Mountain

Know that there is within yourself all healing that may be accomplished for the body. How well are you willing to cooperate with the divine influences which may work in and through you? The applications are merely to stimulate the atoms of the body. Based on Edgar Cayce reading 4021-1

While vacationing in the mountains, David took a hike before supper. When he walked into the cabin two hours later, he was bleeding from head to foot. He had slipped and fallen over 100 feet down a mountainside.

A Cayce-oriented doctor, who was vacationing with David and his wife, put a stitch in his scalp wound and then went to town to buy castor oil, something Cayce recommended for a wide variety of healing purposes. David's wife helped him get undressed and into the tub to soak and clean off the dirt. He had bruises and cuts all over his body, a swollen foot, and hands so scraped and sore he would not allow anyone to touch them in order to clean them.

When the doctor returned, he put castor oil on the cuts and wrapped them in bandages. They simply poured oil on his hands and wrapped them, hoping infection would not set in before the pain subsided enough so they could clean off the dirt.

The treatment worked. No infection developed, and a cast was put on his foot the next day. Today he has no scars except for a small one on his elbow.

APPLICATION: Do some reading about home health care treatments that your family can use.

Four Months at the Gym

Each difficulty has its place, and the body mentally, morally, socially must use each for its own development.

Based on Edgar Cayce reading 900-44

Mary's New Year's resolution had gotten off to a good start. She had decided to spend this year working on the recommendations in the Edgar Cayce readings to balance the physical, mental, and spiritual aspects of her life. She had just finished her four-month emphasis on the physical. She had worked out faithfully at the gym and was in better physical condition than she had been in years. Then she woke up one morning and found a lump in her breast.

She immediately made an appointment with her doctor. She and her friends prayed, and a couple of her friends went with her to the doctor's office to await the results of the tests. Everything turned out fine.

As Mary reflected on this experience, she decided to look upon it like a dream. She wrote down her feelings and interpretations. One of her feelings was that she was mortal—a situation like this could happen to her as it could to anyone else. She also realized she had turned to prayer and friends for support. She has incorporated them into her life more since that experience.

Finally she realized a new reason for keeping fit. Keeping fit didn't mean she wouldn't have problems. It meant that if something did happen, she was as strong as she could be physically to meet the situation.

APPLICATION: Look at what you do to keep in good health. Examine your ideal for staying healthy and take steps to change your health habits if you need to.

Giving New Life

Do not let regret become a part of your experience. Put your purpose, your faith in the promise of God. God will take away your burdens. Based on Edgar Cayce reading 2390-7

Judy enjoys the Edgar Cayce readings about Egypt. In the years she has been studying these, she has discovered ideas that can be applied in her life today.

One reading on Egypt talked about the people who worked in one of the temples. One woman was a confessor. People would come to her with problems, guilts, and errors that they had committed. She knew what to tell people to help them lay their burdens aside, make amends where necessary, and go on living their lives. Another reading talked about how Jesus was also able to do this with people when He lived many thousands of years later.

As Judy read these words, she realized this is also what she is called to do. When people come to her who are afraid or feeling guilty, she knows now that part of her response should be to help them lay aside what is bothering them. Then they can feel renewed and go forth with new hope in life.

APPLICATION: Think of someone you know who is carrying a burden of guilt, fear, shame or other emotional burden. Do one thing you can do to help them release that pain.

Vision Quest

Look then into your own heart, your own mind. What is your desire? What is your purpose? What—and who—is your ideal?
Based on Edgar Cayce reading 1722-1

Rosemary's yearly vision quest was only three weeks away, and she was beginning to focus on issues for which she wanted guidance.

Vision questing had become an annual event for her, and over the years she had developed a ritual that met her needs. Prior to her three days alone, she would go through a three-day apple diet. Then she would pack her Bible, two or three other inspirational books, and a few clothes in a suitcase. After a two- or three-hour drive she would arrive at the site she had selected.

Spending the next three days alone, she would meditate and pray for guidance on current issues. She would try to re-focus her ideals. She watched her dreams closely, many times waking up two or three times a night and writing down notes. She never failed to get images that addressed her concerns. When she returned home, she would share her thoughts and dreams with her husband to get his insights.

This ritual has become an important way for Rosemary to get a sense of her ideals, goals, and directions for the year.

APPLICATION: Do what you need to do to find time to reflect on your ideals and direction in life.

Using, Not Abusing

Know yourself and your ideal—spiritually, mentally, and physically.   Based on Edgar Cayce reading 2487-2

Max had struggled in his life with the appetites of human nature and with desires of the flesh—the use of material goods as well as sexual issues. He didn't find helpful the moralistic views that denied the value of these desires, and he didn't like the idea of "if it feels good do it" either.

In the Edgar Cayce readings he found a balance that helped him make decisions. These readings didn't call him to deny himself completely some of the material things that bring pleasure to life, but—on the other hand—they warned him not to be self-indulgent or overly materialistic.

Learning to affirm all the positive aspects of this material world, Max realized that desires had their place in his experience. He made it his aim to use these desires properly.

Seeking this balance has become Max's goal. He has tried to set spiritual, mental, and physical ideals and to act so that the physical and mental desires are spiritualized—meaning they are lived out according to high ideals. In this way the desires are not abused but used in their proper way.

APPLICATION: Look at how you are expressing physical and mental desires. If you are not expressing them according to your highest ideals, begin to change.

How to Catch a Cold

Keep the constructive mental attitude. Never resentments, for these create within the system secretions that are hard upon any circulation—especially a portion of the liver activity.

Based on Edgar Cayce reading 470-19

Do you ever wonder why you catch colds at unusual times of the year?

Clara read in the Edgar Cayce readings that negative attitudes have a negative impact upon the body. According to the readings, these attitudes affect the liver, creating a toxicity by causing an overacid condition which can make one susceptible to diseases like a cold. Clara found this difficult to believe until she experienced it.

One summer she found herself coming down with a cold. She looked at her life and realized neither the weather nor her sleep patterns nor her eating habits seemed to be able to account for this. So she examined her inner life.

She realized she had been in a "slow burn" over a situation she was hanging onto and not resolving, and she'd been carrying some resentment toward another person as a result. After she resolved the situation, her cold symptoms went away.

Now when Clara begins to be bothered by resentments, she either resolves them or focuses her mind on positive attitudes until the situation can be handled in a more constructive way.

APPLICATION: Think of a resentment that you are hanging onto and take a step to resolve the situation.

Being Transparent

This is the attitude for a soul to take: The surrender of self that self may be a channel of blessings, not to any force or source but to God, for the Creative Forces to manifest through.   Based on Edgar Cayce reading 488-6

Bill remembered seeing a documentary on Mother Teresa of Calcutta and Dom Helder Camara, an archbishop in Brazil. They appeared together for the international press during a conference they were attending. As they walked in with all the cameras on them and surrounded by reporters, Bill was astonished at the radiant glow that seemed to surround them. He could feel the love, the warmth, the presence of God emanate from that film.

He learned later that these two had shared some thoughts together just before that appearance. Mother Teresa was concerned about her ego being caught up in the glitz and publicity that accompanied this kind of international coverage. She expressed her concern to Dom Helder and asked how she could protect herself.

Dom Helder said that every time he found himself in a situation where his ego might become too involved, he would pray, "God, make me transparent." In other words, he would pray for the power to put his ego out of the way and let God shine through.

They walked into the press gathering with these words on their minds. On film months later Bill could still see God shining through the transparent, loving beings who faced those cameras.

APPLICATION: The next time you feel your ego in the way of your being a channel through whom God can work, say to yourself, "God, make me transparent."

What Is God?

Love one another and thus fulfill the law of God, for God is love.   Based on Edgar Cayce reading 524-1

Sylvia was dissatisfied with the image of God with which she had been raised. She began asking questions and searching for other ideas about God, and finally found one that spoke about love being the primary quality of God. She liked this thought and her relationship to God changed because of it.

When she got married and her children began asking about God, she would talk about God in terms of love, in terms of God caring for each child, and in terms of God wanting to have a close relationship to each person. In their mealtime prayers the family would also include ideas like learning how to love each other better and how to share and help others.

She believes her children have a much more positive concept of God than she was raised with and a feeling that God is close to them and really does care for them.

APPLICATION: Do something that tells another person what God is to you.

A Time to Unite

Though there may be many approaches, cooperation in the activities brings the harmony of the universal activity.

Based on Edgar Cayce reading 1297-1

This was not going to work. The staff was pulling in at least three different directions. Diversity of opinion was welcomed for a while, but now Debbie knew it was time for everyone to unite. They all had a common ideal and a common goal, now they needed a common plan of action.

Sometimes, particularly after a heated meeting like the one they had just had, Debbie wondered if it wouldn't be a lot smoother if they all had the same astrological sign or were matched by personality tests. However, she quickly reminded herself that the team would be highly unbalanced. The organization might end up with a staff that was one extreme or the other — too practical or too imaginative. The organization needed all types of people in order to have good, creative tension and a meshing of ideas.

But there came a time in the decision-making process when the staff had to agree upon a process for implementing an idea, even if the process were not the first choice of some. There came a time when the diversity had to unite behind a unity of effort if the team wanted to accomplish its goal.

APPLICATION: Point to an area of your life where diversity is preventing something from getting done. Do something to move the people involved toward unity.

When People Are Ready

It is necessary that patience be exercised so that you may know the hope, the knowledge, the understanding of God's ways in the earth.   Based on Edgar Cayce reading 262-26

After college Arthur spent time rather aimlessly going back and forth from California to Missouri looking for jobs. During one of his visits in Missouri some friends introduced him to *There Is a River*, the biography of Edgar Cayce. Some incidents in the book spoke to his life experience, so he did more reading. For six months he read Edgar Cayce books and put his world view together.

His newly found understanding and the sense of purpose he was discovering excited him, and he became a zealot. He assumed that if everyone knew about this material, they would find the answers to their questions. Whenever he talked with people, he talked about the Cayce material. He was angered and disappointed to discover that some people didn't find the ideas exciting and didn't want to listen to him.

After several months of this fanaticism, he finally realized that he had to let others be and follow his own journey. The Cayce material had come to him when he was ready. It would come to others if they needed it, or they would find their answers in another way.

APPLICATION: When you find answers to your questions, don't force others to accept your answers as if they were their answers.

Serving God from the Heart

Where shortcomings do exist in the experience, those who are wise use same as stepping-stones to real development, for less and less of self and more and more that the body, the mind may be used as a channel for the glorifying of God on earth.

Based on Edgar Cayce reading 1150-1

For twelve years Rabbi David did penance. He fasted regularly and followed rigid disciplines. However, feeling he still lacked something, he went to a rabbi who was called the healer of souls.

This rabbi shook hands with all his guests except Rabbi David. From him he turned away. Rabbi David was so hurt that he left. He thought about it and decided the master must have mistaken him for someone else, so he returned that evening. The same thing happened. So he left and wept and decided not to return to the rabbi's house.

But when the time came for the evening meal at which the rabbi would teach, Rabbi David could not resist and crept up to the window to listen.

The master began, "People often come to me for healing. Some have fasted for as long as twelve years and feel themselves worthy to receive the holy spirit. They come to me to find what little they lack in order to bring the spirit on them. The truth is that all their pains are as nought. Their service did not rise to God but to the idol of their pride. Such people must turn from what they have been doing and begin to serve from the bottom up with a truthful heart."

Rabbi David heard these words. Weeping, he entered the rabbi's house where he was greeted warmly and with open arms.

APPLICATION: Correct your shortcomings to glorify God and not to glorify yourself.

Suicide and Forgiveness

When you condemn, so are you condemned. As you forgive, so are you forgiven.   Based on Edgar Cayce reading 3457-1

When Carol awoke, she could vividly see the scene from her dream. Her father had been standing at a sink taking some pills. The dream had confused her, so she spent time talking with other people, trying to figure out what it meant.

A few weeks later as she was coming back from a walk on the beach, a lady tried to give her a booklet on bereavement. Carol told the lady she didn't need it. The lady insisted she did. Carol said she didn't and didn't take it. Two days later her father committed suicide.

Carol received much-needed support from friends at that time. Given her conservative church background which considered suicide an unpardonable sin, she's not sure she could have pulled through without that support from her friends.

One of the most helpful ideas she received was a forty-day forgiveness prayer for her father and herself. Even though she didn't understand her father's actions, she was to pray for forgiveness for him and for herself. This was a real catharsis. It helped her to let go and not continue to blame him or anyone else for what happened.

APPLICATION: The next time you are faced with a personal tragedy you don't understand, try saying a forgiveness prayer for yourself and the other people involved.

Tell Your Story

Keep ever in that attitude that in your service something is given out that arouses helpful hopefulness in the experience of the individual or group you would help.

Based on Edgar Cayce reading 887-3

Denise moved to upstate New York in the late '60s. Shortly after her move, *The Sleeping Prophet*, an Edgar Cayce biography, was published. A reporter in the area found out that Denise's experiences using Cayce treatments after an accident were related in that book. He wrote several articles about her in the local newspaper. As a result she experienced a number of very interesting discussions and responses to her presence in the community.

One day, sounding a bit panicky, she called her mother. A couple was coming out to see her in a short while. Their daughter had multiple sclerosis, and they wished to talk to her about the Cayce concepts. Denise wanted to know what to tell them since she didn't feel like an expert on the readings.

Her mother told Denise that all she had to do was tell them the readings did exist and that she knew the people involved. Most important, she was just to tell her own story because she could testify to the truth of her life.

When the couple arrived, Denise told her story and answered questions as best she could. Afterward the couple thanked her for giving them hope of finding a way to help their daughter.

APPLICATION: At the next appropriate time, tell your story of how you found hope in your life so others may find renewed hope.

Healing Comes from Within

Know that all strength, all healing of every nature is the changing of the vibrations from within—the attuning of the Divine within the living tissue of a body to Creative Energies. Whether it is accomplished by use of drugs or the knife, it is the attuning of the living cellular force to its spiritual heritage. Based on Edgar Cayce reading 1967-1

Pauline firmly believed that no one healed anyone else, that all healing comes from within, so it is there for people to claim. Knowing this, she did everything she could to keep herself healthy and attuned to the Creative Forces. She followed a healthful diet, exercised daily, got six to seven hours of sleep each night, and maintained a daily meditation routine.

All this did not mean that she avoided outside help when it was needed. She had learned not to be fanatical about ways of staying well. She used to try to fight off illnesses without medication. However, after battling an episode of strep throat for several days she knew she needed help. She took the penicillin and then continued to do what she needed to do with diet and rest.

This experience had taught her that at times she needed outside incentives to help re-attune herself. However, she had to view those aids as just that—as outside helps to assist her body to re-attune so that the body could heal itself.

APPLICATION: Diet, meditation, and willpower are not always enough when fighting an illness. The next time you are ill, be open to whatever can help the body heal itself.

God's Power for Life

In humanity's experience there come those periods of doubt and fear and of the loss of hope. Then to all there should be the reminding of that Easter morn.

Based on Edgar Cayce reading 5749-13

Although it was spring, on this morning the air was filled with death. Mary's hopes and the hopes of many of her friends had been destroyed two days ago when their teacher and friend Jesus had been crucified. Walking to the tomb to complete His burial, she was filled with despair.

When she heard a cry from one of the women in front of her, she at first could not understand what the woman was saying. But as her eyes followed the woman's pointing finger, she saw that the stone covering the entrance to the tomb had been rolled away. Running ahead of the others, she entered the grave first and saw that the body was gone.

As the others ran back to the city to report the theft, Mary knelt outside the tomb and wept. When she felt a presence beside her, she assumed it was the gardener. Through her tears she asked about the body of her master.

Only when she heard a voice speak her name the way no other voice could say it, did she look closely at the figure in front of her. Then, filled with amazement, she uttered the only word that would come to her, "Master."

A few seconds later she, too, was running back to the city, but she carried a message much different than the one the other women had carried. Hers was filled with joy and the power of God that had just made her whole world come alive in a new way.

APPLICATION: The next time you feel saddened and defeated, be alert for God's surprising power to bring new life.

Loving God Where You Are

Whether in home, in the street, in the marketplace—these are but channels or places or opportunities where one may apply the law, "You shall love the Lord your God with all your heart, your soul, your body, and your neighbor as yourself."

Based on Edgar Cayce reading 524-2

Sandra, a young woman in a church group, walked excitedly into her pastor's office one day and announced she was going to seminary to become a minister. She and her pastor discussed what was involved and how she should prepare herself in college. However, in his closing remarks, he said that she didn't need to go to seminary and be ordained in order to become a minister. She could minister to people in whatever occupation she chose.

Eventually Sandra chose secretarial school. She has found plenty of opportunity to minister to people. Her sensitivity to others allows her to respond to their needs. Thus she expresses God's love for them at times and in places where they don't expect to find it.

APPLICATION: Regardless of the job you have, express God's love for others by the way you treat them.

God's Abiding Presence

*God keeps the conditions such that an individual soul may—
if it will but meet or look within—find indeed God's presence
abiding ever.* Based on Edgar Cayce reading 518-2

Peter has always found God to be an abiding presence. In his meditation he feels that God's nearness comforts and sustains him. At other times he has felt God as a friend, a companion, a support structure around him.

However, at the transition moments in Peter's life is when this sense of presence has been most helpful. He remembers at the close of his college years when he was job hunting and getting away from the security of school life that God felt very near.

Peter remembers the days he was giving up one career and beginning another. That was scary. What if the move didn't work out? What if he and his wife couldn't find jobs right away? All these fears could have prevented them from moving, even though they had both lost their enthusiasm for their former careers. During this time, though, both he and his wife felt God surrounding them, giving them courage and support.

This presence of God has given them a foundation and a touchstone and a constant feeling of "It's going to be fine. I am with you."

APPLICATION: The next time you feel worried, distraught or alone affirm that God's presence abides forever.

The Difficulty of Waiting

Know that God's ways are not past finding out. Be not in the shadow of doubt and fear. Know that in God's time and way the desires of your heart—that are in accord with the divine way—will be brought to pass in your experience.

Based on Edgar Cayce reading 262-53

In the midst of a job transition Marcia decided to move to Virginia Beach. She had been offered work all across the country but felt that the Beach was the place she should go. Unfortunately there were no job offers in that area. Still she felt so strongly about the place that she moved there without a job. She believed she would be led to the right position within a few days—or a few weeks at the most.

After several weeks, job possibilities did begin to open up. Marcia went to several interviews, but none of them seemed right. One possibility after another all turned out to be big disappointments when she would look into the details of the job or see the work place.

Those weeks became one month, then two months. She felt frustrated and wondered why the process was taking so long as she was trying to be open to God's guidance.

Then, one big offer came her way. She was hesitant at first. It was a position usually offered to someone with two or three years more experience than she. She felt overwhelmed. However, after meditating on it and talking with several people, she felt this was what God wanted. She took it—with a bit of fear and trembling.

She feels God has been with her since she began that job and believes this is where she is supposed to be.

APPLICATION: Think of a place in your life where you are still awaiting God's way or will. Affirm again that in time you will be shown the way.

The Way of the Cross

The way of the cross is not easy, yet it is the tuneful, the rhythmic, the beautiful, the lovely way.

Based on Edgar Cayce reading 1089-6

This mother's story tells of the way of the cross, which is to do as Jesus did—receive the anger and hatred of the world, transform it, and return love.

The year before Anna's son, Paul, gave up drugs was one of the most painful ones of her life. For long, lonely months Paul lived in a world of hostility and depression.

One afternoon he was sitting in the kitchen when she walked in. Before she could say anything, he went into a tirade and unleashed all his anger and hatred at her. He accused her of ruining his life and said she was filled with ugliness.

At that moment Anna gathered up all the love she could. She felt his anger flow toward her and prayed that she could be a channel for God's love to flow back to her son.

Finally after 10 or 15 minutes he stopped. He paused. Then he said, "What I said isn't true. All the ugly things I see are part of me."

Anna knew her son had just taken a big step because he had admitted his own responsibility for something.

Paul's return to full life was not immediate or without troubles, but it was steady. In all those days it was the transforming power of God's love that enabled Anna to be there with him.

APPLICATION: Next time undeserved anger or hatred is directed at you, call upon God's transforming power which can enable you to receive anger and return love.

Guidance in Visions

In visions there is often the interbetween giving expressions that make for an awakening between what has been turned over and over in the mind and what the self holds as its ideal.
Based on Edgar Cayce reading 262-9

Carla had entered a graduate degree program in hospital administration. Even though this position wasn't her ultimate career goal, her inner voice had said she should do this.

When her third year began, she needed supervised work in some institution as part of her studies. She talked to one professor about her rather vague career ideas. He suggested gerontology—long-term care for the elderly.

Only one facility, a nursing home, would take student interns. She applied there as well as at another hospital because she wasn't sure she would be accepted at the home. She received an offer from the hospital but also visited the nursing care facility before making her final decision.

While touring the home, she had a psychic vision. She began seeing people's auras and spiritual bodies. Some of these spiritual bodies seemed partially outside the physical bodies. She didn't understand what that meant.

As she meditated on this experience later, she realized she was seeing people in transition from this life to the life beyond. She realized then how important it was for these people to have good care so that the transition could be made as easily and as comfortably as possible.

She chose the long-term care facility for the elderly and has not regretted that decision.

APPLICATION: The next time you have a major decision to make, look to God to give you guidance as you go about your daily life.

The Universal Oneness

All concepts of the worship of the Law of One arise from the same emotions—the seeking to be at one with the Creative Forces.   Based on Edgar Cayce reading 1857-2

Diane loved to talk about her world travels, especially her visits to religious sites.   In the Middle East she worshiped in Muslim mosques, in Israel in a Jewish synagogue, in China in both Christian churches and Buddhist temples, and in Japan in Shinto temples. In the Buddhist temples she actually got down on her knees like the worshipers around her, as if this posture were the natural one for her to take.

In England she happened to be riding on a train with several nuns. They began a conversation, and she discovered they worked in a hospital and were also involved in healing people as she was.

In all those experiences she felt comfortable and at home.   In all places and with all religious people she met, she sensed a oneness of purpose even though their external forms of worship varied immensely.

Her experience has convinced her that the Spirit of the one living God is indeed the source behind all the varieties of worship and religious expression she has witnessed.

APPLICATION: Look beneath the surface of another person's religious practices and see what that individual is really trying to express with those practices.

Choosing Growth

Q. Would a separation of any sort be helpful?
A. This must be a choice within self. Self's own development
is in jeopardy. Choose.   Based on Edgar Cayce reading 845-4

Rosemary's marriage had been ending for at least two years. She and her husband were fighting constantly. As a result of the counseling she was getting, she wanted to change how she related to people and change her goals for her life. However, her husband didn't approve of her new plans and resisted her efforts. Finally, she filed for divorce.

When the divorce was granted, she experienced a variety of mixed feelings. A part of her was relieved. She could now begin a new life. The other part of her felt as if she had failed. She wondered if she had not tried hard enough, if part of her lesson in life was her marriage and thus she should have stayed with it.

Almost two years later she began reading the Edgar Cayce readings. She found many instances where he told people to work on problems and not run away from them. However, she also found times when he spoke about the need for a marriage to break up if the relationship had become so stifling that people could no longer grow in it.

Reading these words reassured her that she had tried her best, but she had needed the divorce in order to allow space for both her and her husband to grow in new ways.

APPLICATION: Where in your life are you being stifled and can no longer grow? Take a step to find a new way to grow.

A Trip to Hell

Opportunity depends upon the use of it. Every experience and condition are useful experiences, and these are either made as stumbling blocks or as stepping-stones.

Based on Edgar Cayce reading 1424-2

A woman had a dream in which a wise man came and told her she could see anything in the world that she desired. She decided she really didn't know what heaven and hell were like, so she asked to see these places.

Immediately she was conducted down below to a large banquet room. Long tables were piled high with food and the aroma was magnificent. All the residents of hell were seated at the table with fork in hand. They looked like normal people except that their arms no longer had elbows and so couldn't bend. Even though the food was there, they could not put their forks into their mouths. The cries of frustration and anger were intense.

Suddenly the woman was transported to heaven. Strangely enough, she found herself in a similar banquet hall. The tables were also piled high with food and a magnificent aroma filled the room. As she looked, she saw that the people were in the same condition as in hell. They sat with fork in hand and had no elbows in their stiffened arms. But instead of crying out in anger, the people were singing and laughing. These people were busy feeding each other across the table.

APPLICATION: Where does your life appear to be a bit of hell? Take a step to change it into a bit of heaven.

Facing Life Together

In putting into practice what you know to do, in being led by what has been given to you, your contributions may aid others who seek to know God's presence and the harmony, the peace that comes with abiding in God.

Based on Edgar Cayce reading 262-33

For Cullen it was more than just a coincidental set of circumstances.

He had been involved in a weekly discussion group for only three months when he received an injury that required several months of slow recovery. The group was very supportive and helped him through some discouraging days.

While he was recovering, one of the women in the group was suddenly deserted by her husband. She had two teenage boys to raise and now had to get a job. This meant finding someone to take care of the boys after school until she got home from work.

Cullen helped her find a house not too far from his. The boys came to his home after school because he was well enough to be out of the hospital but still unable to go back to work. The boys gave him the company he needed at that point in his life, and he could be a father to them.

Later they took trips together. They grew with each other during those years and have maintained their relationship with each other to the present day.

Cullen believes that they each had to face these disruptions, which occurred at the same time so that each could give the other the courage to face what they all had to face, together.

APPLICATION: Find a way to get the support you need and then give your encouragement to someone else.

Right-Brain Decision Making

Ask self in your conscious self, "Shall I do this or not?" The voice will answer within. Then meditate. Ask the same, Yes or No. You may be very sure if your conscious self and divine self are in accord, you are truly in the activity indicated.
Based on Edgar Cayce reading 2072-14

William discovered that in his business, using only analytical decision making didn't give him the insights he wanted. After some searching, he found another approach that gave him new and unexpected insights.

This technique involved a meditation exercise. When William was faced with a series of options with none of them standing out as best for the moment, he thought a bit and made a tentative decision. Then he meditated and took that answer into his meditation. He listened for a response from within to see if the decision felt right or if something came up in meditation to imply that the decision was not the best one.

If it felt wrong, he made another decision and repeated the process.

Sometimes even if the decision felt right, he would double-check. He would temporarily assume the opposite stance to see if this second decision felt wrong during the meditation exercise.

William struggled with this process because it went against his usual analytical thinking. However, when he took time to use it and trust the results, he found it helpful.

APPLICATION: When making your next major decision, pause and try the exercise mentioned in the story.

Prayer and Relationships

Pray about it, for you may be given that which may be help-ful. But apply it and seek to use your abilities in constructive ways with your associates.

Based on Edgar Cayce reading 5732-1

Debbie and Nancy found themselves together in a church study group. They took an immediate dislike to one another and didn't know why. For a while neither of them said a word to the other.

When the group was told to divide into prayer partners, Debbie for some unexplainable reason approached Nancy and suggested they be partners. Nancy said no because she felt that Debbie didn't like her at all. In fact, she was think-ing of quitting the group because Debbie was there. Strangely enough, Debbie had also considered quitting.

A few days later in meditation, Debbie picked up a feel-ing that in a past life her child's death had somehow been caused by Nancy. She prayed about that and immediately felt that a portion of the dislike and hatred had lifted from her.

Some weeks later the two women were with each other during a church session. They prayed together, then both felt the tension between them lessen.

They are still not good friends, yet they are able to attend the same church study group and be in the same room with each other now without feeling any antagonism.

APPLICATION: Choose a difficult relationship with some-one. Take steps to work with that person and continue to pray about the difficulty.

The Turn Around

The errors become as stumbling stones to be turned into step-ping-stones, into those characters and ways as are the more perfect.   Based on Edgar Cayce reading 843-9

It was in an upper room when Peter made the biggest promise of his life. "My Lord, I will never leave You, regardless of what others may do."

Jesus, admiring the spirit but also understanding human frailty, prepared Peter by saying, "Tonight, Peter, before you hear the rooster crow, you will deny you ever knew Me."

It was only a few hours later in a darkened courtyard outside the governor's house that Peter did a complete turn-around.

"You were with the man Jesus," accused one man.

"I was not," replied Peter.

"I know you were," said a woman.

"I say I wasn't," answered Peter.

"Your accent gives you away," stated a third.

"I don't even know this man Jesus," proclaimed Peter.

At that moment he heard the rooster crow. He turned and stared straight into the eyes of Jesus who was standing on the balcony. Peter felt nothing but shame and fled.

Later on when he realized the eyes staring back at him had reflected only loving understanding, he turned around again. Less than two months later he found himself in the center of Jerusalem, telling a crowd of several thousand people the story of this great man of love.

APPLICATION: Name something in your life for which you still feel guilt and shame. Now look into those eyes of loving understanding and release the guilt.

Pain from the Past

*Overcome that fear and dread in yourself. That is the karma.
That is what is to be conquered in yourself, for this applies to
the soul in its secular, physical, mental, and spiritual body.*
Based on Edgar Cayce reading 2842-2

Visiting China sent shivers down Anne's spine at times.
Some of the sites felt familiar, and some of them felt like
home. So when her leg problems started up, she couldn't
understand why. As she struggled with the pain during the
trip, she kept getting the feeling of being in a pattern she
couldn't escape. She felt stifled.

One morning as she awoke, she found herself half
dreaming of a previous lifetime. She remembered living in
China when a paralyzing fear had been a part of her life.

At that time she had been a second son in a family. In
that era of history it was the first son who got all the attention and all the encouragement. As that second son, she was
well taken care of but frustrated at being unable to do anything. She could feel this son's resentment and desire to
break away and also the opposite tugs of security; staying
with the family or "walking out of the house" and going to a
different part of China where he could start a new life.

She felt this second son had chosen to stay at home and
had not walked away because he feared moving forward.

Anne feels this is why her leg pains occur in her present
life. It's a reminder that she is facing a decision: whether or
not to move forward and take a chance or stay in a place of
security.

APPLICATION: Name an area of your life where you are
afraid to move forward or take a chance because of loss of
some security. Take one step to overcome that fear.

A Reason to Get Well

Would there be a definite plan, a definite goal with an ideal to be worked toward, then we may find quite a different attitude, quite a different condition develop for the physical and mental body. Based on Edgar Cayce reading 1000-10

Marilyn, who had been ill for two years, had been to many doctors and specialists. None of them could give an accurate diagnosis. However, as she lay in bed crying one night, she heard a voice inside her saying, "Know that I am with you."

Two days later her sister mentioned two books she had found helpful, *There Is a River* and *The Sleeping Prophet*. Marilyn didn't do anything about that comment at first, but three days later she was standing in line at the grocery store and happened to look at the book rack. There in front of her were both books. She decided this was a message, and she bought them. She started to read them and couldn't put them down. Then she began to read more books about Edgar Cayce.

One day in her reading she came upon an episode in which Edgar Cayce asked a man, "Why do you want to get well? Just so you can go out and live the same life you have been living?"

This made Marilyn think. Did she want to get well just to live for herself? Or did she want to live for God? She decided she wanted to live to do God's work on earth. This became her ideal throughout her healing and has remained her ideal since then.

APPLICATION: Ask yourself why you want to live. Examine your answer. Are you happy with your answer? If not, take one step today toward changing your answer.

Creating a Team

*Know that whatever there may be within yourself, that ability
is only lent you for what you may make of it—not to the glory
of yourself, but to the glory of God who gives all things to you.*
Based on Edgar Cayce reading 815-3

As part of his work, Nick manages people. He knows that he
has an ability to take people and incorporate them into an
already functioning team. However, Harold was a real challenge.

A member of one particular group, Harold refused to cooperate. For several weeks a constant tug of war had been
played out between them. So one night Nick sat down alone
to meditate on the situation. After a few minutes he realized
how personally he was taking this. No longer was the group
the central concern, but his concern had become his ego
which was determined to get Harold to cooperate.

Nick began changing his attitude. He focused on the
good of the group and not on the pride of his own ego. In a
few weeks Harold and the group were working well together.

From this exprience Nick realized that he couldn't worry
about his ego while trying to create a working team. He had
to set it aside and direct it toward a goal higher than himself.
This attitude applied whether he was managing people in
his business or organizing groups of people to work together.

APPLICATION: Do whatever you do for the glory of God and
not to glorify yourself. See if this changes your attitude toward groups with whom you are working.

Perfect Love

To express love in your activities to your neighbor is the greater service that a soul may give in this earthly sphere.
Based on Edgar Cayce reading 499-2

On each Day of Atonement a famous rabbi would recite the special prayer that recalled the service of the High Priest in the Temple in Jerusalem. However, in the middle of the prayer he would not say, "And thus he spoke," but instead he would say, "And thus I spoke." This rabbi had not forgotten the time when centuries ago his soul had been in the body of a High Priest in the Temple.

Once he told his followers, "Ten times I have walked in this earth. I have been a High Priest, a prince, a king. I have been ten different kinds of noblemen. But I never in all those times learned to love humanity perfectly. So this time I was sent forth to perfect my love. If I succeed, I will not need to return again."

APPLICATION: Do one thing to show you are learning how to express love for your neighbor or your family.

From Fainting to Nursing

Day by day is there shown the way. Hence the changes would be only greater determination in self to be used by the influences of the Infinite to become a channel of blessing to others.
Based on Edgar Cayce reading 423-2

The voice came so clearly that Nancy thought at first someone was speaking to her. However, she soon realized it was her inner voice that had said, "You are going to be a nurse and work here." Nancy was only a receptionist at the health care center. This was a dramatic change in direction, but inside the idea felt right.

She went home and told her husband. He asked her if she were sure of this. They both looked at the two elementary school-aged children and the one-year-old and thought about the child on the way. Nancy nodded, "Yes." She was certain.

The nursing profession was in her family, but her mother couldn't believe Nancy's new career plans. Nancy was the type who could faint by simply *reading* a medical textbook without seeing the pictures. When her children got cut, she often passed out and had to rely on some other adult to help.

However, she applied to nursing school shortly after the baby was born. The program received 500 applicants and she was one of the 50 selected for an accelerated two-year program.

She did very well and even orthopedic surgery didn't bother her.

APPLICATION: Name something you couldn't do earlier in life for whatever reason. If you have a reason for doing it now, give it a try and see what happens.

God in the Gym Class

Trust in God, not in self—and don't be afraid of other people or what they'll do! So live, so act, as to be able to meet what is said, thought, or done in any of the situations that may come about.   Based on Egar Cayce reading 5475-7

Jane began to feel connected to God because of experiences in physical education class in her sophomore year of high school. Her teacher was a former gymnast and demanded that her students be good at that sport, too. When they did not meet her expectations, she would criticize them in front of the whole class. Jane was not good at gymnastics and these criticisms hurt her deeply.

After suffering through this for several weeks, she told her mom what was going on. Her mom gave her a little prayer to say. As Jane got ready for gym and during class, she would occasionally say, "God give me the strength to handle this."

This affirmation calmed her and helped her handle the criticisms better. At the end of the semester it also gave her the courage to talk to the teacher privately. She told the teacher how much her criticisms hurt and that they didn't help her try harder at all. Her teacher apologized to her during that conversation.

Jane realized that the strength and courage she was now receiving came from a power higher than herself. Her life-long personal relationship with God had begun.

APPLICATION: God is ready to meet you in any situation in life—particularly in ones that are painful to you. Pray for the awareness of God's presence in one area of your life.

Facing Death

Death is separation. Yet it is but the birth into opportunities that—if they are embraced with the Christ, the Truth, as your guide—will bring joy and harmony into your experience.

Based on Edgar Cayce reading 1776-1

Patrick saw in Gladys a courageous woman, who had a strong conviction that life transcends what we call death and that souls continue to grow on the other side. The way she lived her last days on earth demonstrated this. Her example convinced Patrick that this belief can influence how a person lives the last days.

For six years Patrick had known Gladys Davis Turner, life-long secretary to Edgar Cayce. At one summer workshop his son John had sung "I'll Be Seeing You," a song that she particularly enjoyed.

One day Patrick received a call telling him that Gladys was in a coma and was not expected to live much longer. He decided to fly down to see her. First, he traced his son's hand on a piece of paper, then wrote the words to "I'll Be Seeing You" on it. He attached a rose to the paper and took them to give to Gladys.

The day he arrived Gladys was temporarily out of a coma. They talked and talked, and he presented her with his gift. While they continued their conversation, Patrick cried and kept Gladys busy finding tissues for him.

As he left, he turned to say good-bye once more and heard her singing to him, "I'll Be Seeing You."

Gladys passed on a few days later.

APPLICATION: The next time you are faced with the death of a loved one affirm that life goes on and that you will see this person again.

Dreams and Warnings

From the spiritual or divine there may come dreams that show that the higher forces are desirous of warning or aiding individuals in their activities.

Based on Edgar Cayce reading 257-138

Nancy's doctor was going away on vacation. Since she was still recovering from ear surgery, he gave her specific orders to keep water out of her ear for the next six weeks.

During his vacation Nancy needed a check-up. Doctor Williams was called in. He looked at her ear and said that everything was fine, so Nancy could resume her normal activities even though only three weeks had passed.

The night before this check-up, however, she had had a dream about Doctor Williams. She dreamed that the two of them were going uphill in a jeep. They had almost reached the top of the hill when the jeep slipped back and tipped over. The driver, Doctor Williams, blamed Nancy for the accident.

Because of this dream Nancy asked the nurse who had been in the room during the examination to refer her to another doctor. The nurse agreed to do so immediately.

The night before this appointment Nancy had another dream. She saw a newly tarred roof. However, one small white spot in the roof had not been covered completely.

The next day Doctor Peterson examined her ear and discovered that a tiny hole had developed in her eardrum. He immediately patched it up. However, if Nancy had resumed normal activities, she could easily have gotten water in her ear and the infection would have begun all over again.

APPLICATION: Begin to watch your dreams for clues to your physical health and well-being.

Turning Toward Love

Humble yourself that you may bring to the consciousness of others that love that is so near that only those who have turned their face the other way do not see or comprehend.
Based on Edgar Cayce reading 1401-1

A shepherd had lost a sheep. Only one sheep from a flock of a hundred. Yet the shepherd left the ninety-nine and went looking for the one stray. He looked until he saw, caught among the thorn bushes, that one frightened lamb.

This was Matthew's story. Matthew remembered his days as a proud tax collector when he lorded his power over his countrymen. Then he remembered those lonely nights when he sensed something was missing, but he was too afraid to tell anyone. So he used his pride-filled power even more forcefully to cover his fear and loneliness.

On the day when this storyteller, Jesus, walked across the courtyard to where Matthew was sitting, Matthew turned his head away and tried not to look. Then Jesus spoke only a few words, "Matthew, follow Me."

The words lifted Matthew's pride from his soul. The words brought Matthew back into the arms of the loving shepherd and into the humble service of spreading His love to others.

APPLICATION: Where in your life is pride separating you from others? Turn to the love of the One who can open your life to love.

The Importance of Unconditional Love

In love all life is given, in love all things move.
Based on Edgar Cayce reading 345-1

Anne was sitting with her mother listening to a lecture on parenting. The speaker had excellent insights into parent-child dynamics and especially highlighted certain parental behaviors that have long-range effects on children. As Anne's mother sat there, all she could think of was "What have I done to my kids?"

On their way home that night Anne was talking about what she planned to do differently with her children. Then she turned to her mother and thanked her for teaching her about unconditional love.

This surprised her mother, who began mentioning all the times she had done the negative things about which the lecturer had spoken.

After about a minute Anne interrupted her mother and said, "Mother, those instances aren't a thimblefull in comparison to the way you taught us unconditional love. Your example of nonjudgmental love overshadowed for me all the incidents you just mentioned."

APPLICATION: Begin to show unconditional love to someone about whom you care.

The Power Source

Jesus is the Friend that sees in the daily walks of life that the associations become opportunities to know that His promises are sure.
Based on Edgar Cayce reading 412-9

Jim had had a big argument with his boss. Then when he had arrived home and needed someone to talk to, he had learned that his wife was away for the evening. Now sitting in a chair and thinking, he felt very discouraged and depressed. He began to wonder about the wisdom of their recent move. He felt like a failure, as if his life wasn't going to amount to anything. He was worthless and that was that. Then the tears came.

After several minutes of crying, Jim remembered a reverie a friend had introduced him to: "Letter from Jesus."(See January 17.) He took himself through that reverie. The letter he wrote at the end encouraged him, gave him hope, and urged him to be patient. He felt better when he finished the letter, but he also felt incomplete. He needed to do something else but didn't know what.

Then he saw his guitar. He picked it up and began playing. He had played for many years and could play well. However, he always played other people's music and had never felt creative enough to write his own songs. Yet, in a few minutes he found himself playing a new tune and writing words that expressed his new-found hope and light in the midst of darkness. In his moment of despair a new creativity had emerged because he had turned to a greater source of power than himself.

APPLICATION: In joy, in sorrow you can seek Jesus for a Friend. Try this the next time you need a friend.

Listening to the Inner Voice

Depend more upon the intuitive forces from within. Do not harken so much to that of outside influences but learn to listen to that still small voice from within.

Based on Edgar Cayce reading 239-1

Where can you go to find help in making life-changing decisions?

This career decision was not an easy one for Maria to make. She had two options that attracted her. For several months she had been investigating the amount of schooling each would demand. She had researched the future of both jobs as far as potential income and demand for service in that field. She had spoken with professionals in those fields and friends whom she trusted to give good guidance. She had even consulted a couple of psychics and her astrological chart. The end result was confusion and indecision. Neither option stuck out as being "the right one."

Finally Maria realized that through all this she had not meditated on the issue. So, after several meditations for guidance, she clearly picked one option as best for her. After that inner feeling emerged, all the external information she had received took its proper place and fit together into a coherent picture.

She followed this inner voice and is now successfully and happily pursuing that career.

APPLICATION: Pick one decision you are trying to make. Take it into your meditations over the next several days and try to attune yourself to what your inner voice is telling you.

Honesty in Relationships

Virtues can be misplaced, misused.

Based on Edgar Cayce reading 3178-1

Marian was getting upset even if Anne wasn't. Ironically it was Anne who should be upset. Marian had just told her what decision to make and knew immediately she had gone too far. But there was Anne, sitting calmly and smiling just as she always did in situations like these.

This particular part of Anne's personality really bothered Marian. She agreed with Anne that people should emphasize positive thinking in dealing with others. However, in cases like these, she felt Anne was being dishonest with her and with their relationship by not showing her angry feelings.

Marian knew that Anne would very shortly be involved in behind-the-scenes, passive-aggressive behavior that was venting the anger she would not consciously express. This made Marian feel that their relationship was superficial and trivial because Anne, always so positive, did not give honest feedback.

Marian knew that most people were not positive enough in their lives, but she also had learned the value of reacting honestly in relationships she really valued.

APPLICATION: Choose a situation in which positive words are hiding feelings that you need to acknowledge to the other person. Do something to begin expressing those feelings.

A Reverence for Life

God seeks all to be one with the Divine, and all things were made by the Creator. That which is the creative influence in every herb, every mineral, every vegetable, every individual activity, is that same force you call God—and seeks expression!   Based on Edgar Cayce reading 294-202

Dr. Albert Schweitzer taught throughout his time on earth a reverence for all life. One day while clearing underbrush with a native near an African village, a harmless tree frog was spotted. The native raised his machete to continue hacking away, prepared to kill the frog if it didn't jump away quickly enough. Dr. Schweitzer saw the frog and ordered the man to stop. He then rustled the vines so that the frog jumped away to safety.

The native was upset and confused. Dr. Schweitzer calmly explained to the man that this frog was a part of God's creation just like he was. The frog had life, which should be valued like all human life. After a few minutes, the two men continued to work, the native appearing unmoved by anything the doctor had said.

A few weeks later Dr. Schweitzer, this same native, and several others were digging post holes to build a stockade for the animals of the village. As two men raised a heavy log to drop it into a hole, this native called out, "Stop!"

He then knelt down and reached into the hole. Lifting out a small lizard, he set it on the ground and watched it run safely into the forest.

APPLICATION: Look at a part of nature to which you never felt especially close. Treat it with the same reverence for life with which you treat someone you love.

A Chief with No Power

Keep to attitudes of helpful hopefulness so that the opportunities given may be used in service to others.
Based on Edgar Cayce reading 849-25

When Susan first began work at the clinic, a psychic told her that one day she would be offered the position of head nurse. When that opportunity came, she was to take the job. She thought this prediction was not likely to happen but remembered the advice.

Within a couple of years the job was hers. However, she discovered she had all the responsibility but no power. At that time the clinic had just started experimenting with a team-management approach. The doctor and other senior staff members now made all the decisions that previously head nurses had made. Susan, however, had the responsibility to carry out those decisions. It was a frustrating situation but a good learning experience.

Susan knew she tended to be blunt and speak her mind. She also knew she could at times be authoritarian. Having to carry out decisions others had made taught her to modify her bluntness, do what was asked, and be a servant leader.

APPLICATION: Name a situation in your life—at work, in the community or at home—where you have considerable responsibility but sometimes lack power or authority to make changes. Ask yourself what you are learning from the situation.

Another Day, Another House

Whoever would be the greatest among people will be the servant of others. Learn what that means in life, and the life will be worthwhile. Based on Edgar Cayce reading 4185-3

After working with a particular family for almost three months, real estate agent Paul had lost track of how many houses he had shown them. The pattern was predictable by now. If the wife liked it, the husband would find something wrong with the basement. If the husband liked it, the wife would find something wrong with the kitchen. If the husband and wife were somewhat satisfied, their children would complain about the lack of room.

The one house that they all had liked had a price that was more than they wanted to pay even though they could afford it. They made an offer that Paul knew would not be accepted. Instead of responding to the owner's counter offer, the family decided to keep looking.

One thought had gotten Paul through these weeks. He had learned that when there is this much conflict, a family really needs to find the right home or it will not be happy. This family needed patient help to find that home.

At a time like this he needed to put his ego aside and find a neutral spot within where he could be open to listening and receiving a family's needs. He needed to be caring and patient. If he himself were in this situation, he would want the same treatment, so he was willing to be patient with this family. Two months later the right house was located.

APPLICATION: The next time that people you work with begin to try your patience, attempt to find a neutral spot within to listen and be receptive to what they need.

Following Your Dreams

A dream is but attuning an individual mind to those store-houses of experience that have been set in motion.

Based on Edgar Cayce reading 262-83

Carl is convinced that he has found a great way to gain new insights into decisions he has to make at work. Last year he had three companies bid on a project. All three were within a few thousand dollars of each other, and all had good reputations. He didn't know which one to choose. Then one night he had two dreams that he felt clearly guided him to one of the companies. He chose that company and was pleased with the results.

Following that experience he began to pay closer attention to his dreams. If he found two or three dreams leading him in one direction, he used these insights along with his analysis of the situation to help him make a decision.

Recently he had to decide whether or not to begin negotiating with a firm for a major building addition. Several dreams lent themselves to an interpretation he didn't like. His rational mind was taking him in another direction so this time he did not follow his dreams. Three months later he discovered that many months of work could have been better spent if he had listened to these dreams more closely.

Carl still struggles with the question of exactly how much he should depend upon dreams for guidance, but he is rapidly learning that they do provide accurate insights into decisions he has to make.

APPLICATION: The next time you have a decision to make, watch your dreams for several nights and see if you get any insights from them.

God Won't Force It

Behold I stand at the door of your heart, of your mind, of your consciousness, and knock. If you will open, I will enter and abide with you. Based on Edgar Cayce reading 3051-2

Talking with His disciples one day, Jesus told a story. A man went out to sow some seed. Some of the seed fell on the hard path where the birds immediately flew down, picked it up in their beaks, and ate it.

Some of the seed fell on soil that was rocky. It began to grow but did not have enough good soil. So it died. Some of the seed fell on good soil, but weeds were also in that soil. The seed grew up, but so did the weeds. Soon the weeds took up most of the space and choked out the seed.

Lastly some of the seed fell on good fertile soil where it grew and produced a good harvest.

Explaining this story to His followers, He said, "There are many messages in a story like this one. One of them is that God can't force a seed to grow and produce a harvest when the ground isn't open and prepared to receive the seed."

APPLICATION: Name a part of your life that needs to be more open to receiving God's seed. Take a step to open that part of your life to God.

The Victory

There are no shortcuts to knowledge, to wisdom, to understanding—these must be lived, must be experienced by each and every soul. Based on Edgar Cayce reading 830-2

It was finally over. For years they had struggled together, gone from surgery to surgery and doctor to doctor. But to no avail. In the end the cancer was too strong.

Now Evie was alone. John had died and she could not help but feel beaten. They had tried so many treatments. Medical research had made so many strides and helped so many people, why couldn't John have been one of them.

For several months following his death, she lived without enthusiasm for life. Finally Evie decided to visit a well-known psychic and share her feelings about being beaten and John's having lost his battle for life.

The psychic's impressions were different. She suggested that John's soul needed to learn faith, courage, and patience, and that John had chosen this illness as a means to gain those insights. Having completed this task and having learned these qualities, he now felt that his soul's purpose was completed. The psychic stated that John's death was not a defeat, but the final step that brought the lesson for this life to an end. She asked Evie to rejoice in his victory.

It took several months for Evie to accept this idea. But she felt a great release and surge of new desire for life when she woke up one day and could affirm John's way of death as the right conclusion to his life.

APPLICATION: The next time you are tempted to view death as a defeat, see if you can view it as the end of the lesson for this lifetime.

That's Not My Job

Know your ideal, then ask not as to what others are to do for you as the ideal—but what you would do for others.

Based on Edgar Cayce reading 1977-1

One division of the company for whom Tom worked was involved in selling mail-order books. When Tom had been hired as general manager of the business, he had consulted with others on a shipping policy. They had decided that service to the customer was their ideal. Their way of implementing that was to make sure every order was processed within three days.

Under normal conditions the regular shipping department had no problem meeting this deadline. However, at certain times, like before Christmas, orders were heavier than usual. This meant either delays in processing or getting extra help in the shipping department.

So Tom for the past two days had left his desk and was in the shipping department picking books off shelves and placing them with an order form. This freed up other workers to stuff the orders in envelopes, stamp the envelopes, and get them mailed out on time.

To some people it seemed strange to have a general manager pulling books off shelves. However, to Tom and his colleagues in management this was a natural response to their ideal of service.

APPLICATION: Living up to ideals sometimes means doing jobs one normally wouldn't do. The next time a job needs doing that isn't part of your normal responsibility, think about your ideals as you decide whether to help do it or not.

The Prophetic Dream

For life and death are one, and only those who will consider the experience as one may come to understand or comprehend what peace indeed means.

Based on Edgar Cayce reading 2399-1

Although Cindy didn't realize it, the dream she had just written down would become a reality within a month.

She dreamed she had been called home because something was wrong. She thought about her grandmother. When she arrived at her grandmother's house, she was fine. Then she went to her home. She was greeted by Grandpa Ed who had died five years ago. He looked well, and she asked why he was here. He said he had come to get her Grandpa John.

Cindy wanted to run back to get her grandmother, but Grandpa Ed said it was not her time yet. However, Grandpa John had to come now. Otherwise, he would not have another chance for five years. Then he would be in a nursing home.

Together they went in to see Grandpa John who was sleeping peacefully in his bed. There the dream ended.

The next week she was visiting her mother and told her about the dream. Three weeks later she received a call to come home. Her Grandpa John had died suddenly.

She felt sad, but she also knew Grandpa Ed had been there to meet him and help him through the transition.

APPLICATION: The next time you dream about a significant event happening to someone you know, write it down and see if it does happen.

Moving Through Hardships

Individuals have hardships or surroundings that are over-powering, overwhelming. If these are held on to as crosses, they will remain as crosses. If they are met with the spirit of truth and right in their own selves, they should create joy for that is what will be built. Based on Edgar Cayce reading 552-2

Every Sabbath the rabbi would dance before his disciples. As the students watched, his face would glow with a radiance that came from deep within him. They knew that every step he danced was filled with profound spiritual meaning and that in some mysterious way he was influencing the world around them.

One evening while he was dancing, a bench tipped over and landed on the rabbi's foot. He had to pause for a while because of the pain.

Later on the disciples asked him about this incident and what it might mean. He replied, "As I remember it, the pain made itself known because I interrupted the dance."

APPLICATION: Name one problem, burden or setback you are hanging onto in your life. Do something to begin to turn that into a stepping-stone for future growth.

Keeping on Track

*You may not know God, nor God's love, until you have truly
manifested that love in your dealings with others.*

Based on Edgar Cayce reading 257-199

Maureen believes that spiritual growth involves demonstrat-
ing love and care for others. So the best way for her to keep
track of that growth is by examining her relationships to
people. If these are nurturing, then she knows she is on the
road to fulfilling her purpose in life.

She looks at how she is relating to her spouse and to her
children. Is she giving them time? Is she listening to them?
Does she feel a connection with them or a distance?

Then she examines how she is relating to her co-workers,
her friends, and her neighbors. Does she feel any resentments or is she harboring any grudges? Does she feel some
tension that she has not begun to work out with them? Is
she envious or jealous of them? Is she trying to walk over
them to improve her position?

There will be problems and tensions at times in these relationships, Maureen knows. But if she is honestly and
openly working with these issues, if basically her relationships are harmonious and cordial, then she knows she is on
the right track of spiritual development.

APPLICATION: The next time you want to check on your
spiritual growth, sit down and examine your relationships
with your family members, friends, and co-workers. Take
steps to improve these relationships where necessary.

Breaking Out of Old Habits

Only that which is creative grows.

Based on Edgar Cayce reading 4083-1

Bert, a young art teacher, was struggling with the meaning of creativity in his art classes. As he read the Edgar Cayce readings, thoughts about dealing with habits seemed to repeat themselves. He finally decided that he should define creativity as "acting, but not out of habit."

He began to focus his classes more around creativity, using art as a foundation. He sensed that people expected art to be new, unusual, non-habitual, and would feel more at ease in doing something out of the ordinary when creating art works. He encouraged his students to be relaxed and to do what they felt like doing, to let their imaginations run freely. He suggested that they be non-judgmental in the beginning so that the ideas could be developed before being evaluated.

Students not only did more creative work, but they also discovered that their lives in general became more creative. The emphasis on breaking free of habits in class helped them break free of habits in other parts of their lives as well.

APPLICATION: Some time during the next week do something that breaks you free of an old habit.

A Moment of Silence

Your prayer, your supplications have been heard, and they are brought before that throne of mercy, light, peace, and harmony. Based on Edgar Cayce reading 1301-1

Karen walked into the office and found that everything was in chaos. Several issues had surfaced during the last three days and decisions needed to be made quickly on some of them. People were waiting to see her, and one look at her calendar told her the day was not going to get any easier.

She closed the office door, sat in her chair, and prayed for help. Her prayer was, "God help me to handle all this. Let answers come to my mind as I face each issue. Let answers come through other people who also have insight into what to do." Then she sat quietly for about five minutes before opening the door and facing the day.

This little prayer and moment of silence always helped her relax and become more open and more alert. This time alone in silence also helped her focus more on each issue as it came along rather than feel overwhelmed by the thought of all the issues she had to face in a day.

APPLICATION: The next time an overwhelming number of decisions and issues face you, pause and seek guidance from a higher source of strength.

I Wonder What Will Happen

As we take God with us in our activity, we are fit for every problem.   Based on Edgar Cayce reading 641-6

It was time for Sarah's special survival technique again. She had learned to handle the stress, think more clearly, and make better decisions by putting herself in what she called the "witness state." In this state she detached herself from ego involvement and became more objective.

Today the stress came from a major construction decision. Her job involved overseeing the building of a new addition to the firm even though she had primarily been hired to administer the facility and not build it. Unexpected problems developed for which she had never been prepared, and the issue could cost the firm close to $100,000.

Sarah relaxed and tried to see the situation from the viewpoint of the "witness state," the Higher Self. As she looked on, she asked herself, "I wonder how I will get through this one? I wonder what I will learn? I wonder what attitude I will adopt in this situation?"

This inner reflection helped alleviate the stress, but it also helped her realize she was not alone. In this state she could open herself to God and to her Higher Self in order to receive a power greater than what her ego could give her. In this state she could feel God's presence and knew that God, who could see a broader outcome, would guide her as she made her decision.

APPLICATION: The next time you are in a stressful situation, go into the "witness state" and open yourself to this higher power.

The Dream Sign

How often have you envisioned in a symbol or in a dream those very things that happened to you later?

Based on Edgar Cayce reading 1537-1

How do you know if your life is on the right path? Dreams can give clues to this.

Christine knew her dream had been an important one. She saw herself in the library of a new building. She was standing in a glass-enclosed room giving out membership cards to people who were joining some organization whose name she could not read. She knew she belonged there.

Shortly after this dream, she got involved in a nonprofit organization in her community, then joined a prayer group sponsored by this organization.

A year later, the organization began constructing a new building. When it was completed, except for some interior work, the prayer group was invited to come in and pray in each room as a way of dedicating the building to the service of God and humanity. She was moved by the experience but didn't have any other strong feelings.

After the building was completed, she went early one day to take a private tour. The receptionist took Christine to the portion of the new building that was the library. She walked into the library, turned to the left, and found herself facing the glass-enclosed room she had seen in her dream several years earlier.

Christine knew now she was on the right path for her life.

APPLICATION: Dreams can be signs that you are on the right path in your life. Keep a dream log and see if you have dreams about places or situations you later experience.

The Peace Pole

Peace within self first must be found, then in the associations with others. Then we will find harmony in a life which will bring not only a better place for others to live but more harmony in self's own experience.

Based on Edgar Cayce reading 5230-1

Marian's idea came from a fairly recent Japanese tradition. Every year a group of people meet at a special mountain in Japan to pray for peace. They encourage others around the world to pray as well and to put up reminders to others to pray for peace. As reminders of this, they recommend peace poles. Each has inscribed on it in four languages the words "May Peace Prevail on Earth." Every person who then sees one of these poles builds for a few seconds a thought about peace.

Marian discussed this idea with some of her relatives, and they decided to do this at a family reunion. She and her husband purchased a pole, and at a special time all the family members gathered around to pray and reflect on the need for inner peace and world peace while the pole was being planted in the ground.

Instead of this being a controversial idea, the pole became the symbolic momento for this family reunion. Members gathered around it to have their pictures taken. The farmer on whose land it was placed even made it more sturdy by encasing it in concrete. It now stands as a hopeful sign of peace on the family farm.

APPLICATION: Any group of people can do something to show a desire for peace. In a group of which you are a part decide together what you can do and then do it.

Messenger of Life

The entering of every soul is that it may become more and more aware of the Divine within, that the soul may be purged and made a fit companion for the glory of the Creative Forces.
Based on Edgar Cayce reading 578-2

Jonah was confused. All the trouble God had put him through to get him to Nineveh had resulted in his looking like a fool. He hadn't wanted this assignment in the first place. He hated bringing messages of doom and destruction. That's why he had tried to run.

But God wouldn't let him go. No, God had pursued him, caused a storm, and watched while Jonah had been thrown overboard. Finally Jonah had consented to preach God's news of destruction. And what was happening now? The city was going to be saved! Jonah wanted some answers.

At this point God interrupted Jonah's self-pitying reverie to bring him words of understanding and life.

"Jonah, I called you because the people of Nineveh needed a warning, not because they needed destroying. They had to be told of the consequences if they did not change their ways. My ideal was not to destroy but to save.

"But sometimes people need to hear a frightening message before they change their ways. Even in these cases my message is not meant as a proclamation of unalterable doom. My message is a call to new life."

Jonah was still feeling his bruised ego, but he knew he would much rather celebrate life than gaze on death . He knew he could now be God's messenger for life.

APPLICATION: The next time you need to speak tough words to someone, say them not to destroy but to help someone grow.

When Your Friends Change

Let the spiritual be the guide—the material will take their place.   Based on Edgar Cayce reading 288-37

At first Carl and Paula just wondered why the Simpsons hadn't called for several weeks. However, when Paula called to suggest that they all meet at some time for dinner, the Simpsons said they were busy every evening that Paula suggested. Paula and Carl considered this strange and began to wonder if they had insulted them in some way.

They examined the last six months of their lives. Six months ago they were going to cocktail parties every weekend. They went out with the Simpsons and several other couples regularly, but now they saw only one of these couples.

When they looked for reasons for this change, they realized that six months ago they had gotten involved in a metaphysical discussion group. They also noticed they had slowly stopped attending cocktail parties. They now preferred to talk with friends over dinner or attend lectures and discuss them.

Paula and Carl finally concluded that they hadn't done anything to the Simpsons. They had begun a new spiritual journey for themselves. Their interests had changed. Now their friends were people with interests in metaphysical subjects. It was just the old fading away to make way for the new.

APPLICATION: As you travel a spiritual journey, you will find interests and friends changing. Affirm this as a part of your new journey through life.

Accounting for Your Life

Do not fret about tomorrow or what another does. You shall give an accounting of the deeds done in your body, not in someone else's.　　　　Based on Edgar Cayce reading 3213-1

When the answer finally came, it seemed so simple that Ted couldn't imagine why it had taken him so long to figure it out. For years he had asked about his purpose in life. He had found some of the answers along the way, but something always seemed to be missing. Suddenly the answer was right in front of him and it had to do with the job he had done all his life—accounting.

He had graduated from college with a degree in business and received his license as a certified public accountant. For many years he had successful businesses.

Then he had worked as treasurer for an organization. For over twenty years he was responsible for the accounting of all the receipts and expenditures of that organization.

However, Ted also knew he was on earth to learn something else about his life. He had finally realized that he had come to learn to be accountable for his decisions and his actions.

As he reflected on his life, he noted some regrets, some moments he wished had never happened. However, he also remembered other moments of love, caring, and compassion. He was ready to assume responsibility for it all.

Perhaps he *had* learned, and that's why the answer to his question had come at this time.

APPLICATION: For what event in your life do you hesitate to be held accountable? Take one step to begin assuming responsibility for that event.

Accepting Responsibility

Karma is self being met—not a karmic debt between people but a karmic debt of self that may be worked out in relationships that exist in the present.

Based on Edgar Cayce reading 1436-3

Melinda believed that karma defined a type of relationship that existed between people. However, according to what she was reading now, karma was within a person. It was an internal energy pattern that gave a person a tendency to react to people or situations in a certain way. People had to make conscious choices to overcome and change these internal patterns and tendencies.

She understood this when she thought about herself and her father. She remembered how she used to get so angry when her father said certain things or treated her in a certain way. Then one day in the midst of an argument over something he had said, she had decided she was going to respond to him in a different way. She stopped the fight and spoke kindly to him. Her anger quickly disappeared. She had changed a pattern.

What she was now reading related to her own experience. Karma was something within her that was triggered by external events. Only she could change those energy patterns. She couldn't blame another person for her karmic reaction, but had to accept responsibility for her own responses.

APPLICATION: Name a situation in your life that you think is karmic. Realize that karma is within you and begin to change yourself if changes need to be made.

The Place of Ritual

Get the truth of fasting! True fasting is casting out "I would have done," and replacing it with "As You, O God, see fit, use me as the channel." Based on Edgar Cayce reading 295-6

When a rabbi once stated that fasting was no longer of value, his pupils asked him, "Didn't your teacher fast?"

The rabbi told this story: "My teacher used to take six loaves of bread and some wine with him at the close of the Sabbath. He would go off to be alone with God for the week. When he was ready to return on Friday, he would pick up his bag and find it quite heavy. He would open it and be surprised to find all six loaves of bread in it.

"This kind of fasting is allowed because for my teacher fasting was a byproduct of his search for God and not an end in itself."

Rituals and special acts lose their value when one's attention is so focused on them that they become ends in themselves. When the deeds are done naturally, without undue emphasis placed on them and as steps to better serving God or others, they can have value in spiritual growth and transformation.

APPLICATION: Examine the "ritual acts"—prayer, worship, gift giving—that you do. If they have become empty rituals, do something to re-establish them as steps to expressing love to God or to others.

Helpful Confrontations

If one's urges are directed to helpfulness, they may become that which will make life more worthwhile, more optimistic, more joyous, more harmonious in all of its relations.

Based on Edgar Cayce reading 811-2

In his college art class, Mike liked to help students improve their grades. On their assignments he would write down the grade and make comments. Then he would hand the assignment back. Students could make the corrections suggested and return the assignment to get their grades raised.

Anne, a student, didn't understand this approach. She only saw that she was getting a grade and being asked to do the work over again. Her work was piling up on her and she thought she was being penalized.

Her parents heard about her frustration and notified the college. Following a call from his department head, Mike invited Anne to come in and talk with him.

He was angry that the issue had come to his attention in this way. However, he also knew that his ideal was to be helpful and caring toward his students. Before the session with Anne, he spent some time focusing on his ideal and not on his emotions. His attitude of concern in explaining his system helped Anne understand what he was doing. Her attitude toward him and her behavior in class changed dramatically, and she received very good marks at the end of the semester.

APPLICATION: Think of a situation that may lead you to a confrontation with someone. Begin to create an attitude of helpfulness and caring toward that person.

Seeking the Light

Q. What was the form that seemed to be made up of light that appeared at the close of the meditation?
A. The attuning of self to the high vibrations of love and life and joy—and is that which heals and keeps peace among all people.
Based on Edgar Cayce reading 5749-10

Carla loved to listen to Andrew lecture on meditation. Often he would take time after the talk to just sit and chat with people about this topic.

She noticed that as he spoke, he would tell people to seek a white light. She didn't understand what he meant. One night in bed before going to sleep she kept asking herself over and over, "What is the light we seek?"

Early in the morning she woke up suddenly. She had had a powerful dream. She had seen a point of light. Around the light was a series of concentric circles. Occasionally a streak like lightning would come from the center point and pulsate outward. It was so powerful that it awakened her.

For Carla this light was the force, the energy called God or the Creative Forces. It was this energy people were seeking. It was too intense for her to bear at the time, so she woke up. But it was this light that kept calling her, so she continued her journey toward it.

APPLICATION: Pick out a quality you associate with light, such as understanding, warmth, cheerfulness, etc. Begin to express this quality in your life.

Setting the World in Motion

For marriage the standard would be as God has given—there must be the answering within each that their spiritual and mental desires are one.   Based on Edgar Cayce reading 1173-11

He had to admit he had had some reservations about this approach, but it appeared to be working. Frank was rapidly falling in love with Jennifer.

Frank had decided several months ago he was ready to get married, but at the time he didn't know any woman he would consider marrying. A friend recommended that he set the universe to work for him.

He was to write down his ideals for a marriage relationship, all that he had to offer, and the characteristics he thought he would develop in a relationship. Then he was to write down what he wanted in a spouse. While doing this, he was to ask the universe to send him someone who would complement his ideals and fit what was on his lists.

He was to take this task seriously. This was not the same as going to a cafeteria and nonchalantly asking for a little of everything. The items he wrote on these lists were to come from deep inside him.

Frank took a few weeks to do this and then kept himself open to meeting people and letting his intuition guide him. After a few months, he was beginning to have some doubts, but he kept at it.

Within six months he had met Jennifer, and their relationship appeared to be everything for which he had hoped.

APPLICATION: The next time you want something that's important, put the universe to work for you and then keep open to its time frame.

The Gift of the One Talent

Each act of each body helps to bring about God's kingdom in the earth, or adds to that which prevents it from becoming manifest in this material plane.

Based on Edgar Cayce reading 911-6

Jesus' story had confused Esther. She could understand why the man who had used ten talents ($10,000) to make ten more talents had been rewarded. The same with the man who had multiplied five talents into ten. However, she thought it unfair that the man who returned the one talent should be treated so harshly. Some people can't do as much as other people.

On her way home, she passed by Timothy's house. She liked Timothy and felt sorry for him. He was crippled, so he could not help his father in the fields. She wondered how he could be so happy, knowing that he could never help his family.

In front of Timothy's door she stopped to listen and smiled. Timothy was playing his flute. His parents, brothers, and sisters were laughing and dancing as he played. The cares of their poverty and hard day in the field were forgotten.

Timothy could do so little for his family, but he *could* play the flute. How sad their lives would be if Timothy refused to use the gift he did have. As Esther thought about this, she began to understand the story she had heard. Even a single talent is not to be buried.

APPLICATION: Use one of your talents today to bring a bit of God's kingdom into someone's life.

Changes Do Happen

*Be patient! You've had years and years of the disturbance.
Don't expect it to be cured in a moment and be of a perma-
nent nature.*   Based on Edgar Cayce reading 716-3

Over the years Kate's relationship with her father had healed
considerably. They both thought the earlier tensions had
been overcome. Then one night at supper something was
said, and the old patterns surfaced immediately. For several
minutes she and her father had an intense argument in front
of her two children.

Later they talked, but some of the tension was still there.
Her father maintained that nothing had really changed.
They were still the same as they had been ten years before.
However, Kate said that that wasn't true. She remembered
that ten years ago she had really felt angry at times like
these. Tonight she didn't feel that intense anger. She only
felt regret at the words that had been spoken.

Kate realized that their relationship *had* changed, but it
was not yet perfect. They would continue to have moments
when the old patterns would surface again, but she knew
that they could meet them in new ways if they chose to do
so. A lot of healing had occurred.

APPLICATION: Think of a relationship where changes are
occurring slowly. Affirm the changes that have been made,
and do one thing to continue the positive growth.

Learning by Living

Life in all its experiences is a practical application of the concept of God or Creative Energy in the lives of individuals as they deal with others.   Based on Edgar Cayce reading 1206-3

Back in the late fifties Janet attended a month-long seminar during her vacation from teaching. While attending the program, she decided to make the most of her experience by getting involved in an intense small-group program called a "project group."

This meant that for those weeks she would spend many hours outside the lecture time with a group of people she had never met before. They had breakfast together, worked together— painting, building, or doing whatever needed to be done to improve the facilities where the seminar was being held—and they played together.

The group was also involved in several disciplines, such as getting up at 2:00 a.m. for an hour of meditation.

The group members did all their waking-time activities with one another, including attendance at the seminar lectures. If a group member was late, everyone else waited for that person to show up before beginning anything.

She learned through practical experience how to apply cooperation, friendship, patience, and many other spiritual disciplines. Through this experience she learned that these principles do work. After this month, she was able to return home and begin applying them in her daily life.

APPLICATION: Take one principle, such as patience or cooperation, and begin to apply it in your life.

Coping with Fears

Do not let things which may not in the present be understood weary the soul, but know that sometime, somewhere you will understand.   Based on Edgar Cayce reading 5369-2

How can you help your family members understand and cope with some of their fears?

Jill was only six and had not had a bad experience with the police, but she was really afraid of policemen. When the family was driving along in the car and she would spot a policeman, she'd panic. She would immediately check the speedometer to make sure her dad was not speeding. Then she would check to be sure that everyone was wearing a seatbelt.

Her parents believed in reincarnation and understood the impact of emotions that carry over from one life to another. They raised the issue of past lives with her and suggested that maybe she had had a bad experience with a policeman in a previous life. They never said that this was the only explanation, but simply offered it as a possibility.

This idea didn't erase Jill's fear completely, but it helped her to relax and not to panic every time she saw a policeman. As they reinforced this thought, she became more and more able to control her response to her fear.

APPLICATION: Name a fear you have that you cannot trace to an experience in this lifetime. Think of a possible past-life experience that might account for this fear.

Weeping for the Victims

As Jesus gave, you may ever feel in yourself, "Who made me a judge of my neighbor?"

Based on Edgar Cayce reading 3213-1

The news pierced David's heart as if the spear had been driven into him. His son, his beloved Absalom, was dead.

Sorrow and anger fought within him. His first cry was one of grief: "O Absalom, my son, my son." His next cry was about to be one that would order the death of the man who had killed his son. David felt himself torn in half.

What had happened? Absalom had been a promising youth if an ambitious one. He had led a rebellion against David, so he was not an innocent victim. Still David had loved him, loved him because he believed Absalom could have changed. It was that love that caused so much grief.

But David could not punish the man who had killed Absalom because that soldier had killed a man who with his rebellion had destroyed many innocent lives. Was the soldier's act a deed of justice or of revenge? Did the soldier kill on the battlefield because he believed David would never order Absalom's death later?

David was torn. How could he judge what he did not understand? He would not continue the killing by punishing the soldier, but he would not hide his tears either. He would weep for one who had been lost and would cry his tears of love and grief. And he would embrace the soldier who had killed believing that he was serving his king.

APPLICATION: The next time you read of a tragedy, try to suspend judgment and feel compassion for all persons involved.

Picky, Picky

There do arise periods when little petty disturbances call for the quick retort; find rather the fault in self, if there be one. If there is not according to the standard of your ideal, open not your mouth.　　　Based on Edgar Cayce reading 262-24

Marion learned several lessons from her first marriage that she now tries to avoid in her second. One is to talk a lot with her husband and not get caught up in arguments that are not really important. She avoids these kinds of disagreements by checking her own quick words and not setting into motion cycles of friction. She used to express her feelings about every little item that irritated her. However, she discovered that some situations aren't worth arguing over when she tried the following experiment: Instead of speaking out every time something happened that irritated her, she decided to keep quiet. At that point she also wouldn't fuel her irritation, but would wait a day or two to see if she were still irritated enough to say something.

She discovered that many of the things no longer bothered her after a day or two, and they didn't even bother her when they reoccurred. Those disturbances that persisted, however, she brought up later for discussion. Then she and her husband could look together at what could be done. Thus, a lot of petty, destructive arguments have been avoided through using this technique.

APPLICATION: Pick out something that someone close to you does that irritates you. Try this experiment to see if the irritation will go away or if it is really worth discussing.

An Idea Whose Time Was Right

Faint not at waiting, for in patience you become aware of your soul.
                                                        Based on Edgar Cayce reading 2144-1

As Gloria looked back, she was amazed at the series of events that had brought her to this new venture.

In her senior year in high school six years ago, she had done some questioning of her family's religion. She had read books on Eastern thought, reincarnation, and yoga. She had felt that she might find some answers to her questions, but she did not really pursue it.

Only two weeks ago she had been watching TV—a special on Nostradamus. She was intrigued by this man who could predict so much about future events and felt her soul being pulled toward something she didn't fully understand. For her it was almost a rebirth experience.

Now here she was sitting in an airport stranded because of a snowstorm and engaged in a conversation with someone she hardly knew. They had begun talking about the special. Then they spoke about earth changes. He had mentioned Edgar Cayce and was talking about Cayce's view of earth changes, reincarnation, and those other ideas she had dropped six years ago.

Gloria sensed that a whole new chapter in her life was opening up to her. She didn't know where it would lead, but she knew this time she wasn't going to give up the search.

APPLICATION: Sometimes ideas are introduced and then go undeveloped for years. Identify an idea important to you that has been dormant for a while and is now ready to surface and be used.

God's Gift of Laughter

*For know only in those whom God has favored is there the
ability to laugh, even when clouds of doubt arise or when
every form of disturbance arises.*

Based on Edgar Cayce reading 2984-1

Richard's nature is to laugh and joke. During his recovery
following a shooting accident, his humorous nature gave
him courage and hope. It also helped him recover more
quickly and touched the lives of the patients and the hospital
staff around him.

In his job Richard also finds it necessary to be humorous.
Sometimes in meetings when he feels that he and his co-workers
are getting too serious about themselves, he will
crack a joke and maybe be a little irreverent about who they
are. Some people take offense at this action and see it as not
taking work seriously. However, he continues to do it because
he thinks people need to laugh at themselves in order
to put all things in the right perspective.

Joy, happiness, and laughter are meant to be a part of
humanity's heritage from God.

APPLICATION: The next time you feel you are taking something
too seriously, take time to find something humorous
about the situation and have a good laugh.

Finding God

As has been given, those who love their neighbors may indeed through patience become aware of their souls.

Based on Edgar Cayce reading 752-1

A merchant once came to a famous Jewish rabbi to complain that another merchant had built a shop right next to his.

The rabbi responded, "You think your shop is what supports you? You are setting your heart upon it instead of upon God who is your true support. Perhaps you do not know where God lives?

"Remember how it is written: 'Love your neighbor as yourself: I am the Lord.'

"This means that you should want for your neighbor what he needs just as you want those things for yourself. In doing this you will find God."

APPLICATION: Think about what you need. Then pray for three other people that they may receive what they need from God.

The Power of Patient, Loving Care

There must ever be that prayerful attitude that in the ministering, in the care there may be done that which will not only make for an attitude of helpful hopefulness for the patient but that there may be gained patience, kindness, endurance, and consistency in the attitude of those about the patient.

Based on Edgar Cayce reading 552-1

When Sheila and her three-year-old daughter, Mary, were in an auto accident, Mary's foot had been badly cut. But doctors managed to save her leg and another operation corrected some of the damage. However, the main tendon had been injured, causing her to drop her foot down at each step she took.

A few years after the accident, a different doctor saw Mary limping along behind some other children. This doctor told Sheila that she had better get to work on her daughter or Mary's leg would atrophy and she would eventually lose the use of it. He advised the mother to see Gladys, a woman familiar with the Edgar Cayce readings, and get her advice.

Working from memory, Gladys pulled out some readings. The two women put together a massage treatment that consisted of peanut oil one night and camphor oil the next. For several years Sheila and her husband took turns massaging Mary's leg and encouraging her progress.

One day Sheila looked out the window and noticed Mary leading a group of children on roller skates. She knew then that they could stop the nightly treatments. Today Mary can ski. Her leg has not been a handicap to her at all.

APPLICATION: The next time you help treat someone, remember the ideas of hopefulness, patience, consistency, and kindness.

Jesus' Rules

*There has come a teacher who was bold enough to declare
Himself the Son of the living God. He set no rules of appetite.
He set no rules of ethics other than, "As you would that people
would do to you, do so to them" and "As you do it to the least
of these, you do it to your Maker."*

Based on Edgar Cayce reading 357-13

Carolyn was reliving the conversation in her head.

"Randy!" Carolyn had exclaimed. "Do you realize how intolerant you sound when you say that? You imply your way of meditation and spiritual growth is the only way for people. You remind me of some of the religious leaders you complain about."

"What do you mean?" Randy had asked.

"You know," Carolyn had continued. "The ones whom you say set rigid rules and have a list of specific dogmatic statements that people have to believe in order to have the 'truth.' You always accuse these people of feeling so superior to others, but I sense a similar attitude in what you are saying."

Randy had then responded, "I don't get your point. What are you trying to say?"

Then Carolyn answered, "Randy, your excitement over the path you have found is leading you to set up similar rules and legalisms only in a different form. Jesus did not set down religious legalisms to be used to divide people."

At that point Randy had walked away. She hoped she hadn't ruined their friendship, but she knew she had to help him question what he was really saying.

APPLICATION; What attitude do you have about another person or group of people that separates you from them? Take one step toward changing that attitude.

Body Care

The soul finds self in the material world experiencing those physical conditions within the body imprinted from a previous experience.   Based on Edgar Cayce reading 900-289

Tim and Don were discussing reincarnation when Don made the comment, "It's like buying a new car. When one car wears out, you throw it away. Then you get a new one."

Tim thought about that a few seconds and said, "No, that's not exactly what I believe. When people buy a new car, there is no relationship between the old car and the new one.

"However, a soul doesn't just return to a new body. I believe there is something about our bodies that carries over from one lifetime to another. I guess I believe that the way you treat your body in one life influences the kind of body you will have in the next life. If you take care of it, you create energy patterns that carry over."

"You mean," Don interrupted, "that if I eat right, do some exercise, and maybe get a massage every once in a while, I am not just helping my body in this lifetime? I am creating something for the next one?"

Tim nodded, "Yeah, I think so."

APPLICATION: Do something you consider preventive health care for your body and think about its influence on you for many years or lifetimes to come.

Turning Around

Don't feel sorry for yourself if you have chosen the wrong road—turn around.   Based on Edgar Cayce reading 462-10

One day a man picked up a newspaper and saw the announcement of his death. The newspaper had, of course, reported the death of the wrong man. However, being curious, he decided to read the epitaph to see what people thought of him.

To his dismay the paper called him "the merchant of death" because he had invented dynamite and had made his fortune selling weapons.

Pondering this description, he decided he really didn't want to be known as the merchant of death. At that moment the focus of his life changed. He devoted the remainder of his life and his fortune to helping people and working for peace.

Today this man is not remembered as "the merchant of death" but as Alfred Nobel, founder of the Nobel Prizes for outstanding human achievement in literature, the sciences, and world peace.

APPLICATION: Think of one aspect of your life with which you are displeased and take a first step in changing that part of your life.

Knowing What You Believe In

Know in whom you have believed and believe that God is able to guard what you have committed to God against any condition in your experience.   Based on Edgar Cayce reading 262-17

There were crucial times in her life when Patricia found it important to know in what she believed. There were times when she had to reaffirm her belief that service to others was one purpose of her life and that God would walk with her through the troubles she might encounter. She needed to have this solid rock upon which to base her decisions, particularly when the decision did not always seem like the most rational one. This was one of those times.

Patricia had to decide whether or not to help Marjorie who was terminally ill and had requested that Patricia stay with her. She had not had a good relationship with Marjorie for several years and was surprised Marjorie had asked for her help. Now she wondered if she could overcome the estrangement of those past years and care for Marjorie.

Being able to reaffirm service as one of her ideals and knowing she could trust God to help her through the rough spots enabled her to respond positively to Marjorie's request even though her friends strongly advised against it. The situation worked out better than she or others anticipated it would, and she and Marjorie healed their relationship considerably before Marjorie died.

APPLICATION: Make a decision today that requires some trust in God to help you follow through on it.

Coming Home

As conditions, opportunities present themselves, so accept them, and—as these work their way—the conditions, the things necessary for the development will present themselves.
Based on Edgar Cayce reading 307-3

Randy's leaving home for the West Coast had not been an escape. He had needed room to grow, to get away from the home town where everybody knew him and his family. He had needed to find out who he was in a world where things weren't handed to him.

For the most part he had used those years on the West Coast wisely. He had a few regrets, plus some stories he wasn't going to pass on to family members. However, he had also experienced a different world and a series of different jobs. He had tested the values he had been taught and discovered for himself which ones applied to him.

Now as suddenly as the urge to leave home had struck years ago, the knowledge that he had to return home was confronting him. It was time "to go back to school" again. That's the way he saw it. He needed to go back home to learn some lessons he could not learn anywhere else. He needed to live out who he had become among family members and friends who might have different expectations or goals for him.

He was returning home to communicate with his family on a different level as a different person—his own person. The issues were not easy to work on, but now he knew that home was where he had to be to live the life he had to live.

APPLICATION: Think about the time you left home. Affirm that necessary growth step and what you have become since then.

Start Over Again

Each and every development in the physical, in the social, in the mental plane has its place, each and every reverse—each and every mount surmounted.

Based on Edgar Cayce reading 900-214

Paula's goal had sounded so exciting at the beginning of the new year. She was going to work consciously on the physical, mental, and spiritual parts of her life this year — just as the Edgar Cayce readings recommended.

Her plans called for a concentrated effort on the physical during January to April, effort on the mental from May to August, and effort on the spiritual for the remaining four months. Naturally she wasn't going to ignore her mental and spiritual life for the first four months, but she was going to concentrate on the physical at the beginning.

But she encountered some unraveling of this plan in late April when she had some health problems. This difficulty seemed ironic to her since she had just spent four months focusing on exercise and diet.

The readings helped her put this situation in perspective. They spoke about obstacles. They seemed to know that on the path of spiritual growth one would encounter obstacles that might slow down progress, but they said to work through the obstacle and then start in again.

She also realized that four months was not a long time. Progress in these areas of life did not come overnight. She decided to modify her expectations and not rush her growth in any of these areas.

APPLICATION: Think of an obstacle that has slowed down growth for you in some area of your life. Take time to learn the lesson it has to offer you and then move on.

The Strange Summer

There have been the attempts on the part of the body physically and mentally to adjust itself. Give the time. Be patient.
Based on Edgar Cayce reading 716-3

It had been a strange summer. Sandy was constantly experiencing unusual phenomena. Sometimes when she walked into rooms, the lights would dim for a second or so. Even though an inner feeling inside her kept telling her it would pass, she was wondering what was going on.

In a discussion with her neighbor, Francine, she finally mentioned these occurrences. Francine asked if Sandy had been doing anything different. Sandy mentioned she had begun meditating in late spring, but that was all. Francine smiled a bit and asked if anything else had been happening to her. Sandy admitted she occasionally reached for the phone before it rang and knew who was calling.

Francine said meditation helped people attune their bodies to different levels of consciousness. Sandy was evidently making these attunements quickly. This helped Sandy realize she was not going crazy. She was going through a growth stage that would lead her to some beautiful experiences.

APPLICATION: Meditation can produce changes in a person's ability to perceive the world. If they happen to you or someone you know, affirm them as part of positive growth.

Words of Encouragement

Anyone can find faults. It is the wise person who finds that which encourages another in the turmoils and strifes of the day. Based on Edgar Cayce reading 1449-2

Jack's teenage brother, Bob, had been difficult to control for the past three years. However, their parents really got worried one evening when Bob became irrational. They called Jack and the three of them managed to calm Bob down. Later that evening, Jack recommended that his parents get Bob some counseling help immediately.

Because Jack knew something about the Cayce readings and about his brother's eating habits, he wondered if part of Bob's problems might stem from the food he was eating. He gathered information and talked to the psychiatrist Bob was seeing.

Fortunately this doctor was open to exploring many avenues to helping patients. He ordered some tests, which surfaced a chemical imbalance in Bob stemming from too much sugar and not enough vitamins. The doctor recommended a strict diet along with vitamin supplements and continued counseling.

Over the next several months the only time Bob had severe relapses was when he went off his diet and refused to take care of himself. During those episodes Jack was there to encourage and support him and give him a vision of what his life could be like in the future.

APPLICATION: Do something to encourage someone who is experiencing turmoil in his or her life.

It's the Law

Each soul constantly meets itself. Would that each soul would but understand that those hardships which are accredited so much to others are caused most by self. Know that in those you are meeting yourself.   Based on Edgar Cayce reading 845-4

Carolyn looked back at the past five years and realized how much she had learned. The idea of universal laws had been so helpful. But at first that concept had bothered her because it sounded as if some legalistic God was keeping score. However, as she came to understand that these laws were there to help her and not punish her, her attitude changed.

Her first lesson involved "like attracts like." She had harbored anger at someone for years. Periodically she would make comments behind that person's back. However, she became outraged when she discovered that two other people were doing the same to her.

When someone told her about this law, she decided to try a new approach. She stopped talking about this other person and tried to release her anger. After she did this, she learned that others had quit talking about her as well.

As she not only released the anger but also replaced it with forgiveness and thoughts of love for this person, she found the wall between the two of them breaking down. Eventually they started speaking to one another. This enabled her to see that universal laws were for her benefit. She could use them to send out and attract love, healing, and new opportunities for growth. She now saw that they could make her life richer.

APPLICATION: Like attracts like. Look at your life and become aware of the positive things you are attracting to yourself because of what you are sending out.

Her Heart Opened

*Whoever holds grudges for those activities that have brought
contention in the life makes the way rough and hard for self.*
Based on Edgar Cayce reading 585-2

Nancy was having a difficult time with someone at work.
Several situations had occurred which had left her full of
bitterness and resentment. Since she saw this individual
almost every day, she realized she had to work on herself in
some way to resolve her anger.

When she asked others for advice, several people recommended the forty-day forgiveness prayer. In this prayer, said
once a day for forty days, she would ask the other person as
well as herself for forgiveness. At first she thought this was
silly. Since regular prayer and meditation were not doing
any good, why should forty days of the same prayer make
any difference.

However, as she looked at the prayer, she realized she
was not dealing with "should's" or "ought's." The prayer
focused solely on forgiveness in order to remove barriers
between people. She decided to try it.

She was amazed that at the end of forty days a weight
had disappeared from her life. Her attitude toward the person had changed completely and even the relationship had
changed. Her heart was now open in a way it had never been
before, and she knew healing had taken place.

APPLICATION: If you have a difficult situation in your life
that you want resolved, the forgiveness prayer is a tool you
can use.

God Looks on the Heart

With what yardstick do you measure others? That which is creative and of God or that which is of your own making?
Based on Edgar Cayce reading 3128-2

Samuel was fed up and so was God. Saul had disobeyed God for the last time. If he kept this up, he would bring Israel to ruin. It was time to act.

The next day Samuel was on his way to Jesse's house. By taking a cow along he was implying that he was going to make a sacrifice. Samuel knew God had told him to find a new king for Israel.

When he arrived he met seven of Jesse's sons, one at a time. The first was tall, strong, and commanded authority by the way he looked. God said, "No, people look at the outer appearances, I look at what is in the heart."

Samuel went on to the second son, then the third, and so on until all seven had been seen. "Have you no other sons?" he asked.

The eighth son, David, was watching the sheep in the fields. A messenger went for him.

He arrived, and Samuel looked at him. Even without the voice of God speaking, Samuel knew he had found the right one. As David knelt and Samuel anointed him, Samuel's heart felt what God's eyes could see. Inside David was the heart of a servant of God.

APPLICATION: Learn to see with your heart. The next time you evaluate someone, listen to your intuitions and feelings. Don't rely merely on appearances.

Getting Ready for Baby

Let my body, my mind, be such as to keep attuned to the best that may come as a channel of blessings to others.

Based on Edgar Cayce reading 1523-7

Carla and Bill already had two children and weren't planning on having any more. They had made this clear to Richard, a friend of theirs; however, Richard kept insisting that they look at the Edgar Cayce readings on pregnancy and preparation for parenthood. Finally, they did.

They were impressed by the ideal-setting, the disciplines, the diet, and the idea of attracting a soul who could serve the world in a positive way. They decided one more child would be fine and for the coming year followed all the suggestions.

They set a common ideal for what they wanted. They were aware of their emotions and didn't have any serious arguments or disagreements. Carla gave up beef, pork, and her favorite soda. Both of them meditated daily. Fortunate to have an open-minded obstetrician, Carla shared her dreams with her doctor to see if they offered guidance.

They had a healthy girl. By age six the child had decided to be a doctor, and she later went to college for medical training.

Although no additional children came after this one, they continued to set ideals as a couple, follow disciplines, watch their dreams, and meditate. This enabled them to nurture other visions to successful conclusions as well.

APPLICATION: Name a vision of yours you want to see fulfilled. Imagine it is an embryo in you that needs the best of care. Set ideals, meditate, watch your dreams, and take other steps to nurture that vision.

When Mistakes Are Made

Why berate or belittle those who attempt to do the best?
Based on Edgar Cayce reading 4061-2

Anita walked into the middle of a chaotic work situation. The managers in her division were arguing about a recent decision they had made. As it turned out, they had not made the correct decision, so now everyone was trying to blame someone else or the people in other departments for not following through correctly.

After listening to what had gone wrong, Anita told them that at this point she didn't care who was right or wrong. She wanted to get on with the job. Whatever was needed to be done to correct the decision would be done by all of them together.

She never did try to determine exactly where the problem originated because the basic decision had been incorrect. Through experience Anita has learned that at times like these it is better for the entire department just to take the corrections and not to make one person feel guilty for the entire snafu.

APPLICATION: The next time something goes wrong, try to help make corrections without laying blame.

For a Worthy Cause

Purpose is of the making of the individual as souls seek the Father, and communion with God means doing, applying self to the duties—material, mental, and spiritual—as is known. Based on Edgar Cayce reading 99-8

Alice had only been retired a year when she was asked to be on the board of directors of an organization she had belonged to for just three years. She and her husband talked about it. She was enjoying her freedom, but she also felt she wanted to help this organization in any way she could.

Having served on other committees and attended board meetings in connection with her career, she knew that it could be frustrating. People would disagree about the direction in which the organization should go. Undoubtedly, there would be some personality conflicts. However, she had experiences in world travel, management, and policy making. She knew that part of her ideal in life was to use, wherever she could, those skills and talents God had given her.

She accepted the position. Though there were moments of frustration, overall she enjoyed the camaraderie of the board members. Instead of finding it draining, she found it exhilarating. Even when she didn't agree with all the decisions, she knew she was contributing to an organization that was trying to live out a similar ideal to hers. Being on this board gave her a new sense of purpose in her retirement.

APPLICATION: Take steps to begin contributing your skills and talents to an organization or group you believe expresses your ideal.

Where to Find Your Treasure

Know that the answer to every problem, to every question is within self.
Based on Edgar Cayce reading 2438-1

After many years of poverty in Cracow during which he had never doubted God, David, a devout Jew, had a dream. He was told to go to a bridge in Prague and look for a treasure. After he had dreamed this dream for the third time, he went to Prague. Unfortunately, the bridge there was guarded night and day and he did not dare start digging. Nevertheless, he would go there every day and walk around until evening.

Finally the captain of the guards asked if he could help him. David told him about the dream. The captain laughed and said, "For this dream you walked all the way to Prague? Why if I believed in my dreams, I would leave today for Cracow, for the house of a Jew named David, and dig under the stove in his kitchen for such a treasure."

David hurried home. He dug under his stove, found the treasure, and built a House of Prayer.

APPLICATION: The next time you are tempted to seek outside yourself for the key to finding meaning in your life, begin by seeking within.

Why Do You Want to Be Psychic?

Psychic abilities may be developed dependent upon what the individual seeks as the ideal or guide. There is one way, but there are many paths. Based on Edgar Cayce reading 3083-1

Many times when people came to Edgar Cayce to ask how they could develop their psychic powers, he would respond with the question, "Why do you want to be psychic?"

Walt looked at this question as an invitation for him to examine his motives. The way he answered this question would give him a clue as to what his experience would be. In the same way that wishes and desires shaped his dreams, so motives and purposes could shape the psychic experiences he was seeking.

Walt remembered the story of a couple who wanted $20,000. They didn't really need it for a specific reason other than they wanted to attract money to themselves to see if the experiment would work. One day they had an automobile accident. The settlement they received was $20,000.

This story reinforced what Walt's experiences taught him— that motives and ideals can dramatically influence the results of trying to develop psychic powers.

APPLICATION: As you try to develop your psychic abilities, write down your motive and ideal so you know clearly why you are making the effort.

Revelation

In the Book of Revelation the visions, the names, the churches, the places—all are but emblems of those forces that may work within the individual in its journey through the material to the entering into the glory.

Based on Edgar Cayce reading 281-16

Allen found what he had been searching for when he read the Edgar Cayce readings on the Book of Revelation. In all the discussions about this Book in which he had participated, people had looked at historical events to interpret its symbolism. But the readings internalized everything.

As he read, he shared ideas with members of his discussion group. They looked at the Book as a study of the experiences and changes each soul goes through as it returns to God. Instead of seeking for some historical figure to be the anti-Christ, for example, they looked at themselves as being the anti-Christ. Whenever they were going against God's will, they were being the anti-Christ.

The group discussed the battle of Armageddon as the battle of wills within each person. The struggle was between the will of the ego and the will of God or the Higher Self.

Some of the other symbols in the Book had to do with opening the spiritual centers in the body as souls moved along their spiritual journey to God.

Allen was excited. As he studied, he began to see how other external objects and events in life reflected what was going on in his internal life. He now viewed the world in a totally different way.

APPLICATION: Many external happenings and situations are reflections of what is happening inside us. Look around and find a situation that is mirroring what is going on inside you. Tell yourself what this teaches you about yourself.

The Doors Opened Wide

The outcome of any development is according to the use the soul makes of opportunities and the ideal with which the soul entertains those opportunities.

Based on Edgar Cayce reading 2630-1

When doors started opening for Helen, they opened in every corner of her life.

A few months earlier she had gotten interested in metaphysics. She began reading books on the subject and thought briefly about moving to a city near a major metaphysical center. However, she really hadn't given this serious consideration. She had also decided that she was going to give up looking for a husband and dedicate herself to her search into metaphysical studies.

Then suddenly her roommate walked in and announced she was leaving to get married. Helen began thinking that maybe the move she had been casually dreaming about would be a reality sooner than she thought.

She decided to see what might be available for her in this other city. Taking a few days off, she visited there and asked someone at the center for the name of a real estate agent who might show her some houses. She received a name and, during the next few months as she looked for housing and finalized her plans to move, she realized she was falling in love with her agent.

A few months after she moved, they were married. She now had a new home, a new husband, and a new spiritual journey that was reshaping her life.

APPLICATION: When one door opens, several others frequently follow right behind. Be alert for doors opening in your life in the near future.

The Otter's Children

Each soul should come to this realization—God is not mocked. Whatsoever a soul sows that must it also reap.

Based on Edgar Cayce reading 5343-1

The Otter ran to the King crying, "O King, you want peace and justice among the creatures. But there is no peace."

"Who has broken the peace?" cried the King.

"The Weasel," cried the Otter. "I dove into the water to hunt and left my children in the care of the Weasel. While I was gone, my children were killed."

The King called in the Weasel who said, "Alas, it was an accident. I heard the Woodpecker sound the alarm to defend our country. In my haste I trampled the Otter's children."

The King called for the Woodpecker. "Why did you sound the alarm?"

The Woodpecker replied, "I sounded the alarm when I saw the Scorpion sharpening his dagger. This was an act of war."

When the Scorpion appeared, he said, "I began sharpening my dagger when I saw the Crab preparing his sword."

The Crab said, "I saw the Lobster swing his javelin."

The Lobster said, "I began to swing my javelin when I saw the Otter coming toward my children to eat them."

The King turned to the Otter and said, "You, not the Weasel, are the guilty one. The blood of your children is upon your head. Whoever sows death shall reap it."

APPLICATION: Stop as you get ready to do something important and think about the possible consequences of your actions.

Starting Out Slowly

As the breath of life was breathed into the body of the first man, so breathed Jesus the breath of love and hope into the experience of those who were to become witnesses of Him in the world.   Based on Edgar Cayce reading 5749-10

Are you a bit uneasy when it comes to telling others about your spiritual journey?

One couple felt awkward and shy when they began to find meaning in the Edgar Cayce readings. They liked what they were learning, but they wanted to meet others involved with the information to feel more secure about the ideas. So they decided to attend an out-of-state conference. Living in a small town, they didn't want people to know where they were going, so late at night they drove out of town—just in case the conference participants would turn out to be strange, and they'd then have further explanations to make to their neighbors.

But they were impressed. They met genuine, sincere people who could think for themselves and ask intelligent questions, as well as be compassionate and caring. Right then, the couple decided to return next summer for a retreat on the subject of knowing yourself.

By the time the first conference was over, they didn't care who knew about their trips or about what they were reading. Their attitude toward themselves, toward their marriage, and toward others had changed. They were willing to share their experiences now with anyone who wanted to know.

APPLICATION: If you're hesitant to tell others about your spiritual journey at this point in your life, don't feel guilty. Keep looking for the appropriate time to share, knowing that the proper time will come.

The God Who Cares

This is the message you shall carry—there is a loving God who cares. And God may walk and talk with you. This you may experience in your own life.

Based on Edgar Cayce reading 254-95

Even though she was meditating and reading as many books as she could find on the Edgar Cayce material, Patty wondered for a while if some of these statements were really true. One day she found out.

She was Christmas shopping at a mall and looking for a certain matchbox car. In fact, she was so involved in her search that she did not even notice a man walk up beside her.

Suddenly she had an uneasy feeling, as if someone were telling her she was in danger.

She looked around and saw this man who was looking at her in a strange way. She hurriedly left the toy store, ducked into another store close by, and allowed the man to pass by.

This happened at a time when several people had disappeared mysteriously from local shopping malls. Although she might have overreacted, she was glad she had heeded the voice within. She had listened because of a Cayce quote she had read that said that help would be there when you least expected it from a loving God who cares.

APPLICATION: Begin using this affirmation, "God cares and will walk and talk with me."

Unlimiting Yourself

Know this within: the spirit of the Master's love gives each soul the knowledge to do what is necessary for that soul to develop.   Based on Edgar Cayce reading 452-7

Sandra had been fighting limitations since she was a child. All her life she had struggled with those imposed on her by her family, by society, and by herself. She remembered that in growing up her parents would tell her what her abilities were and what her career choices should be.

She remembered teachers telling her that she had limited intelligence and could only expect to go so far. Sadly she had accepted those statements for many years.

When Sandra began working with the Edgar Cayce readings, she saw that her own patterns of doubt were now imposing limitations on her. So she began to put her trust and faith in God. It was not her limited self she was going to allow to blossom, but the power of the Creative Forces using her as a channel to meet the challenges in her life.

She went on to graduate school, taking one of the most demanding programs in the university. She graduated at the top of her class, won major awards, and received top job offers.

Now in meeting challenging situations, she doesn't think in terms of limitations on herself or the circumstance. Instead she opens herself to God. She sees God going with her and the Universal Forces working through her to accomplish what needs to be done.

APPLICATION: Think of a limitation you are imposing on yourself. Do one thing today to place faith in God and act to overcome that limitation.

The Risky Journey to Life

The greater forces should be exercised in placing that faith, that confidence, that purpose in God—the Giver of all good and perfect gifts.   Based on Edgar Cayce reading 2888-2

Abraham was living a secure and comfortable life. He had a wife, a job, and a good reputation in his community. He had his family near him and a good future in front of him.

One day the voice inside called, "Abraham, it's time to leave this place. I have a new land to which to lead you. I won't tell you all the details, but I will tell you that you will have children and give hope and new life to many people. All along the way you can count on me to be with you."

For many days Abraham thought about these words. Was he really willing to risk everything he had for something as vague as some unknown land? Could he believe that this voice had a power that could be present to help him regardless of whatever he encountered.

Finally he decided to follow the call. For many years he wandered from place to place. He fathered his child. He experienced the presence of the power behind the voice. He found new life for himself and others. He never reached the land but found the journey worth the risk.

APPLICATION: Name an area of your life where you may have to take a big risk and leave familiar security and territory behind.

Beginning the Day

Be a well-rounded body.   *Take specific, definite exercises*
morning and evening.   Based on Edgar Cayce reading 341-31

Because of her age Agnes cannot do vigorous exercises, but she still does some simple daily ones. She has a morning routine that helps her begin the day alert and ready to work.

First, she does stretching exercises, stretching like a cat by putting her hands upwards as high as she can. She does this two or three times.

Then, she stands by an open window and breathes in fresh air for several seconds. She follows this with a head and neck exercise. All these bring circulation to the brain and upper body so it has plenty of blood to begin the day.

When Agnes began this routine two years ago, she wasn't sure it was helping her much. So she got a little lazy. For two weeks she slept in later and didn't leave time to exercise before going to work. After three days she began to be lethargic and didn't feel as alert or feel she could think as clearly as she had the week before. After two weeks she could tell she was getting up more slowly and feeling tired for the first few hours every morning.

She decided to go back to her routine, get up fifteen minutes earlier, and begin the exercises again. Within a week she could feel the difference. Since then, she has been faithful to her routine.

APPLICATION: Get up fifteen minutes earlier in order to do a few stretching, wake-up exercises to prepare your body for the day.

Sing Him to Sleep

Music becomes a means of expression that bridges much of that which may bring beauty and harmony into the experience.   Based on Edgar Cayce reading 412-9

As a parent of a four-year-old son, Norman has tried pre-sleep suggestions several times for such conditions as bad dreams and behavior problems, or simply to create a positive sleep atmosphere for David.

On one occasion Norman put the words of these suggestions to music because the Edgar Cayce readings spoke about music being a bridge to the unconscious that would help to empower the words being used. He picked out a tune that David was familiar with and made up words appropriate to the issues for the evening.

Norman was never sure if these were really making an impression on his son. However, he has noticed now that David asks for these songs occasionally. He will say, "Daddy, sing 'David is a good boy.'" Since he was now asking for them, Norman knew that at some level his son's soul was benefiting from these musical suggestions.

APPLICATION: During the next several days spend five to ten minutes a day sitting quietly with some relaxing music and notice its effects on you.

Unexpected Surprises

Each experience builds the ability of the individual—either mentally, spiritually, or physically—to make application in whatever may be the next experience.

Based on Edgar Cayce reading 2489-1

Looking for God in your life can bring you the unexpected.

Ever since Ron has been consciously looking for God's activity in his daily life, some unusual sequences of events have occurred. One such experience involved his business.

Ron received a unique contract which required specialized skilled labor to do the job. He called the qualified people he knew, but they were all unavailable. After a few days he didn't know who else to call so he told God his need and decided to be alert for God to act.

A few days later he was engaged in a conversation with John, a longtime friend. The conversation had nothing to do with business, but as John was leaving, Ron felt he should mention that he needed someone with a particular skill. John gave him Bill's name and phone number.

Ron had heard of Bill, but Bill's phone number was unlisted so he had not been able to contact him. Ron called and discovered that Bill was about to move. However, after listening to Ron's offer, Bill changed his mind about moving and joined Ron's business.

To Ron, looking for God in one's daily life means being alert and taking advantage of the unexpected surprises.

APPLICATION: Look at each experience today as something that is preparing you for a future experience.

Doing What Needs to Be Done

*Good is creative, is constructive without the thought of self,
but that others may know peace and harmony in their experience.*   Based on Edgar Cayce reading 1877-1

The word was all over the city. At least one night a week for
the past two months Rabbi David had been seen entering
the house of a known prostitute, staying for about an hour,
and then leaving.

That afternoon at Rabbi Samuel's house everyone expected to talk about this news. Instead the rabbi asked how
far one should go to help another person.

Students offered a variety of quotes from the scriptures
and their own opinions. Finally Rabbi Samuel spoke and
said, "If you desire to help someone caught in mud and filth,
it is at times not enough to stand by the mud hole and reach
down. There are times when you must go into the mud pit,
grab hold of the other with your hands, and pull that one
and yourself out into the light."

Then he dismissed them.

A few days later people learned that the woman had dis-
continued her business and had moved to her brother's
house in a different city to start her life over. Rabbi David's
discussions with her had changed her life.

The students then understood Rabbi Samuel's words
that sometimes it is necessary to go where we might not go
and do things we might not ordinarily do in order to help
other people.

APPLICATION: Look at the people around you whom you
know. Risk getting your hands dirty and doing some things
you might not ordinarily do in order to help someone.

Being Where You're Supposed to Be

Let the approach be made in humbleness of heart, seeking not that of self but as your Lord, your God, would have you do. Pray earnestly, pray sincerely.

Based on Edgar Cayce reading 1125-3

It had been three years since her auto accident, and complete recovery had been slow. Now her doctor and her friends were encouraging Amy to go back to work for her own good. However, she was hesitant even though she didn't understand why.

A next-door neighbor told her that her boss, Mr. Andrews, needed a new secretary. Amy's responsibilities in this job would be similar to what she had done before so there would not be a lot of pressure to learn new skills right away. Amy agreed to go for an interview. However, she went to the interview knowing she was going to refuse the job.

Mr. Andrews listened to her and accepted her decision, but he did ask her to do a few hours' volunteer time for him today, if she would. She agreed. She also agreed to return every two or three days to help out with some typing.

A month later Mr. Andrews called and asked Amy to work full time. Before going over to talk to him, Amy did something totally out of character for her at that time. She fell on her knees and prayed about it.

In spite of the fact that it looked like a lot of work, she agreed to try it for a week. Everything seemed to come so easy. Amy knew after a few days that this was where she was supposed to be and that God had worked through this slow process to get her there.

APPLICATION: Pray today that in all you do, God's will can be done in your life.

Emptying Self for God's Work

*In Jesus and in the study of His example in the earth is life
and that you may have it more abundantly.*

Based on Edgar Cayce reading 357-13

How can you look at Jesus as a pattern for your life?

Sally turned to the Bible to find out more about Jesus when she first read this statement: "Jesus is the pattern for each individual's life." As she read the Bible looking for insights into this idea, she discovered characteristics of Jesus she had not realized before.

She noticed His acceptance of people. She saw that He showed no bigotry or prejudice. To Him a person's position in society or the amount of possessions was not important.

However, she also noticed that Jesus pointed beyond Himself. He was always acknowledging God and giving God and the Spirit the credit for working through Him. He did not take the credit Himself.

When Sally now works with people, she finds herself trying to follow Jesus' pattern in this important way. She tries to set her ego aside and attune herself to a greater oneness with the Spirit so that it is God's Spirit at work in her.

For Sally the idea of Jesus being the pattern involves the task of emptying herself, setting ego aside, so that a greater power can work through her.

APPLICATION: Pick out one characteristic of Jesus and apply it to your life.

Reaching Complete Agreement

For a body, mind, and soul being in oneness of purpose brings harmony into the body as a whole.

Based on Edgar Cayce reading 3250-1

Do you ever have times when you think you have accepted something and later discover that a part of you really hasn't?

Jill began running a slight fever, which usually indicated that she was getting sick. Since it might be the flu, she lay down to rest and found herself very relaxed.

She asked herself why she was running a fever. An intuitive response told her she was pregnant. She continued this internal dialogue and learned that she had the fever because a part of her had not accepted the pregnancy. She also learned that she would continue to have a fever once a month until she really accepted and wanted this child.

For the next month she consciously affirmed her desire to have this child, but next month the fever reoccurred for three days. Still she continued working on affirming her pregnancy, but the fevers kept occurring until the fifth month of her pregnancy. Then they ceased.

Jill doesn't know what finally changed within her. However, this experience taught her that parts of her do not always consent to what she has consciously agreed to, so now she tries to affirm her decisions at all levels of her being and to be alert for signs when this is not happening.

APPLICATION: Think of a recent decision you made that you felt your whole being may not have accepted. Either continue to affirm your decision until you feel total acceptance or re-examine it to see if your subconscious is sending you a wiser message.

The Miser

Giving—that is the law of love. Giving in action, without the force shown or reward for that given.

Based on Edgar Cayce reading 3744-4

There was a rich man who never gave to any charity. He never gave bread to a beggar nor contributed to any philanthropic organization. The people called him the Miser.

There was in the same village a poor shoemaker who was very generous. He responded to every cry for help, and no one was ever turned away from his door empty-handed.

One day the Miser died. The elders of the village had him buried at the edge of the cemetery.

As the days passed, the rabbi heard disturbing news about the shoemaker. He no longer gave alms to beggars, and he refused every charitable group that came to him asking for assistance. He was claiming he had no more money to give away.

The rabbi called in the shoemaker. "Why have you suddenly stopped giving to needy people?"

The shoemaker told his story. "Years ago the one you called the Miser came to me with a large sum of money and told me to give it to those who needed help. He made me promise I would never tell where the money came from. Every month he would replenish what I had spent."

The rabbi called the villagers together and told them the shoemaker's story. "This one we called the Miser has truly fulfilled the scriptures, keeping his alms-giving a secret."

When the rabbi died, he asked to be buried near the edge of the cemetery, next to the one called the Miser.

APPLICATION: Give anonymously to some person.

Losing Isn't Always the End

You only fail if you quit trying.
Based on Edgar Cayce reading 3292-1

Daniel's work includes presenting proposals for expansion, so that the business can branch into new areas. There are times when his job becomes frustrating because other people who have decision-making ability do not share his vision and his dreams. Several times he has worked for months on a project only to have it voted down.

At those times he finds it tempting to quit. Then he ponders the quote from the Edgar Cayce readings, "You only fail if you quit trying." This thought helps him realize that the final vote does not determine the validity of his efforts. Even if others think that his ideas are wrong, he does not feel as if he has failed, because he continues to try and to work for something in which he believes.

Daniel had his approach affirmed when his last project was voted down. He had known for several weeks that the vote would be close and that several board members would strongly oppose him on this issue. But he kept working on it because he believed in it.

After the negative vote, he became discouraged. However, two weeks later the project was resurrected in a new and better way. So his efforts were not in vain. An idea will come true that would not have happened if he had listened to his opponents and dropped the project weeks before.

APPLICATION: The next time you feel you have failed, focus on the value of your efforts and not on the results.

Talking Without Talking

If the problems of the experience today are taken as an expectancy for the unusual and that which is to be creative and hopeful and helpful, life becomes rather the creative song of the joyous worker.   Based on Edgar Cayce reading 1968-5

It wasn't that Audrey didn't enjoy her work. She did, but it was frustrating. She never knew how important verbal communication was to her until she began working with mentally handicapped children who couldn't communicate in this way with her. After days like today, she wondered if she would be able to communicate with them at all.

One girl had really gotten upset today. Obviously she had wanted something, but nobody could figure out what. This made the girl frustrated and so angry she started throwing things. Unfortunately she had to be put in her room.

That night Audrey dreamed of this girl. She and the girl were communicating, but they weren't talking. Audrey didn't know how they understood each other, but they did.

When she woke up, she realized the dream was telling her about other ways to communicate. The next day she tried to listen to everything the little girl did. She watched every gesture she made and tried to recall every toy with which the girl had ever played.

In the afternoon when the little girl seemed to want something, Audrey knelt down in front of her for a few moments. Then she had a feeling about a particular doll. She helped the girl find the doll, and smiled as the little girl warmly embraced it.

APPLICATION: There are many ways to communicate with people. Begin observing how people communicate with you without using words.

The Power of Positive Eating

Whenever you eat, see it doing what you would have it do. See the food as taken to fulfill a purpose that will better do what the body, the mind, the soul has chosen to stand for.

Based on Edgar Cayce reading 341-31

Carla was doing it again. She was eating a second piece of pie. She knew she was eating foods that weren't good for her, but she didn't know how to stop.

Then she read some health tips in the Cayce readings such as: Drink eight glasses of water daily. Eat a fresh salad every day because lettuce is a blood cleanser, carrots add vitamin B_1 which the body cannot store, and celery is good for fiber and the nerves. These all made sense, but it sounded like it could become a boring routine.

However, Carla quickly discovered that she could keep the routine from getting stale by having positive thoughts as she ate. She began to think about bringing vitamin B_1 into her body when she ate the carrots. She thought about cleansing the blood when she ate the lettuce. These thoughts influenced her attitude about what she was eating, but she also knew they were influencing the way her body received and used the food. So her thoughts were as important as the food was to her health.

Carla also discovered that these thoughts overcame her desire to eat those foods that were unhealthy for her. She found herself automatically reaching for foods that were good for her. Within a few weeks she could pass up a pie without giving it a second glance.

APPLICATION: At your next meal tell yourself that you are eating this food in order to give your body nourishment to better live out your purpose in life.

The Money Will Be There

Your daily acts will bring the realization of the ideal being manifest in you as well as in others.

Based on Edgar Cayce reading 262-12

This year Steve was president of a local nonprofit organization. He decided he was going to make some changes in the annual picnic held to thank volunteers.

The year before he had heard some staff complaining. They were saying that they did all the work—providing food, setting up, and serving. Then they didn't even get help cleaning up. Steve decided to turn the event into a catered picnic and invite the organizational staff as guests as well.

He realized his plans would go over the budget allotted for the event. Therefore, he had to get extra money somewhere. He kept telling himself that the money would be there if he kept his ideal of "thanking those who served."

At the picnic people were told of the changes that had been made and the incurred costs that were not yet covered by income. As a result of some fun fund-raising activities held at the gathering, they not only met their budget but were also able to contribute $4,000 to the organization's operating income.

APPLICATION: Be sure of your ideal. Then work on completing a task without letting doubts dissuade you.

Called by Name

Know in whom you have believed, that your God may call you by name as you enter into God's service day by day.

Based on Edgar Cayce reading 262-32

Ellen's discussion group decided to try a discipline of calling everyone in the group by name when they greeted each other. She found this meaningful, so she decided to try that throughout the week at work.

She went to school to begin her work week and try out her new discipline. The first colleague she saw she opened her mouth to say "hello" and suddenly realized she didn't know his first name. By the end of a few days she realized she hadn't known the names of almost one quarter of her staff associates. This discipline helped her learn their names, but it also made these people more personal.

Ellen soon realized that the staff, too, was picking up her discipline. All of them were now using first names when they talked to each other. No longer were morning greetings and acknowledgments routine. They were talking and relating to real people. The entire feeling among the staff changed because they now called each other by name.

APPLICATION: Begin using other people's first names every time you greet them.

The Cycles of Life

Individuals in the earth move from cycle to cycle in their own development. They have taken this or that road in meeting certain conditions. And one experience at one portion of the life is as a lamp or guidebook. When they have come to the crossroads again, there is another experience or another lesson.
Based on Edgar Cayce reading 993-4

Sandra was frustrated with herself. She had faced the issue of jealousy about two years ago with Susan and thought she had conquered that tendency in herself. Now the problem had surfaced again, but this time with another person. After two weeks of wondering why she had those jealous feelings about Marian, she realized it was time to get some help.

She immediately went to talk with a good friend about her frustration. After listening to her story, he told her something that became for her the key to understanding her dilemma. Life is like a spiral. We each have several central issues to work on in this life. As we meet the issue the first time, we respond in one way and, we hope, have learned something.

However, we don't usually learn what we have to learn the first time we face and deal with the issue. So later on, when we are ready to confront the issue again, we meet the problem in a somewhat different way. Maybe we will learn a little bit more. We continue to face the issue each time in a slightly different way until we have learned the lesson that we need to learn.

APPLICATION: The next time you confront an issue you know you have dealt with before, make sure you are facing it in a way that shows growth and soul development.

Treating Others with Respect

Work where you are. As was given to those who were called, "The ground upon which you stand is holy." Begin where you are.
Based on Edgar Cayce reading 4021-1

Now that Frank was leaving his job, he took time to look back on his career as manager of a gasoline service station. He had known from the start that this would not be his life's work; however, he had also believed he was in this job for a reason. He had decided to work with one of the spiritual truths from the Edgar Cayce readings, "Work where you are," to see if he could apply the readings in his job.

His approach had been to work alongside people, never asking his employees to do anything he himself wouldn't do. He had frequently worked with them, treating them like co-workers and not as if they were just there for him to boss around. As a result, he had gained their respect.

Because Frank had been honest with them and had encouraged them to be honest with others, the station attracted customers who would drive miles out of their way to stop there. Frank and his mechanics would look at those cars carefully. They didn't sell people what they didn't need and would alert them if it appeared a new part or new tires would be needed in a few months. They didn't try to force others to buy then but to be prepared for the future.

As he pondered these things, he realized he had done a good job of living out what the readings said about treating people with respect and dignity. He had "worked where he was" to apply the readings in his everyday life.

APPLICATION: "Work where you are" to treat people with respect and dignity.

The Dreamer

Let the approach be made in humbleness of heart, seeking not that as of self but as your Lord, your God, your Savior would have you do.   Based on Edgar Cayce reading 1125-3

While he stood there waiting, he reflected on his life. Many significant events could be marked by his dreams.

He had come down to breakfast one morning glowing over two dreams. The first one contained an image of him as a star. He had seen the sun, moon, and eleven other stars bowing down to him. The second concerned harvest time. He had set a sheaf of wheat in the field and the sheaves his brothers had made bowed down to his. He felt pleased with his interpretations of those dreams, although his family's anger over his pride had somewhat spoiled the moment.

Much later, in prison, he had interpreted dreams for two of pharaoh's servants. Their dreams had come to pass.

Now he was standing before pharaoh. He knew pharaoh's dreams were important ones, and he knew something about himself now as well. He had learned about humility and God's presence in his life.

When pharaoh asked if he were the one who had interpreted his servants' dreams, Joseph answered, "Only God can interpret dreams. But tell me your dream. God will give pharaoh a favorable answer."

As pharaoh spoke, Joseph could sense the insight coming from the divine power that had sustained him for these past several years. God's answer would be ready for the pharaoh.

APPLICATION: The next time you are looking for answers to a question, know that those who open to God with sincere hearts will find answers.

Listening to the Still, Small Voice

Learn to listen to that still, small voice from within. In that voice comes the impelling influence that must be the basis of our actions. Based on Edgar Cayce reading 239-1

How do you react when your inner voice calls you to do something at an inappropriate or inopportune time?

Having learned to listen to her inner voice even when it speaks at inconvenient times or asks her to do something that would usually be considered unacceptable, Marian found herself one morning taking a detour on her way to work.

While she had been driving along, her inner voice suddenly told her to visit a friend. She knew she would be late for work if she did and so kept driving. She told herself she would go after work. However, the voice would not let up, so she finally went to see her friend.

Marian found Angie depressed and suicidal. She had been having drinking problems and was just beginning to realize the true condition of her life. Without asking Angie's opinion, Marian told her she would take her to an AA meeting that night and wouldn't even listen to any of Angie's excuses for not wanting to go.

That evening Marian took Angie, and Angie has been going ever since. Angie said later that that early morning visit and that first AA meeting were real breakthroughs for her.

APPLICATION: If you are doing something today and your inner voice calls you to do something else, stop and listen carefully to what it is saying.

The Ending Is Not Like the Beginning

You are in the present experience more far-reaching in the influence you have, in the opportunity you have for making the earth a better place to live in for those to come.

Based on Edgar Cayce reading 4047-2

Where Mary had begun was certainly not where she was ending up. She remembered vividly that her interest in earth changes had first awakened her curiosity in metaphysical subjects and brought her to the Edgar Cayce readings.

However, the more she read, the more she became aware of how people can strongly determine the world around them. People influence not only their own lives, but their thoughts can also actually influence the earth.

Instead of focusing now on the gloom and doom and drama of the changes, she found herself wondering what she could do to heal the earth and bring peace to a troubled planet. Her prayers became more frequent and more focused on healing. She became aware of the energies she was sending out and tried to bring herself to a point of inner peace so she could radiate this peace to others.

In her spiritual growth group, she found herself encouraging others to do their part. She quoted the scripture passage that said, "The prayers of one man saved a city," in order to tell people that each individual was important.

She had begun by focusing on the drama of earth changes. Now only a few months later she was talking about healing the earth and seeking peace. Her interest had certainly been transformed in a very positive way.

APPLICATION: Do one thing—even if it's a small thing—to make the community where you reside a better place in which to live.

The Power of the Subconscious Mind

The subconscious mind is a portion of the mind of the universal forces—that has been builded, made, or come into existence through an individual's experience in the earth.

Based on Edgar Cayce reading 195-31

Tim had been asking himself the question for over twenty years—"Why was the subconscious mind more powerful than the conscious mind?" Ever since he had become interested in both reincarnation and psychology, he had wondered if there were a connection somewhere. Now the answer lay right in front of him.

The morning paper announced a lecture on *The Search for Bridey Murphy.* Within the article was a quote from the Edgar Cayce readings saying that "the subconscious mind is the mind of the soul." He decided to attend that lecture and see if he could learn more about this guy Edgar Cayce.

That evening began Tim's metaphysical journey that helped him explore the depths of his own subconscious mind. His journey taught him the source of many of his interests, the possible background for many of his emotional responses to people and places, and even why he had chosen the occupation he had in this lifetime.

As he explored this link between reincarnation and the power of the subconscious mind, he became less afraid of it and more willing to listen to and respond to its guidance.

APPLICATION: Your subconscious mind is a storehouse of thousands of years of experience. Affirm its value as you further understand its purpose in your life.

Getting What Is Needed to Grow

Let each budget time. Let each give so much—for the necessary activities for the supplying of the needs in their relationships.
Based on Edgar Cayce reading 480-20

After Mark and Sandy had been married for a year, they came to a crucial decision-making point. They had both finished college, but they knew they needed advanced schooling to pursue their particular careers. They also wanted children. They had to decide which to choose first.

The advantages of going to school first could mean a better financial base upon which to raise a family. On the other hand, having a family while they were this age appealed to them. They opted to have children now.

Over the past 10 years this has meant struggling to keep life in balance. Mark is careful that he doesn't spend too many evenings away from home attending meetings or completing unfinished work at the office. This choice may have hurt his career advancement a bit, but that is not a major concern for him.

They both make sure they take time for each other and for their children. Spending hours at sports events, helping with homework, or chaperoning trips are acceptable aspects of their schedules. They watch school grades and behavior patterns to be sure the children aren't feeling neglected.

Their guiding ideal is to be sure that every member of the family gets what he or she needs to grow. This has not always been easy, but they have never regretted the choice they made.

APPLICATION: Do something to be sure that those you care for get what they need in order to grow.

Heading into the Lion's Den

It is for this purpose that a soul enters a material life— that it may put the will, the glory, the purpose of God first and foremost.
                                    Based on Edgar Cayce reading 2081-1

The lion's den—those thoughts sent shudders through any man, even one as strong as Daniel. And that terrifying death would be so simple to avoid. All Daniel had to do tomorrow was kneel to a powerless idol.

But Daniel wasn't afraid of the power or lack of power of that idol. Daniel was concerned about what kneeling before it would mean. To do so would be to acknowledge that something other than the God of Israel deserved his faith and his worship. That Daniel could not do.

Even in times of trouble and testing when he had been punished for his faith, Daniel had still found power coming from his God. That power had not helped him avoid pain or persecution every time, but that power had always given him the strength to endure it. If tomorrow were to be the day of his death, Daniel knew his God would be with him in that moment and beyond.

Daniel's decision had been made long ago. Tomorrow would only be one more day of living faithfully for his God.

APPLICATION: The next time the easy way means you have to deny your principles or ideals, choose your ideals.

Every Dream Says Something

Dreams may be used as lessons for a more perfect under-standing of forces manifest in the physical world.

Based on Edgar Cayce reading 136-12

When Connie woke up, she knew she had had another significant dream about her sister. She rolled over in bed, grabbed her pen, and immediately began to write down what she could remember. She was glad she had changed her way of recording dreams.

Until recently Connie had kept track of the dreams she considered important. However, only if this dream had left a strong impression with her did she write it down the next morning. Then someone spoke to her about all dreams having insight into issues she was working with every day.

She thought about this. She also was aware that her sister was very important to her and began to wonder why she didn't dream about her if that relationship was significant.

So Connie began to write down every dream she could remember. When she woke up in the middle of the night, she wrote down the dream because she knew she would not remember it the next morning. She discovered that she had a dream about her sister every two or three nights. These dreams gave her significant information about everyday issues because of what her sister represented to her.

Her dream journal now contains three or four dreams a night, and her ability to understand the daily issues being addressed in her dream symbols is improving rapidly.

APPLICATION: For the next month try keeping track of every dream you have. Look for recurring symbols and ideas that speak to daily issues in your life.

Waiting for the Questions

Become as a companion so that there may be the seeking by the developing mind for counsel, for guidance.

Based on Edgar Cayce reading 759-12

Sally's first day at work was a memorable one. She had accepted the job not knowing exactly what this company's business really entailed. However, she had assumed it had something to do with oceanography because it was near the ocean and the word *research* was in the title. The man who hired her wouldn't tell her either what they did.

The first day on the job, she opened some mail and found a request for a "black book" because someone wanted help with psoriasis. A check was enclosed. That day she opened several letters talking about various diseases, and some of them mentioned the name Edgar Cayce.

She finally asked who Edgar Cayce was. Her boss wouldn't tell her. Instead he gave her two books to read— *There Is a River* and *The Sleeping Prophet*. He said they weren't required reading but that she could come back and talk to him when she had read one of them. She devoured them in a week and wanted more and more to read.

Only later did she realize what he was doing. She was to get interested on her own. She was supposed to ask questions so she would learn when she was ready.

It worked. She has been working with the Edgar Cayce material for over twenty years now.

APPLICATION: Describe an instance in your life where someone opened a door to a new field of learning and then allowed you to progress at your own pace. Take one step to do that for someone else.

The Experience Made the Difference

Know what within self, from one's experiences in the earth, is prompting the desires of the heart.

Based on Edgar Cayce reading 1043-1

Harold didn't know how it had happened. One minute he was a happy seven-year-old boy standing with his back to the fireplace feeling warm. The next minute his pant's leg was on fire and he was screaming for his mother. Fortunately she was standing nearby and put out the fire, but not before he had a burn from his ankle to the top of his thigh.

Instead of rushing to a doctor like most mothers would, his mother immediately contacted Edgar Cayce for a reading on how to treat her son. A medical solution and way of applying it were recommended. His mother followed that treatment, and the burn began to heal.

When Harold could walk with the use of crutches several weeks later, he noticed that his leg would not straighten out. It was bent backward at the knee. His mother again went to Edgar Cayce for a reading. He recommended some massages and another series of treatments.

By the end of four months Harold was an active seven-year-old again. He never had to have any skin grafts, never had any infection, and has never had problems since with that leg.

This experience made Harold investigate the Edgar Cayce readings further when he got older. He has found many guidelines for his life as a result.

APPLICATION: Be alert for experiences that make you see life in a different way and encourage you to set off in new directions.

The Gift of a Whistle

*What a body or a soul does with the knowledge or under-
standing that it has makes for development for that soul.*
Based on Edgar Cayce reading 476-1

Rabbi Abraham was staying as a guest in the home of Rabbi
David. Late one night Rabbi David heard strange sounds
coming from Rabbi Abraham's room. He went to the door
and listened. Rabbi Abraham was running back and forth in
the room crying out, "Lord of the world, I love You! But what
is there for me to do to show You that love. I can't do anything."

Then Rabbi David heard nothing for a few seconds.

Soon Rabbi Abraham began running back and forth
again, repeating those same phrases over and over, "Lord of
the world, I love You! But what is there for me to do for
You."

Then, there was silence again. For a minute nothing was
heard. Finally, Rabbi Abraham blurted out, "I know! I can
whistle! Lord of the universe, I shall whistle something for
You." So Rabbi Abraham began to whistle.

APPLICATION: Use one of your talents or gifts—that you
usually don't think of as a talent—to express your love for
God.

Silent Communication

The spirit or soul of those who are in accord or may be attuned makes for a unison that becomes harmonious in its every relationship. Based on Edgar Cayce reading 1135-4

It had happened to her again this morning. Gloria was sure Mike must have sensed it this time, so she decided to call him that evening and ask.

Ever since they had gotten engaged, Gloria had felt herself growing closer and closer to Mike. Especially in her meditations she felt as if they were communicating at a deep soul level. The first time this had happened she had considered it a strange experience and didn't tell Mike. However, when it happened two days later, she called Mike to tell him. He admitted he had been meditating about the same time she had, but he had not experienced anything like that.

Then it began to happen even when they weren't meditating at the same time. Mike would laugh it off when she called to tell him what she had sensed. However, even if Mike did laugh at these experiences, she enjoyed them. It made Gloria feel even closer to him, knowing that in some way they were communicating at a soul level even though consciously neither of them knew what was occurring.

If this were happening, perhaps it meant that they were special people to each other. That gave her all the more confidence that their upcoming marriage would work.

APPLICATION: People who are close to each other often learn to communicate without words. Pick out a special person in your life and be alert to the ways you communicate with this person without using words.

Making Up Is Hard to Do

*"Love ye one another" and thus you will fulfill all that is in
the purpose of Jesus' entrance into the earth—to replace hate
and jealousy with love and hope and joy.*

Based on Edgar Cayce reading 5749-10

Brenda usually didn't get into arguments like the one she
had had with Sarah this evening. But tonight had just been
the culmination of what had been building up for months.

When she joined Sarah's discussion group, Brenda knew
problems might develop. Both tended to be powerful
women with strong opinions. However, Sarah was also a
good teacher so Brenda had spent several months learning
without arguing or disagreeing. During the last month,
though, Brenda had begun to express her own views. This
led to disagreements and finally to the big argument tonight.
Brenda decided not to go back to that discussion group.

For over a year the two didn't speak to each other. Then
Brenda began to realize she wasn't living what she was
teaching others about the Edgar Cayce readings' approach
to solving conflict and dealing with anger. When she finally
called Sarah, she found Sarah ready to talk as well.

They had several long, honest discussions about what
they liked and disliked about each other. They affirmed
each other and became friends again. When Brenda moved,
it was Sarah who organized her going-away party.

APPLICATION: Name someone you have not seen in a
while because you had a disagreement. Take a step to release the anger so you can view the relationship in a new
light.

The Big Picture

Be joyous, be happy in God's love.   God has loved us from afar.   How much more when we try, though we may stumble and fall!   Based on Edgar Cayce reading 262-83

As a business administrator, Carolyn faces stress daily. If it isn't major decisions, it's the little things that keep mounting up minute by minute throughout the day. The Edgar Cayce readings have helped her handle the stress with the following ideas.

One, she tries to maintain a sense of humor by having two good laughs during the day. Sometimes she even laughs at how seriously she is taking everything, just to help her keep things in perspective.

Two, she remembers that life is continuous. What good she does today will continue, even if it appears to bear no early fruits. If she makes a mistake, she can always come back and try to correct it as much as possible. She knows that holding on to her ideal will also allow God to work with her mistakes.

Finally, she takes time to look at the big picture. She will mentally project herself several miles into the air and look down on the business. This enables her to see the overall efforts and directions of the business. It also allows her to see the relative insignificance of some of the smaller irritations that are currently facing her. This enables her emotionally to detach herself a bit from those irritations and be more objective in making decisions.

APPLICATION: The next time you feel small items mounting up, take time to laugh or see the bigger picture in your life.

The Apple Stand

To bring hope, to bring cheer, to bring joy, to bring a smile again to those whose face and heart are bathed in tears and in woe is making that divine love shine—shine—in your own soul.   Based on Edgar Cayce reading 987-4

Three businessmen were rushing through the crowded station to catch their commuter train home. They bumped into an apple stand and sent apples rolling all over the floor. Without looking back, they raced on as the young blind boy who was tending the stand began to crawl around to retrieve his apples.

The train was just ready to depart when the first two men jumped on. However, at the last moment, the third man stopped abruptly and didn't jump on the train.

He turned and walked back through the station to where the blind boy was still attempting to gather his apples.

"Here, let me do that," he said, putting down his briefcase and getting on his knees to retrieve some of the apples that had rolled under a bench.

After a few minutes he had finished putting the apples back in place. Pulling a ten-dollar bill out of his wallet, he handed it to the boy saying, "I hope this will make up for any damage or inconvenience we might have caused you."

As the man walked away, he heard the boy say, "Golly, mister, are you Jesus Christ?"

The man stopped and stood still for a few moments, thinking about the words he had just heard.

APPLICATION: The next time you realize you have been insensitive to someone, stop and do something to show you care.

A Worshiping Community

The church is the living Christ. Make association first with that, and whether it is in this, that, or the other name—Christ you serve and not a church.

Based on Edgar Cayce reading 2823-3

Marian and Steve weren't getting anything out of the church service they were attending. However, they felt a need to gather with people and worship in a community. They knew that just meditating at home would not meet their spiritual needs or help them reach out to others in need.

After asking around and trying several churches, they found a small group of 10 people who were meeting together. Steve and Marian felt at home immediately. They liked the support they witnessed members giving to each other. They appreciated the prayer time when people could express out loud their current needs and concerns.

As they attended for several weeks, they noticed that the people would occasionally meet outdoors or in a home instead of the room they rented.

They liked this flexibility and change of location when it was done for a good reason. They liked how the pastor addressed ideas such as reincarnation in the sermons and used inclusive language for people and God. Feminine images and masculine images, abstract images and more physical images were all used. They felt these terms painted a more complete picture of God.

They knew with this group of people they had found their worshiping community.

APPLICATION: Find a group of people who can nurture your spiritual growth and give you loving support.

The Result Is Peace of Mind

Let my ways seek to know what You would have me do day by day. For only in You may there come the peace, the harmony that make life worthwhile. Based on Edgar Cayce reading 792-1

The peace of mind Esther has today did not come overnight. Forty years of working with the Edgar Cayce readings has led her to this stage in her life. She sums it up by saying, "If I take care of today and do the best with what I have, I will have laid the foundation I need to meet what tomorrow brings."

She has peace of mind in relation to the world around her as she thinks about the earth changes she believes are coming. She has a serenity as she observes her aging and what that might mean. She doesn't know how either of these issues will impact her, but she does know that she will find the strength and courage to face what she has to face and learn what she has to learn from any experience that will confront her.

She also has peace of mind in relation to future lives. A life reading she had received from Edgar Cayce mentioned an incarnation in which she had regressed. The reading did not go into detail because it said she was not dealing with those issues in this present life. However, she knows she will face them some time in the future. When this happens, she knows she will have the ability to meet those experiences as well.

For Esther peace of mind has been the result of her life-long spiritual journey.

APPLICATION: Look for ways you can find peace of mind as you approach your life.

Finding Self-Acceptance

All life, all activity emanates from a spiritual source. As these are seen, felt, and experienced by the body, they may be used as stepping-stones for the proper understanding of those influences in the experience of the body.

Based on Edgar Cayce reading 665-2

The first time Joyce and Gary attended Judy's spiritual growth group they looked ill at ease. After they had attended a few meetings, they told their story.

Joyce had had several psychic experiences when she was a young girl which had troubled her. Her parents could not accept them and would not help her understand them. As a result, she looked at herself as abnormal and blocked these experiences whenever she could.

When she got married, she told her husband, Gary, about these experiences because they were happening again. Gary loved her, but he did not understand what was happening to her either. In addition she was now having trouble sleeping. She would have strange feelings and see images just prior to sleep, so she was afraid to go to sleep at night.

As other group members shared their stories, she realized that she was not abnormal. Other people had experienced what she had experienced. After only a few months the woman's acceptance and understanding of herself and her abilities had improved tremendously. She was more relaxed, could sleep peacefully, and felt as if her life were starting over.

APPLICATION: When you or people you know have psychic experiences, remember that many people have them and they can be a normal part of our lives as spiritual beings.

Time to Let Go

In the love as may be manifested in the daily activities of every soul, each may show the love which impels the giving of everything within self as a sign of the Maker having spoken with you.   Based on Edgar Cayce reading 262-44

Hannah was filled with gladness and grief. The years had gone by so quickly. It hardly seemed possible that Samuel was old enough to begin his training in God's house.

She could still remember the years before his birth. Month after month she had come to the temple to pray for a child. When she was almost too old, she had come once more with a special pledge to God. If God would give her a son, she would give her son to God.

Her family, her friends, and she herself could hardly believe it when she discovered a few months later she was going to have a child. The joy in the community was intensified when her child was a boy.

The years had passed so quickly since the day of his birth. God had kept a promise. Now it was her turn to keep hers. She had come to the temple to give her son to God.

Her gladness was for the joy she had experienced these last few years. Her grief was for the way her relationship with her son was changing. However, deep inside her she knew Samuel was a special child. He had been given to her for a few years, but he was ultimately God's gift to the people and was needed to prepare for the purpose God had in mind.

She left God's house that day with a few tears in her eyes but with a deep smile in her heart.

APPLICATION: Celebrate the relationships you have with people but be ready to let go when God calls you or the other person to something new.

A Father's Legacy

There is no death to those who look and hold to that given,
"Let others do as they may, but as for me and my house we
will love, we will serve the living God."

Based on Edgar Cayce reading 3416-1

As Peter reflected on those months leading up to his father's death, he realized how important they had been to him. He had been able to spend many hours with his father. He had listened to his father talk about life and the memories of people who had touched him and whom he had touched.

He had also observed his father gradually letting go of physical reality and looking to the spiritual reality that he was sure awaited him. His father spoke of a world where souls continued to grow and learn, where souls continued to love, and where souls would find a closer relationship to God than what they could experience on earth.

Unlike some of Peter's other friends who had felt extreme helplessness and hopelessness when facing terminal illness with a loved one, Peter had not felt this at all. He had felt throughout those months that his father was getting ready to make a transition. When that transition came, Peter would have a feeling of "I'll see you later," and not a feeling of having a door slammed in his face that would separate them forever. Indeed, that was the feeling Peter had as he watched his father take those last breaths.

Peter's life and faith had been touched deeply in those months. It was the greatest legacy his father could have left him.

APPLICATION: The transition we call death is not the end of life. Affirm this whenever you need to.

Looking Back

Do not let those things which may not in the present be understood weary the soul, but know that sometime, somewhere you, too, will understand.

Based on Edgar Cayce reading 5369-2

Dorothy and Bill felt a strong desire to work for a particular organization and couldn't understand why. Working for this firm would mean a career change for him and a minor position for her. Nevertheless, they finally decided to apply.

When they began working for the organization, they were placed at a branch office. Even though they had applied for jobs at the home office and made some connections there, the jobs weren't available. Eventually they received promotions in the branch office and found themselves doing creative work that they could not have done in the home office. So now they knew why the other jobs had not developed for them.

Two years after they began, the question of why they had felt drawn to this business was answered for them. Bill was visiting the home office for the first time and walked around the oldest building in the complex. It seemed familiar in many ways, but something didn't feel right. When he went inside, he saw pictures of how the building had looked before it was remodeled. He knew he had been in this building before the remodeling and sensed that he and his wife had come back to complete work they had not completed in a previous lifetime.

APPLICATION: Name a place that seemed familiar to you the first time you saw it in this life. Have fun speculating on what your past association with this place might have been.

Getting Just Enough

As it has been given, "Show me your faith in your works," in your relationships, in your conversation, in your activity with others.
Based on Edgar Cayce reading 261-50

The retreat was only two weeks away and registrations were only half of what was needed to meet expenses. Frank and Nancy kept reminding themselves that they could afford to cover the expenses and that their ideal was to offer people a good program, but they were still disheartened.

For the two of them this retreat was the culmination of a dream. They had been attending such retreats in other states for several years. They wanted to introduce interested people in their area to a spiritual growth experience so they had decided to organize a retreat.

Since there was no local group to sponsor such a gathering, they paid the $800 deposit on the retreat site themselves. They secured a speaker and began publicizing the event. Now only two weeks away, they had to decide whether or not to cancel it. After two days of prayer, meditation, and discussion about their ideal, they decided not to cancel.

Thanks to the registrations on the first day, all bills were paid. The retreat was a success. A few attendees even volunteered to help plan next year's retreat. Now these yearly spiritual retreats continue to be a highlight for people in that area even though Frank and Nancy have moved away.

APPLICATION: When problems arise in projects you are involved in, take time to focus on the ideal behind the project. Let the ideal be the guide in making decisions about how to handle the problem.

Learning to Love You

*You in your associations and your activities should make of
yourself one who would be a help, a savior, a hope for many.*
Based on Edgar Cayce reading 1709-3

A famous Jewish rabbi told this story of how he learned to
love people.

He was sitting in an inn along with other peasants, drinking. For a long time one peasant sat silent. However, after
having several glasses of wine, the peasant was moved to
speak. He turned to one of the men beside him and asked,
"Do you love me?"

His friend replied, "Of course, I love you."

But the first peasant responded to these words by saying,
"You say these words so easily. But you do not know what I
need. If you really loved me, you would know."

The friend could not respond to this, and the peasant fell
silent again.

But the rabbi understood. To know the needs of people
and to share with them the burden of their sorrow—that is
the way to love people.

APPLICATION: Pick out someone you know. Ask yourself
what that person needs and give one thing that that individual needs.

Finding the Strength

Each soul enters each experience for its needs, its preparation for a greater expression of God's love.

Based on Edgar Cayce reading 1158-2

Carrie was exhausted. Today she had spent many hours again trying to nurse her husband back to health. His illness had been going on for months now, and she didn't know how much longer she could keep up her strength.

When he first began this health regimen, she didn't mind. Carrie was aware that her husband had a serious illness and only the strictest diet and exercise routine would help him regain his health. She willingly threw herself into this plan.

However, her attitude lately was one of resentment. Because he was so weak, she found that she had to do most of the work and provide constant encouragement to keep him going. There was very little time she could call her own.

In an effort to understand the situation further, she sought a psychic reading. The psychic told her that in a past life she had encouraged her husband to live a wild life of unhealthy habits. That life style had led to his early death. Now she found herself in the present situation in order to help reverse some of her actions.

This insight enabled Carrie to see her reason for attracting this situation into her life and gave her renewed strength to face what she had to do.

APPLICATION: The next time you begin to resent doing something you have to do, try finding the strength to change your attitude and do what needs to be done.

Checking Ideals Daily

Know your ideals physically, mentally, and spiritually. Cherish and nourish each of them. As the physical body needs sustenance, so does the mental body, so does the spiritual body. Based on Edgar Cayce reading 5000-1

Ginger checked her ideals almost daily. She discovered this was the best way to keep her life balanced. She made three columns on a piece of paper and at the top of one she wrote "physical"; above the second "mental"; and above the third "spiritual." Then she wrote her corresponding ideals in each column.

Every day she checked to see if she had followed her diet and done her exercises, including her morning stretches. She recalled the number of hours she had slept the night before and whether or not she had allowed time for play and recreation. These were under the column marked "physical."

Under the "mental" column she examined to see if she had maintained an "up" attitude, if she had been thoughtful of other people, and if she had been constructive in her thinking.

Looking under the "spiritual" column, she recalled the amount of time given to prayer and meditation.

If she hadn't done something on the list, she didn't berate herself or feel guilty, but just resolved to do better the next day.

APPLICATION: Try keeping a chart. Check each day to see what you have done toward your physical, mental, and spiritual ideals.

Your Psychic Powers

All *have some psychic powers.*
Based on Edgar Cayce reading 2954-1

Do you ever ask the question, "How can I become psychic?"

Another person had just asked Jason that question and he gave his favorite answer: "You already are psychic. However, you block it most of the time."

Jason explained: "It's like my daughter learning to ride her bike. She saw everyone else her age riding and began wondering why she couldn't. She gritted her teeth and kept trying and trying. She was too tense and couldn't let the natural coordination occur. When I could get her to relax, she could do it easily.

"People are like that. They are psychic but each one in a different way from other people. They just have to pay attention to those areas in their lives where their feelings and hunches appear to be stronger and follow those inner urges more. This will make those feelings stronger, more frequent, and more accurate.

"People have to recognize what is happening naturally and where it is happening. Then all they need to do is to follow it to its natural results."

APPLICATION: Be alert to intuitive thoughts and feelings as they happen. Be aware of what they are saying to you at those times.

Talking to the Trees

Meditate oft. Separate yourself for a season from the cares of the world. Get close to nature and learn from the lowliest of that which manifests in nature, in the earth, in the birds, in the trees, in the grass, in the flowers, in the bees—that the life of each is a manifesting, is a song of glory to its Maker. And do likewise! Based on Edgar Cayce reading 1089-3

An old Indian teacher was sitting with his pupil by the fire. After they had eaten, they talked. Finally the teacher picked up a piece of wood and asked, "What is this?"

The pupil answered, "A piece of firewood."

The teacher looked sad and disgusted. He put the stick down and sat silently.

The pupil tried again, "It's wood. It's a piece of a tree."

The teacher's eyes widened and he nodded, "Better. What's a tree?"

Silence.

Later that night as they lay looking up at the stars before going to sleep, the teacher spoke, "When you see a leaf as a unique part of nature, you begin to see the tree. When you see the uniqueness of the tree, you can begin to see the spirit of the tree. When you can see the spirit of the tree, you can talk to it and begin to learn something."

APPLICATION: Take a walk. Pause to look at a tree, bush or other natural living thing. Look at it and notice how it is different from other similar natural objects around it.

Some Things Can't Be Required

Sow the seed. The choice must be in the individual. To use force is to become responsible, not only for yourself but also for the one that is so induced.

Based on Edgar Cayce reading 954-4

In her job Jenny has discovered that cooperation cannot be forced on someone else. In order for it to work to its fullest, people have to want to work together because they basically believe in what is happening.

She agrees that people may act when told what to do. They may even give lip service at times and do the job adequately. However, if they don't *own* the idea or the goal to be accomplished, their spirit of cooperation will go only so deep. She had a chance to put this idea into practice at work.

After she attended an excellent training seminar at her work place, her boss considered requiring it for everyone. As they talked about this, Jenny agreed that some seminars can be required and can be effective. However, she felt strongly that this type of seminar could only be effective if people *wanted* to attend and try the exercises they were being asked to do. Her boss agreed with her and said he would encourage others to attend but not require it.

APPLICATION: Where in your life are you requiring someone to cooperate. Do something to help the person *own* the goal you are striving toward.

Working Together

When there is combative self-assertion, then egotism and self-ishness rise to the forefront. If the world will ever know its best, it must learn cooperation.

Based on Edgar Cayce reading 759-12

Andrea liked part of the idea presented by Carl, one of her staff members. If done correctly it would make her department look good. However, if this idea were not discussed first with other managers in the organization, it could catch them off guard and cause real problems. Since it was important for all departments to work together for the good of the organization, she asked Carl to take his idea to them for comment.

Andrea's instructions were motivated by unhappy experiences in the organization's past when this sort of cooperative follow-through had not happened. Some managers acted just to get a pat on the back from the president or they did something just so their division would look good even if it meant that other managers were made to look bad. The immediate result was an apparent success for a few people in the company, but the effects didn't go beyond that. Shortsighted efforts like that left a negative sense of competitiveness and distrust in the organization.

When departments could support each other and look for the good of everyone, the long-term results were better for the organization. The more the motivating spirit was cooperation and mutual support, the better the business would thrive. Andrea believed that and practiced it.

APPLICATION: Cooperate with someone to get a task done.

A Matter of Timing

The whole experience of a soul on earth is the coordinating and cooperation of Creative Forces from without to the Divine within, to keep an activity that may bring into manifestation health and happiness

Based on Edgar Cayce reading 1158-8

Sandy has learned one valuable lesson in her life—there is a force at work in the universe that is greater than she. This force has a way of timing events so that important happenings and situations occur at just the right time.

Sandy moved to St. Louis in the early fall. She rented an apartment in an old building. It so happened that Jim, the man who was to become her husband, moved into one of the other apartments in the building about five minutes before she did. He had just broken off an engagement that summer and also decided to move to St. Louis.

They were both interested in finding the right partners, and since they were now living in close proximity to each other, it was easy to get acquainted and let their relationship grow.

Later, as Sandy reflected on the events that preceded their marriage, this timing just didn't seem like an accident to her. Somehow she felt a guiding force in her life that could bring about important situations like these at just the right time.

APPLICATION: Be alert for a "chance meeting" or situation to develop at just the right time for you to take advantage of it. Look at it as coming from a master plan instead of as an accident.

The Doors Keep Opening

The purpose for each entrance is that opportunities may be embraced by the soul for living, being that which is creative and in keeping with the Way.

Based on Edgar Cayce reading 2021-1

Miraculous things happen once people stop running away from their purpose in life and begin to cooperate with the universe in fulfilling that purpose. This was Jack's story.

A series of events led him from a teaching job with which he was dissatisfied to an exciting job with a magazine—a switch he had never considered a possibility. He had to risk, though, by resigning his teaching job first and living with uncertainty for a while. However, his patience kept him on the path until the magazine job came along.

The rightness of this job is continually reaffirmed by unusual events. For example, his work for the magazine has periods of heavy, time-consuming responsibilities followed by slow weeks where almost nothing needs to be done. For two years now special opportunities to travel overseas always seem to fit nicely with times when he could easily be away from the office. He's been able to keep up his work and also make those trips to Mexico and to Europe.

Jack can't explain how all this seems to fit into place, and he doesn't know where it's leading him. However, he says he would be foolish not to recognize that the universe was guiding and leading him to these new experiences. And they all began when he took the risk of leaving his teaching job and following the call that was coming from within.

APPLICATION: Take a step to respond to what your inner voice is calling you to do with your life, even if it means taking a bit of a risk.

Some You Like and Some You Don't

*You are given the opportunity to meet yourself. In the rela-
tionships you have to others, you are to fulfill the purpose for
which each soul enters the earth—to manifest to the glory of
God and to the honor of self.*

Based on Edgar Cayce reading 3333-1

The encounters began at a committee meeting to plan a
campus event. Jack and Bill hadn't known each other until
the meeting; however, they had taken an instant dislike to
each other. During the past three weeks their disagreements
had become so intense they were threatening to stalemate
the committee and prevent it from getting any work done.

It was obvious to Jim, Bill's roommate, that Bill was dealing with a karmic relationship from a previous life, so he
mentioned this to Bill. Even though the two of them had
discussed reincarnation, Bill hadn't related their discussions
to his daily life. However, Bill now had some life experiences
to which he could relate these ideas.

As they talked, Bill admitted that he was jealous of Jack
and didn't know why. But now that he had learned this, he
knew what he could do to eliminate some of the tension in
the relationship.

APPLICATION: Name one person toward whom you took
an instant dislike. Assume this relationship has something
important to teach you and move beyond this first impression.

Christ's Presence in Healing

The consciousness of Christ's presence must be the basis of all healing. "Be not afraid, it is I."

Based on Edgar Cayce reading 281-3

The voice on the other end of the line was desperate. Could Arlene come over and pray for a healing? Arlene asked if the sick woman were able to come to the regular healing prayer group, but Susan was too weak to get up. So, after calling the other group members to ask for their prayers, Arlene went to see Susan.

She sat with her and they both meditated for a few minutes to attune themselves. Arlene found out later that during the meditation Susan had prayed that Arlene be allowed to be a channel for her healing. This helped to explain what Arlene had experienced. During that meditation she had felt that Jesus came, that He merged with her, and through her touched Susan and healed her.

After the meditation Susan, who just moments earlier had not been able to get out of her chair, got up and drove her friends to dinner.

Arlene thinks that this happened because Susan believed that healing was possible. She knew that the source of the healing power for her was Jesus the Christ, and she asked for that power to come into her life.

APPLICATION: Pray for healing for someone and expect the Spirit of the Christ to be present in your prayer.

Giving for Giving's Sake

Give to others service for service' sake that the joys of the knowledge of the source of good may be magnified in the world.　　　　　Based on Edgar Cayce reading 2855-1

Randy was raised in a family who taught that if anyone ever did a favor for you it was because that person wanted something in return. He accepted that and believed that if he himself ever did a favor he should expect a reward in return.

But his attitude began to change when he met a certain young woman. He wanted to get to know her, but she didn't seem too interested in him at first. He discovered that her mother had just had surgery and needed help fixing up her mobile home. So he volunteered to help. He knew his motive at first had little to do with being a helpful person.

He really didn't have much extra money, but he bought a few items to begin the repairs. Then something changed as he worked. Whenever he was nearly out of supplies and neither mother nor daughter had any more money, he unexpectedly had the chance to work overtime at his regular job or he found an extra job. This allowed him to buy a few more house fixtures plus some wood.

As he was experiencing this series of events, he also discovered that his motive was changing—he was enjoying giving. The more he gave from his heart without looking for a return, the more he enjoyed what he was doing and how he was helping.

His early beliefs have been transformed. He now gives because he wants to give.

APPLICATION: Give something to someone today just for the joy of giving.

The Oneness of All People

Life itself is the consciousness, the awareness of that oneness of that universal consciousness in the earth.

Based on Edgar Cayce reading 2828-2

Have you ever experienced a sense of kinship with people from different cultures or countries?

Laura has been fortunate enough to have traveled to many parts of the world. Every place she's gone she's found herself feeling at home in that country. She's felt not only open to the people of that culture, but also a deep sense of oneness with all whom she contacts. She has a sense that she has lived before in all of them, and the positive lessons she has learned seem to surface in this sense of oneness.

She has noticed that this feeling of oneness is even reflected in the photos taken of her with various ethnic groups. In China Laura happened to be wearing the same outfit worn by many of the Chinese women the day they were photographed. Mainly it was her eyes that distinguished her from the others. In Japan, people would stop and look, confused by her blue eyes, and wonder about how this "Japanese" woman got her blue eyes.

All these experiences have made her more and more convinced that we are all expressions of the oneness of the divine universal consciousness.

APPLICATION: Look at every person you see today and tell yourself that we are all expressions of the universal consciousness. Treat people as if they were a part of you.

Serving at Any Time

*Open self in every fiber of your being that the Lord's way may
be done in and through your thoughts and your activities.*
Based on Edgar Cayce reading 272-7

Phil was sitting in his office working hard on a report that
was due in two days when Alicia casually walked in and
began a conversation. Since there appeared to be no ur-
gency in her voice or much importance in what she was
saying, Phil continued to work while responding to her occasionally.

After about fifteen minutes something told Phil to pay a
little more attention and ask some questions. He did. In a
few minutes Alicia began talking about her mother's stay in
the hospital and the results of some tests that had been run.
Although not conclusive, it looked very serious. Alicia was
scared and didn't know what to do. Phil and Alicia then
talked for another hour about what her next steps might be.

Incidents such as these continue to remind Phil to be
aware that each moment may be an opportunity for him to
live out his ideal of service. He can't always pick the time
and place to serve others. God seems to make him available
to serve whenever someone is in need.

APPLICATION: Even a casual conversation may be important. When you find yourself not listening to what someone
else is saying, stop and bring your attention back to that
person.

Beware of Hasty Judgments

Look within. With God ask if your judgment is based only upon the outward appearances.

Based on Edgar Cayce reading 288-37

At first this looked as if it were going to be a normal healing. After all, Jesus had done this many times before. He had been walking through the city streets when a man had yelled from the side of the road, "Jesus, Son of David, have mercy on me." People couldn't keep him quiet, so Jesus had eventually heard him. Now Jesus had walked over to the man and was getting ready to heal him.

Then came the surprising question from the crowd: "Master, whose sin caused this man to be born blind, his or his parents?"

Some of the disciples scowled. This was not an innocent question asked by a curious passer-by. That person knew what he was asking, and the answer could cause quite a controversy.

Jesus looked at the blind man and then at the man who had asked the question. "Why do you think those are the only possibilities?" He asked. "Is it not possible that this man was born this way so that people might see the power of God at work in his life?"

Having said this, Jesus put dirt on the man's eyes and sent him to wash it off so he could see.

APPLICATION: The next time you find yourself judging someone because of outward appearances, stop and ask why you are judging in this way.

God's Unusual Guidance

Those who would gain the more will suffer the more. Those who would attain to a more perfect understanding of the true relationship of an individual to Creative Forces and use them constructively, recognize the unfolding of the mind through the experience. Based on Edgar Cayce reading 5242-1

Mary had invested a large sum of money with a reputable firm. However, her agent made a number of risky investments without asking her permission. Although she received financial statements, she didn't understand them and merely asked her agent what they meant. Only when her money had diminished considerably did she get suspicious.

When she tried to find a lawyer whom she could trust to help her get her money back, she looked for weeks. None of the lawyers she spoke with "felt right." She prayed for guidance—that someone would be sent to her.

Finally she met a young man only two years out of law school. A look at his credentials would have sent most people away, but she liked him. She learned he was originally from Virginia Beach, Virginia—a fact that built a connection of trust for her and that seemed to be the answer to the guidance she was seeking. Through his efforts her money was returned in two months.

As she looked back at the experience, she knew she learned at least two major lessons. She needed to learn about money so she could be a good steward of the money she had. Also, she learned to rely on God to answer prayer for guidance even though God's guidance didn't always come in the most expected ways.

APPLICATION: Find someone who has suffered in life but has come through in a strong way. Ask that person what he or she learned in pulling through the suffering.

The Body of the Future

With what body will you be raised? The same body you had from the beginning, else how could it be individual? The physical dissolves—yes. But when it condenses again, what is it? The same body.   Based on Edgar Cayce reading 262-86

Paul had never met David until they were roommates at a retreat. In their room that first evening Paul saw David rubbing peanut oil on his fingers and other joints in his body. Concerned that David might be suffering from an arthritic condition, Paul asked what was wrong. David told him that everything was fine, but then added, "Even if I knew I were going to die tonight, I would still do this."

As they discussed this further, Paul discovered that David had a belief in reincarnation that was future-oriented. David was in the process of building and preparing his body for the future. He was not waiting to react to a situation, but was being active to determine his future health and well-being.

As he thought more about this, Paul discovered extracts from the Edgar Cayce readings to support this idea. The readings speak about the energy patterns which make up our bodies and about our actions which can influence these patterns. What David was doing was building positive energy patterns now in order to reap the fruits of his efforts later.

APPLICATION: As you live, do something to your physical body to prepare for a healthy body next time.

Learning What You Have to Learn

For each entity in the earth is what it is because of what it has been! So a sojourn in the earth is as a lesson in the school of life.
                                    Based on Edgar Cayce reading 2823-3

Natalie finally could make some sense of her life when she read that she was the author of her own destiny. Now she could look in a mirror and say, "No one else did this to me." She knew she was meeting herself. This concept especially helped her understand her marriage.

She and her husband had talked one evening about separating. They decided to go to a lawyer for some advice. The next day she was in an accident, so they put off all further discussion.

Several times over the next few years, they would bring up the subject again. Each time they did so, something would happen to her physically, and their plans would again be delayed. Finally they decided to continue the relationship — no matter what happened.

Years later she had a dream. She realized during the dream that she had done everything she needed to do and was now free. It took her a while to act on that, but eventually she did get the divorce.

As Natalie looked back at all those experiences, she realized she had something to learn from the relationship. That's why a part of her kept her in it for so long. When she had finally met herself and learned what she needed to learn, she was free to move on to another part of her life.

APPLICATION: Look at a difficult situation in your life. Observe what you are learning about yourself or about life as you work through it.

Mercy on the Lost

For each soul is a part of the universal consciousness, the universal energies that we worship or know as God.
                                    Based on Edgar Cayce reading 1648-1

A disciple once asked a wise Jewish rabbi, "The Torah commands us to love our neighbor as ourself. How is this possible when I know my neighbor has wronged me?"

The rabbi answered, "You must understand what this passage tells us. All souls are as one. Each soul is a spark from the original soul. Thus the original soul is in each soul just as your soul is found in all parts of your body.

"Suppose your hand makes a mistake and hits you. Would you then take something and beat your hand because your hand lacked understanding of what it was doing? Wouldn't such a punishment only increase your pain? So it is with your neighbor who, though part of one soul with you, hurts you because of lack of understanding. If you punish your neighbor, are you not just hurting yourself more?"

The disciple continued, "But if my neighbor is wicked before God, how can I love this neighbor?"

The rabbi said, "Do you not yet understand that this soul came out of God, so every human soul is a part of God? Will you not have mercy when you see one of the divine sparks lost in misunderstanding and almost snuffed out?"

APPLICATION: Look at yourself and everyone you meet today as a part of the Creative Energy we call God. Be aware of your feelings as you see people in this way.

A Good Use of Time

Each shall so live that the Christ (through you) becomes available for all who meet you—whether at table or walking in the street. Based on Edgar Cayce reading 262-50

At school Diane often has very little free time to herself. When she does, she wants to grade papers and get other work done. Often this time is interrupted by students and even former students wanting to come in and chat. She began to resent this intrusion on her time.

One afternoon Carol, a former student, came in as Diane was walking down the hall to a quiet room to get some papers graded. Carol obviously wanted to chat. Diane invited her in and half-listened while she graded papers and Carol talked. After about 15 minutes Diane nonchalantly asked about Carol's sister, trying to sound like she was interested in Carol's conversation. Carol said her sister had died the previous Sunday. That's why she had come in to see Diane.

Later on, Diane reflected on this experience. She realized God was telling her that people come to see her for a reason and part of her calling is to listen when they do.

This experience changed Diane's attitude toward her students and other teachers taking up her free time.

APPLICATION: The next time you feel you are too busy to listen to someone, stop and listen.

The Power Beyond

*Instill in children the Christ principles as the basis for judg-
ments, for decisions in dealing with every problem that arises
within their experience. For as has been given, train children
in the ways they should go—of the Lord—and in their old age
they will not depart from under the shadow of God's hand.*

Based on Edgar Cayce reading 1125-3

Allen was discouraged. He had taken his kids to church, had
talked a lot about the Edgar Cayce spiritual philosophy, and
encouraged his sons to read books like *There Is a River*.
However, there were still problems along the way.

Allen's oldest son, George, got involved with drugs and
alcohol. Allen remembers how George would lie on the
couch trying to fight the temptation to drink. Allen would
talk about what he found important in life, then he would
listen to his son's questions, struggles, and doubts. The two
of them often went hunting together during those days.
They never shot much, but they were together.

Many years later Allen asked George what had helped
him the most during those years. George said that hearing
over and over about a higher self that was within him and
which he could turn to to find strength and the ability to
resist temptation was what helped him the most at that
time. Eventually he discovered he could tap into that higher
self and find for himself the power and strength he needed.

APPLICATION: Do something to demonstrate the Christ
principles to your children or some other young person.

Balancing Life

The life must be a well-balanced life, knowing that the applications of the spiritual, mental, and physical are but the pattern one of another. All must be working in coordination and cooperation. Based on Edgar Cayce reading 349-6

In his business Richard endures a lot of stress. It affects him especially when important decisions have to be made, particularly when two or three are facing him at one time. He also feels stressed out when he attends meetings in which there is a lot of disagreement and the staff can't come to a consensus even after numerous discussions on an item. Budget questions and decisions on what gets funded and what doesn't create tension in him. Finally, stress also arises when hirings and firings have to be done, actions which still do not come easy to him.

When Richard finds himself in these situations, diet, exercise, and meditation help considerably. He can alleviate much of the tension by adhering to a good healthful diet, especially by decreasing the amount of coffee he drinks. He also tries to stick to a daily routine of exercise and fifteen minutes of meditation. He can tell almost immediately when he is or is not following this routine. When he is, he's more relaxed.

Richard couldn't believe at first that diet changes, exercise, and meditation could help so much, but he is convinced now.

APPLICATION: Do one thing to nurture yourself physically, mentally, and spiritually so you can work toward a better balance in your life.

Each One Plays a Part

Each soul who enters the earth has something to contribute.
Based on Edgar Cayce reading 1350-1

An African tribal chief decided to hold a great feast, so he sent word to all the men of the village to come to his dwelling. He declared that all the food would be provided, but each man had to bring a jug of palm wine.

One man wanted to attend but he had no wine. He considered buying some, but then he decided on a way he could get in without it. He would carry water in his jug instead. When the men arrived, they would all put their wine in one big container and no one would know he had brought only water.

On the day of the feast the tribal drums called the men together. They came dressed in their finest clothes, and each carried a jug of wine. As they entered the special tribal grounds, each poured his wine into a big earthen jug.

After all the guests had arrived, the chief motioned for the music to stop and ordered the servants to fill each man's wine glass. Then the chief made a toast and all raised their glasses to drink. Suddenly a gasp of astonishment was heard. The men drank again. What they tasted was not wine but water! Each guest had decided to bring a jug of water, hoping it would not spoil the wine!

APPLICATION: As you go through the day today, stop three times and tell yourself what it is that you are contributing to the situation you are in at that moment.

Living the Message

Only by manifested acts that make for a closer relationship of the soul to that source from which it comes may there come the consciousness of self being at one with the Creative Forces or God.
Based on Edgar Cayce reading 423-3

When Katy got excited about something, she really got involved in it. Her latest interest had become the Edgar Cayce readings. She brought home books to read and talked about the ideas at the table, trying to live cooperation and patience in her life because she knew she had a lot of growing to do in these areas.

At the parties Katy and her husband attended, she openly discussed these new ideas. It didn't bother her if other people didn't agree with her. She was finding new meaning in her life, and she had to pursue this path for herself. All this time her husband listened to her but never said a word in any of those discussions or tried to apply any of the thoughts to his daily life.

One day he asked her why she was getting so much out of this. He himself didn't feel as if he were getting much at all from the Cayce material and wondered why she seemed to be finding a new spiritual dimension to her life.

Katy's response was that one person can't do it for another. We each have to *live* the truth we find in order for the message to really become meaningful in our lives.

APPLICATION: Look at your own spiritual growth. Do something to show you are living the truth you know and not relying on someone else to do the growing for you.

God: Dream Interpreter

If you will but empty yourself of yourself, you may become a channel through which a glorified God may be manifest among people. Based on Edgar Cayce reading 1150-1

Where can you find help in interpreting dreams?

Several years ago Janice found some inspiration for her approach to dream interpretation. She was reading the story of Joseph in the Bible. When Joseph was called in to interpret pharaoh's dream, his response was, "Only God understands, but tell me your dream." Janice noted that Joseph was acknowledging the power of a higher source, but he would listen and be the channel for the interpretation.

One evening during a discussion group Janice tried this approach. Members were sharing dreams. As the group struggled to help Alice, Janice sat still, trying to open up to what God wanted to say. Finally she had the impression that the dream was about some physical symptoms Alice was having. She shared this idea, and Alice responded by saying she knew exactly what she had to do next.

Janice's guideline for dream interpretation has become, "Let me set myself aside sufficiently so I can hear the Spirit and the Spirit can interpret."

APPLICATION: The next time you are asked to help interpret someone's dream, pray for the Spirit to listen and respond through you.

Lifting Life's Burdens

The purpose for the entrance of each soul into the earth is for development that the soul may be a companion with the Creative Forces. Based on Edgar Cayce reading 1641-1

The auto accident had almost killed Carla and had seriously injured her child. For several days Carla lay in a coma. Her daughter had a leg injury and facial cuts that threatened to leave her crippled and scarred for life. As she recovered, she began to ask questions.

During this period she also met people who were discussing the questions she was asking, ones that dealt with suffering. Why do children suffer? What kind of God allows things like these accidents to happen? As she sat and listened to her new friends, she heard words that helped her.

One lady said she believed now that the soul of her sick child chose this illness because he had something to learn, and this was one way to learn that lesson. A man said that he felt his child chose her fatal accident in order to teach him lessons about love and compassion.

No one blamed God. No one talked about meaningless accidents. All of them remarked that they had learned valuable lessons when they began to view events in this way.

It took Carla several weeks before she could begin to look at her auto accident in that way. However, when she did, she began to see what she and her daughter were both learning now about themselves. She also found she could turn back to God for strength to face the days ahead.

APPLICATION: The next time you confront a serious illness or tragic accident, try eventually to see it as a soul's way of learning the valuable lesson it needs in order to grow.

The Sickness of the Soul

The soul may know and experience the truth in the promise that has been given, "I will remember their sin no more." This should be the experience of every soul in the activities in the earth.   Based on Edgar Cayce reading 699-1

The crowd were listening intently to every word He was saying when they heard a noise on the roof. Soon the tiles were laid aside and a paralytic lying on his mat was lowered until he lay at Jesus' feet.

Jesus looked compassionately at the man and realized all the trouble his friends had taken in order to bring him into this room. He searched the man with His eyes and then said, "Your sins are forgiven. Go."

Immediately the crowd reacted. Those waiting for the chance to trap him grabbed it. "How is this possible? Only God can forgive sins."

In his quiet way Jesus answered His accusers with another question. "Which is easier to say, 'Your sins are forgiven,' or 'Stand up and walk'? Know that here is the power to forgive sins."

Turning to the man, He said, "Your sins are forgiven. Your soul is healed. Rise, take up your mat, and go home."

APPLICATION: Pick an area in your life where you are paralyzed because of fear or some other attitude or emotion. Affirm to yourself the words you need to hear to remove your paralysis.

God Is...

First, the entering of every soul is so that it may become more and more aware or conscious of the Divine within, and so that the soul-body may be purged, that it may be a fit companion for the glory of the Creative Forces in its activity.

Based on Edgar Cayce reading 518-2

Are you looking for an image of God that is meaningful to you?

Although only in high school, Peter was already questioning and searching. He was looking for God—at least a concept of God he could find appealing and helpful for his life. One day, almost by accident, he heard someone talking about the Edgar Cayce readings and the idea of "Creative Forces." Peter thought about that and decided he liked that term because it personalized God yet did not put the limitations of a person upon God.

The term "Creative" spoke to him of consciousness with desire, awareness, intent. This meant a being with whom he could have a relationship. The term "Forces" prevented Peter from putting the limitations of a human body or a human being on God.

Peter liked this idea of a loving spirit, an abiding presence that cared for him personally. He felt he could enjoy getting to know this being that wanted to give him direction and help mold him so that he could become a fit companion to and co-creator with this loving spirit.

APPLICATION: Spend some time today writing down what your idea of God is and what God ultimately wants you to become.

You Can Change Yourself

What you ask for, acting and believing in such ways, shall bring you that peace, that knowledge, that understanding which comes only in the acceptance of—and being at-one-with—the divine forces—God manifest among people.

Based on Edgar Cayce reading 731-7

Karen's stormy relationship with her father began in her teenage years. She felt she had to stand up to him or she would be trampled by him and lose her identity. The only way she knew how to do this was to be defiant.

After several years of difficulties with him, she discovered the Edgar Cayce readings. Two ideas spoke to her: the importance of prayer and trying to change yourself instead of trying to change others. She decided to try these.

She began to pray for peace and harmony within herself so that every little disagreement with her father wouldn't trigger her volatile emotions. She knew it was working when the following incident happened.

While she and her father were arguing on the porch, he had to leave for a few minutes. During that time she knew she had a choice. She could fall back into the old pattern or she could change her attitude and respond differently. When he returned, she said she was sorry that just a few words had led to such a bitter argument.

Later on Karen realized none of her identity had been lost with her apology. Since she no longer feared being overwhelmed by her father, they could have open, honest talks without her getting upset so easily. This moment marked the beginning of a new relationship between them.

APPLICATION: Think of a person with whom you are having difficulties. Begin to change one thing about yourself that might help the relationship.

Where Are You Going?

Free will and choice are the gifts of the soul that it may make a closer relationship with the Spirit of truth, of life, of light, of understanding. Based on Edgar Cayce reading 556-1

Life seemed aimless and meaningless to Betsy. She could not focus on a career goal. She felt deeply that she was supposed to do something with her life, but her schooling had not helped her better understand her purpose.

Then she discovered Edgar Cayce's story of the creation and destiny of humanity: In the beginning all souls were created as companions for God. To the souls God gave free will and the right to choose. However, some souls made choices that were not in keeping with God's will. Therefore, their close relationship to God was severed and they ended up living lives that were not what God intended. The purpose of life, she discovered, is to learn to choose wisely so that the relationship to God can become whole and complete again.

This story helped Betsy to see her life like a school, like a learning process. She was on earth to learn to make wise choices that would help her establish a closer relationship with her Creator. Knowing where she came from and that she had the free choice to determine where she was going helped her make decisions that were more in harmony with God's will. Betsy now had a framework around which she could build her life.

APPLICATION: Make one choice that will help you build a closer relationship to God.

Do All for the Glory of God

In the place where you are, in the consciousness in which you find yourself, is that which is today, now needed for your greater, your better unfolding.

Based on Edgar Cayce reading 357-13

One of the disciples of a Jewish rabbi came to him one day and asked the rabbi to teach him how to prepare his soul for service to God. The rabbi told him to go to a devout Jew, Samuel, who at that time was working as an innkeeper.

The disciple stayed at the inn for several weeks and observed all that Samuel did. He did not see any particular holiness in Samuel from the time Samuel said morning prayers until he said his evening prayers. The disciple only observed a man devoting himself to his business.

Finally the day before the disciple left, he asked Samuel, "What do you do all day?"

Samuel answered, "My most important job is to clean the dishes thoroughly so that no food is left on them and to wash and dry the pots and pans properly so that they do not rust."

The disciple returned to his rabbi and told him what he had seen and heard. The rabbi said to him, "You have the answer to your question."

The disciple didn't understand. But later when the innkeeper Samuel became a well-known rabbi, the disciple realized that Samuel had learned how to glorify God in each small task that he had performed as an innkeeper. This had prepared him to find the glory of God in each task which he or anyone else did.

APPLICATION: Look upon what you are doing today as the job you are called to do for the glory of God at this time.

To Stay or Not to Stay

Persistence is wonderful but impatience may destroy all persistency.   Based on Edgar Cayce reading 955-1

Mary was going through a divorce and needed extra money. She asked for a raise at her job where she had not received an increase in over a year. However, the business manager refused her request, saying she wasn't a good nurse.

This made her nursing colleague Audrey furious. Audrey was new at this facility, but she knew Mary was quite a skilled and effective nurse. She also knew the business manager had no written reviews to back up his subjective statement. What's more, there were no raise schedules in place to prevent this type of situation from recurring in the future. This wasn't the kind of place where Audrey wanted to continue working, and she was ready to quit.

Although Mary was grateful for Audrey's support, she was worried that Audrey's indignation would lead her to a hasty decision. Knowing that Audrey believed in the value of dreams, Mary suggested that Audrey look for dream guidance. She agreed to give it a try.

That night Audrey remembered only one short dream, but it was revealing. It told her she could do more good by staying than by leaving.

Years went by. Audrey received several promotions. Eventually she became administrator and instituted reviews, raise schedules, and other needed procedures.

APPLICATION: The next time you feel like leaving a situation, stop and reflect on this question: Is it better for me to stay and work for change or is it time for me to leave?

Dealing with an Upside-Down Life

Let each ask within self: With what spirit do I make this or that assertion? Whose kingdom is being maintained by the attitudes I hold—that of the Creative Energies or that which is destructive? Based on Edgar Cayce reading 263-18

Becky's life was running smoothly. She had a job that brought in extra money and left her evenings free for her family. Then she felt God's call to go to nursing school, even though she still had four children under age ten at home. Her husband was not in agreement with this decision. He liked the house clean and supper on the table when he got home. However, he did not stand in her way.

In those two years of schooling during the day and homework at night, her only social life was the weekly discussion group she and her husband attended. This group sustained her. Every week she would walk in, proclaiming that her world was turning upside down: Her relaxing evenings were gone; her family and school were demanding more time than she could give either of them.

The group listened as she talked about her concern for her family and as she questioned whether her schooling was a calling from God or an ego trip. The group members had no definite answers. However, they kept affirming her ideal and her effort to keep that ideal in front of her.

Her questioning made her sensitive to her family and kept her focused on why she wanted to become a nurse. When she eventually graduated and began work at a special clinic, she knew she had found her answers.

APPLICATION: As you struggle with a decision, keep asking questions about your ideal and find a group to support you, if possible.

Letting the Words Come

Enter into the consciousness of the Creative Forces. "Take no thought of what you shall say, for in the selfsame hour will it be given you." When one has reached and does reach that consciousness of the Divine's activity within, then your consciousness or self-consciousness is laid aside.

Based on Edgar Cayce reading 666-1

When Jeff received a call from a local radio station to be on an interview show, he thought it would be fun and agreed to do it. After all, he had been speaking to small groups about the Edgar Cayce material for several months and felt comfortable doing it.

He began listening to the show a few weeks before his scheduled appearance and was surprised to hear "big name" people from all around the country. He began to feel that he was in over his head.

On the day of the interview Jeff prayed over and over, "Let me be a channel. Let my words be a blessing to someone." This relaxed him. He was able to let go of his ego and really enjoy himself. The interviewer didn't even stick to the specific subject they had earlier agreed upon but instead covered a vast amount of Cayce material. Jeff simply let the words come and spoke what was given to him.

Later, he heard that his interview was one of the best of the year because his answers were short, to the point, and clearly stated. He now appears on that show periodically and continues to enjoy himself. He tries to open himself to be a channel to whatever comes through him on that day.

APPLICATION: The next time you are anxious about doing something, use the prayer in this story to open yourself to being a channel for God.

Speaking Out

True. One must become selfless, but to have knowledge and withhold same from others is not always best.

Based on Edgar Cayce reading 2775-1

Maggie felt as if something were missing in her life, so she decided to get a psychic reading from Edgar Cayce to see if that would give her some insight.

The reading told her of a previous life in early America when religious freedom was a big issue. In that lifetime she firmly believed in everyone's right to freedom of worship.

However, she had let her feelings go too far. Because she feared that she might impose her beliefs on someone else, she often kept silent. The reading told her she had many times remained silent when expressing her opinion would have helped a seeking soul find answers. It recommended that she express her thoughts without compelling others to accept them.

Her first opportunity came during a discussion with Alice, who was talking about an investment she was about to make. Maggie had serious questions about the soundness of this particular investment. She wondered if she should say something, and then she remembered the psychic reading. She spoke up, first affirming that Alice would have to make up her own mind, but then telling her where to check further on the investment.

Three days later Alice came back and thanked her. She had checked and discovered new information that made the investment too risky for her.

APPLICATION: As you speak to others, find a way to express your ideas without compelling others to accept them.

Dreams and Wishes

In sleep the conscious mind feeds that which the subconscious digests; hence, the necessity of the body, the mind, to keep in that line wherein the highest, noblest thoughts will control both waking and sleeping states.

Based on Edgar Cayce reading 900-81

Robert was in love. He had met a girl in his college history class and didn't date anyone else after that day. They had a lot in common and enjoyed just being with each other. He was sure this relationship would lead to marriage.

A number of Robert's dreams pointed to marriage. Even several synchronistic events seemed to be guiding him that way as well. So he was surprised and disappointed when he discovered Gale didn't feel that way.

For several years after this experience he doubted the reliability of dreams and didn't pay much attention to them anymore. Then he read this idea in the Edgar Cayce readings: Dreams can be a reflection of our wishes and desires and not messages coming from our Higher Self.

He thought about his college romance and realized his dreams at that time were just reflecting his ego wishes. He knew now that when he really desired something and wanted guidance about whether it was right or wrong for him, he had to discern the dream message carefully. He needed to look closely to be sure that the message was coming from his Higher Self and not just reflecting what his conscious mind wanted.

APPLICATION: As you work with dreams, be alert for those that may only be reflecting conscious desires and not coming from the highest source possible.

A Time for Renewal

Rest, play, work, think. Keep yourself attuned to the consciousness of life in its entirety.

Based on Edgar Cayce reading 137-125

Do you need a time to renew your spirit and be refreshed?

Returning from her annual week at summer camp, Judy, as usual, felt a great sense of renewal. The camp was primitive, yet she loved it. The old cabins with bunks and screens allowed her to go to sleep hearing the crickets and listening to the wind. The separate outdoor bath facilities reminded her of her appreciation for modern comforts, which could be set aside for a while.

Every day there was an opportunity for her to nurture body, mind, and spirit. The almost vegetarian, sugar-free diet of camp-grown vegetables and other healthful foods cleansed and nourished her body. The program offered her mind new insights and gave her new thoughts to dwell upon. The daily meditations, singing, group prayers, and opportunity for quiet communion with nature fed her soul and helped her re-establish her sense of oneness with nature.

Although she wouldn't choose this life style permanently, she has found that her summer experience refreshes her and prepares her for the kind of life she lives the other days of the year.

APPLICATION: Pick a place you can go to get renewed and refreshed. Make plans to go there as soon as possible—even if only for a day.

Resisting the Quick Sale

Use your opportunities—not as privileges of abuse but as opportunities for service. Based on Edgar Cayce reading 2251-1

Norm could see that this sale could be an easy one. Sitting in front of him was a young couple looking for their first home. He knew from the way they talked that they were ignorant about many of the details of home buying.

He listened to their explanation of what they wanted. In their description were numerous loose ends and some unrealistic expectations. If he played on those and showed them how unreal their expectations were, it would be easy to get them to see things his way. He could probably unload one of several houses he had been carrying for a few months.

However, Norm recognized service as one of his ideals in his real estate business. That meant teaching people, showing them what to look for, and helping them find what would make them happy. It meant correcting false expectations, but helping people find realistic ones for themselves rather than imposing his desires on them. So Norm began to talk.

The first hour went quickly. The couple could see what Norm was trying to tell them. Even though he didn't have exactly what they wanted, he had three homes that would meet some of their hopes. They made arrangements to come back in to take a look at what he did have.

APPLICATION: Do something to be of service by teaching or helping someone find what that person really needs.

Tools for Insight

As we have given in regard to every omen, it is an indication. As to whether or not it will come to pass depends upon what one does about what one knows in relation to oneself.

Based on Edgar Cayce reading 416-2

Sally came in one day and asked Phil what her palm had to say about her future. Before answering her question, Phil took time to tell her that he saw the palm as a tool to help people get a whole view of themselves. In her palm Sally could find an interaction of physical, mental, and spiritual influences in her life. How she would be affected by many of those influences depended on what choices she made.

Then looking at her hand, Phil suggested she listen more to her feelings and trust the path she was on because it would lead her to her desired goal.

While this was not what she had expected, Sally went home thinking about these words. She realized she was trying to decide whether or not to change jobs. A new job promised a little more money, but she felt she should stay with her current job. She did, and six months later an unexpected promotion allowed her to move back to California near her family.

APPLICATION: Do something to show you are working on an insight you have gained about how you can grow in your life.

Shutting Out God

For in the manner you treat your neighbor, you treat your Maker.   Based on Edgar Cayce reading 417-8

Irene's neighbor, Kathy, had a kitchen window that faced Irene's big picture window. Kathy seemed to be constantly in her kitchen waving and smiling at Irene every time Irene walked by her window. Kathy was also constantly calling Irene to comment on Irene's visitors, what time Irene got up in the morning, and even on the delivery of the new piano. Irene finally got fed up with this invasion of privacy and closed the drapes.

Several months went by. Then one night Irene's discussion group talked about this quote, "If you want to know how you stand with God, look at your relationship with other people." Irene began to wonder if she were shutting God out of her life in the same way she was shutting out her neighbor.

The next morning she opened the drapes and saw Kathy standing at her kitchen window. Kathy smiled and waved just like she had done months ago.

Then Irene began to get better acquainted with Kathy, sensed the loneliness in her, and reached out in friendship. This friendship became one that endured through Irene's move to a different neighborhood.

APPLICATION: Look at how you treat your neighbors. What do your actions say about how you are treating God?

Letting Go

Keep in constructive thought. Poisons are accumulated or produced by anger or by resentment or animosity.

Based on Edgar Cayce reading 23-3

Connie and Jane had had a big argument. After a few weeks they had talked and begun to heal their relationship. Connie wanted this friendship. She wanted healing. However, she couldn't let go of the resentment she felt over some of the minor words that were exchanged. She sensed something more was involved and went for a psychic reading to get insight.

The reading told her about an incarnation in which her husband, who had been a spiritual leader, had left her for another woman. She was unable to forgive him and carried this resentment so strongly in that lifetime that its impact was felt in many lives after that one.

Connie knew that she did not trust church leaders or people in power. She always accused them of saying one thing and doing something else. According to her psychic reading, hanging on to resentment has kept her from trusting and forgiving people in many of her lifetimes and has led to loneliness and alienation from others.

With help from this reading she began to see that no matter how justified she may feel in being resentful over a wrong, she must learn to forgive and let go of it or the resentment will only harm her in the long run. She began to apply this understanding, then, in her friendship with Jane.

APPLICATION: Think of a resentment you hold because someone treated you unjustly. Do one thing to begin to let go of that resentment.

Conscious of Consequences

Each soul is accountable to its Maker for what it does with its opportunities at each and every turn of its experiences on the earth.   Based on Edgar Cayce reading 335-2

Having been raised in a conservative church background, Helen asked herself for a long time if God were so loving, how could God condemn people to hell forever. But, as a teenager in that kind of setting, she did not question much and certainly not out loud.

However, when Helen was in her twenties, she did question. She wanted some answers that her previous background did not provide. During those years of searching, she came upon the idea of cause and effect—that everything we do has a consequence for good or for ill. Taken to its extreme, this meant that people could choose to separate themselves from God and the results would be a hellish kind of existence. But it was their actions that put them in that situation, and not God.

As she thought about that idea, she realized she was being told that she was responsible for her life. She then began to think twice before she would say something that might hurt someone. She also began to think twice before acting. She discovered that she could not consciously do some of the deeds she had done before because she had to stop and think about the consequences of her actions.

This idea helped make her more responsible and gave her greater control over her life.

APPLICATION: When you get ready to make a decision, stop and think about the effects it will have on your life.

Always Another Opportunity

Never think that the opportunities have passed. For ever is there set before you a choice to make. It is never too late to begin, for life in its experience is a continuous effort in the making. Based on Edgar Cayce reading 909-1

As a teenager, Daryl questioned religion and the concept of God that he was taught. The upheaval of World War II added to his skepticism. Military duty in the South Pacific wiped out what remained of his belief in traditional concepts.

Following the war, years of alcoholism, self-indulgence, and wandering aimlessly took its toll on his health. Despair, pain, death, and negativity were his companions and the world his enemy. What Daryl wanted to do was die—but for some unexplainable reason, God did not give up on him.

Daryl doesn't know exactly when the change began. All he knows is one day he walked into a church for the first time in 23 years and went to confession. It was the beginning: "This day choose between good and evil."

In time, he studied Edgar Cayce and world religions, began to pray daily, and became involved in Alcoholics Anonymous.

Today Daryl shares with others his message—of a God of love and acceptance, of a God who never gives up and always gives us another opportunity to respond.

APPLICATION: Choose a habit of behavior that you would like to change and always believed you couldn't. Take one step to make a change.

Living by the Inner Call

Do not be overanxious about material things. For the mental and the spiritual aspects and desires should be set in those directions so it may be said, "I will be guided by the influences from the inner meditations and that which is shown me from within."   Based on Edgar Cayce reading 681-1

Martin's job was no longer satisfying. He felt he had to move, but he didn't know where. While visiting Virginia Beach one summer, he knew he wanted to live there. But that would mean finding a job very different from the one he now had, and he had no idea what that might be.

Trying to find an apartment and a job before moving there proved futile. Just one week prior to his relocation, he finally found friends to live with until Labor Day.

Upon arrival, he looked for jobs and apartments. One job interview went well, but the answer was no. One apartment looked promising, but someone else got it. As the Labor Day deadline grew nearer, nothing happened. Then with five days left, he found a part-time job plus an apartment.

Living on savings and on the salary of a part-time job was not easy. Each month he watched his money go out faster than it was coming in. He felt frustration and fear, but deeper than these he felt that what he was doing was right.

Three weeks before his checking account hit zero, he got another small job that gave him enough money for two more months. Two months later, a full-time job opened up at the place he was working, and his monthly income finally began to meet expenses—but not by much.

Martin was just getting by, but he was living by the inner call and his soul knew he was on the right road.

APPLICATION: Take time to listen to your inner voice. What impressions about your life is it trying to give you?

Courage for the Moment

There has ever been the promise that God will guide, guard, and direct those who put their trust in the Lord.

Based on Edgar Cayce reading 257-88

When Betsy became involved with the Edgar Cayce readings, she was immediately attracted to the material on the lives of Jesus. She was fascinated by it and found it extremely meaningful to her. She studied all the information she could find and asked numerous questions. This quest inspired her to begin reading the Bible and return to church activity.

John, a friend of hers, had been invited to speak about Jesus and the Edgar Cayce material at a gathering. Just two weeks before the lecture date, he discovered he had a conflict with another event. He suggested that Betsy do it. She thought he was crazy. It happened that another friend was visiting their area a few days later and he also encouraged Betsy to give the lecture. She reluctantly agreed. However, she told God that if she were going to do a good job, God would have to put words in her mouth and starch in her knees.

When Betsy got up to do the lecture, she realized she wasn't scared. She had turned the talk over to God and God was there. She got through it, received good comments, and continued to give lectures for many years on this topic.

APPLICATION: The next time your courage fails, look for the strength God can give and let God work through you.

The Fall

For each accident, incident or experience should be, in the mental self, as something necessary to fit the individual for greater and better opportunities for service to the Creative Forces or God.   Based on Edgar Cayce reading 1424-1

Matt had just gone through his second divorce. In the settlement he felt he had been treated unfairly so he devised a plan. First, he would go to California to get a new job. Then, he would come back to kidnap his children and take them to his new home. However, just before he was to leave for California, as he was working on a construction job, he slipped, broke his leg, and crushed his heel. He remembers thinking at the time, "If there is a God, why now!"

During his recovery, he bought a copy of *The Sleeping Prophet*, the biography of Edgar Cayce, and read it through. He was intrigued by the ideas but skeptical.

Later, to test these ideas, he put a castor oil pack on his crushed heel for the three to four weeks between doctor's appointments. At his next visit the doctor remarked that he was a fast healer. Matt continued to use the castor oil packs and got back to work quicker than usual. In six months the doctor couldn't even tell which heel had been crushed.

This healing experience convinced Matt to look at other concepts from Cayce. Working with other ideas helped him release his anger toward his ex-wife and changed his life.

As Matt looks at this accident now, he realizes that if he hadn't fallen he would have gone to California. Then he never would have arrived at an agreement with his former wife on seeing his children more frequently.

APPLICATION: The next time an unusual event happens to you, ask how God might be at work in that event.

Getting Another Chance

*If the soul will use self in the mercies of Him who said, "I con-
demn you not—sin no more," the soul may gain much in this
association and relation.*   Based on Edgar Cayce reading 585-2

The crowd gathered excitedly to hear the Master speak. They
hungered for the words of life that gave them new hope and
a new connection to God.

He had just begun when He was interrupted by a yelling
group of men who were dragging a woman with them. They
threw the woman at Jesus' feet and exclaimed, "This woman
was caught in adultery. The law says she should be stoned.
What do You say?"

The crowd was silent. A few quietly began to gather
stones.

Jesus looked at the woman. Then He knelt and began
writing in the dirt. Finally He said, "Let the one among you
who has never sinned throw the first stone at her."

Some walked away thoughtfully; some dropped their
stones, feeling cheated.

When Jesus looked up again, the woman was standing
there alone.

"Is no one here to condemn you?" He asked.

She shook her head. "Your sin is behind you. You have
learned. Do not condemn yourself. Do not condemn others.
Go home to a new life."

APPLICATION: Find someone in your life who needs a second chance. Discover a way to give that person this chance
and still help this individual learn something from the first
error.

Learning to Make Choices

To force issues when in the formative period is to break the will. Train one to depend upon the Divine that lies within.
Based on Edgar Cayce reading 276-2

Jennifer knew how important it was to raise a child without breaking his or her will. A parent has to teach a child how to direct and control a strong will without destroying it.

She decided that the best way to do this was to begin giving her children choices at a very early age, so they would grow up feeling they were using their wills in some way. She would always try to put choices in positive terms, such as you can have this or have that.

Jennifer also taught them that they had choices in reacting to situations or to people's actions. Often she said to them, "You can choose to be happy or sad, you can choose to be angry or be more understanding."

Her system worked better than she realized it would. Now when her children do something irritating, the younger one will sometimes say, "Mom, you can choose to be angry or not, you know."

APPLICATION: The next time something unexpected happens, remember that you have a choice as to how you can respond.

Mending Fences

To hold grudges, to hold malice, to hold those things that create or bring contention, only builds the barrier to prevent your own inner self from enjoying peace and contentment.
Based on Edgar Cayce reading 1608-1

Wanda had had another argument with her sister-in-law. She wasn't sure exactly what the problem was, but they didn't see eye to eye on many issues. Fights like these happened so often and their relationship was so troubled that they decided to stop speaking to one another.

Six months later Wanda's husband got a new job, which entailed their moving to another country. So she knew she would not be seeing her sister-in-law for quite a while and did not feel at all upset by this. However, a few days before they moved Wanda was reading about people regretting certain actions they had done in life. It struck her that she might really feel sorrow later if she didn't at least take time now to say good-bye to her sister-in-law.

The day she was to leave, Wanda drove over to her sister-in-law's home, planning to stay for just a few minutes. It turned out that her sister-in-law's child was ill, and she could not have left the house to tell Wanda good-bye. The two women spent a few minutes together and wished each other well. Wanda felt much better on the way to the airport and did not feel any regrets about their relationship.

APPLICATION: Do one thing to break down a barrier that exists between you and another person.

An Attitude for Recovery

An experience is not only a happening, but what is the reaction in your own mind? What does it do to you to make your life, your habits, your relationships to others of a more helpful nature, with a more helpful attitude?

Based on Edgar Cayce reading 1567-2

Stephanie was furious and upset. She had been ill for several months, and the doctors were stumped as to the cause of her illness. She was frustrated with what she considered to be their incompetence, and she was feeling bitter and alone—as if no one really cared.

Then she read a quote that said, "If you want friends, be friendly. If you want love, be loving. If you want peace, be peaceable." She looked at herself and noted that she was not being very friendly, loving or peaceable to anyone. She began to change her attitude and the way she treated people. Almost immediately she realized that she wasn't really alone. She had family members and friends who wanted to support her, but she hadn't been allowing them to do so.

It took several more months for her to regain her health, but during those months she knew she was loved and supported. She didn't feel alone or bitter. But that change of attitude helped her to learn more about herself during those months of recovery.

APPLICATION: Be friendly to someone, loving to someone, and act in a peace-filled way toward someone.

The Dance of Your Life

God is God of the living way! God is life! God is love! God is music! God is the rhythm of the body in a dance that is a service to God. Though others make slight of your manner of speech, of your body, of your walk, of your ways, hold fast to God, grudging no one, loving all.

Based on Edgar Cayce reading 281-25

A fiddler in a certain village played so beautifully in the town square that his music soared over the village. Children came from the playground, gathered around him, and began to dance. Customers left the market stalls, shopkeepers left their stores, and housewives left their chores unfinished and came to the town square. As farmers trudged in from the fields, they too heard the music and went to the center of the village. Soon the entire village had gathered around the fiddler and had begun to dance.

It happened that a stranger who was deaf and knew nothing about music arrived in the village at that moment. He looked at the villagers in amazement. He saw unattended shops, market baskets lying on the ground where anyone could steal them, and the people moving in strange ways all over the village square. To him all this activity appeared to be the actions of a people who had gone mad. It was senseless.

He left vowing never to return to this village again.

APPLICATION: Though others laugh at you, try to dissuade you, or fail to understand you, follow God's music for your life.

The Ideals Marriage

There are needs for the soul to analyze self, self's purpose, self's desire, realizing that the expression of life is a creative thing and that there must be an ideal—ideal spiritually, ideal mentally.   Based on Edgar Cayce reading 2034-1

Mike and Sandy had both worked with the Edgar Cayce readings before they were married and had found the practice of setting ideals helpful. As they began their married life, they talked about how to work on ideals together.

They decided that at the beginning of each year they would sit down and write ideals for themselves as a couple for the next year. Then throughout the year they would take time to review them. Driving in a car together on trips gave them hours, they discovered, when they could do this review.

In addition, they took the ideals they had written and formulated an affirmation statement, which they could look at throughout the year and which summarized the essence of their ideals. This statement expressed what they wanted their marriage to be like during the year.

Each year they discovered that this practice gave them new insight into another and into what their marriage could become.

APPLICATION: Ideals apply to couples and groups as well as to individuals. Choose a person or group and set joint ideals for the coming months or year.

The Joy of Growing

It isn't the individual who plans for some great deed to be done that accomplishes the most. It is the one who meets those opportunities and privileges accorded it day by day. As such are used, there are better ways opened.

Based on Edgar Cayce reading 1152-9

At first in the spiritual growth group Mark sat quietly and listened. He was shy and introverted and, although he felt comfortable in the group, it took him a while to even participate in the discussions.

However, when the time came to organize all the spiritual growth groups in the area so that they could work better together, Mark was the one to whom people turned. They knew of his organizational skills and challenged him to accept the job. It was scary, but it forced him to use his abilities. He had to get up in front of people to introduce speakers and make announcements. Eventually he became more willing to do this.

Finally Mark began to do more speaking himself and to lead workshops. He even became comfortable enough to participate in skits where he knew people were now laughing with him and not at him.

As Mark looks back on those days of growth, he realizes that this was not his ego reaching out. This was God working in him to develop his individuality so that Mark could accomplish what he came in this lifetime to accomplish.

APPLICATION: Today look at everything you do as a step toward some greater good to be accomplished even though you don't know yet what that may be.

Refocusing

Meditation is not musing, not daydreaming; it is the attuning of the mental body and the physical body to its spiritual source, to the Maker. Based on Edgar Cayce reading 281-41

Do you have a way to harmonize your body and soul as you begin each day?

Tammy begins every morning by getting in touch with her body. She pulls a chair next to the window so she can look out at the trees. Then she says silently to God, "I am here. I need Your guidance throughout this day. Help me to be aware of what is coming to me so that I can better serve You and be loving to others."

She allows this thought to lead her into meditation.

Tammy knows if, after a few minutes of meditation, she is in harmony with God and her higher self. If she isn't, she realizes that she needs to be more careful working with people that day, as she might be less tolerant of and more edgy with them. She also must be cautious in making decisions because her intuition will not be as sharp.

If she does not feel in harmony, she says a special prayer for protection, guidance, and openness so she can be more thoughtful of others.

APPLICATION: Begin your day with a meditation period and see what happens.

The Widow's Grief

Healing others is healing self.

Based on Edgar Cayce reading 281-18

One day a tragic accident took the life of a widow's only son. Her grief was so great that no one could comfort her. Finally she went to the house of the Buddha and begged, "Bring my son back to life. Surely you can do that."

The Buddha spoke kindly saying, "Bring me a mustard seed from a home that has never known sorrow. I will use it to take away the pain from your life."

Immediately the woman went to the richest of the families in the village. Surely tragedy cannot be present in the midst of such wealth, she thought. She knocked on the door and said, "I seek a house that has never known sorrow. Is this one?"

The woman of the house exclaimed, "Never known sorrow! You don't know my life." Sobbing, the woman told her visitor of her pain. For several days the widow stayed, listening and caring for the woman.

Then the widow went to other homes. The same scene was repeated. In each house the widow remained, listening carefully and knowingly to the cries of others. After several months she had become so involved in caring for others who were grieving and in pain that she forgot she was even looking for a magic mustard seed.

APPLICATION: Think of someone you know who is in pain, in trouble, or is sorrowful. Take that person into your thoughts and prayers and then do one thing to help bring some joy or relief into that person's life.

Steps Along the Way

Be not unmindful that as each opportunity is added and applied in self, it will radiate and attract and draw unto the body that necessary to be accomplished by the body for a success. Based on Edgar Cayce reading 1982-2

Stan's job interview did not go well. He had honestly told the personnel director he was "office stupid." It was not an inspiring way to present himself, but he got the job.

After a few months in one position, a job opened on the company switchboard. Stan got it and loved it. He held this job for about a year. Then a job change gave him the opportunity to learn typing, more office skills, and how to take initiative to accomplish his objectives. Within a few months he received more responsibilities that included organizing programs.

When the position as department head opened, he applied. He went to the interview and showed them he was "on fire." He sold himself well and felt very good about this positive image of himself. He didn't get that job, but the interview did lead to another job offer in a different department.

As he looked back on those years, he could see how the series of jobs he held helped him overcome his poor self-image by giving him the opportunity to learn new skills along the way. Each opportunity led to his developing new abilities until he was ready to handle the job he now has.

APPLICATION: Look at all you have to do today as being opportunities to learn and grow.

Trusting the Healing Power Within

Your prayers, your meditations rise as a sweet incense before the throne of mercy and peace and grace. Your efforts on behalf of your brothers and sisters will not, do not go unheeded.   Based on Edgar Cayce reading 1151-14

Fern's granddaughter, Susie, had suddenly become ill. After a trip to the doctor's office Fern's daughter had called to tell her that the baby was hemorrhaging internally and her platelet count was down to zero. The doctors had put a helmet on Susie's head to keep her from bumping it and perhaps bleeding to death.

Fern called a friend who put the baby and the family on the healing prayer list. Then she went to her daughter's home and held Susie all night long, praying. The next morning Susie was not a lot better, but the change in Fern's daughter, Mary, was very noticeable—she came into the room filled with a sense of peace, knowing that eventually everything would be all right.

A new doctor was called in for consultation. This doctor thought that Susie's condition was a reaction to a diphtheria shot and did not recommend transfusions or medication, but believed they should let Susie heal herself. For the next several months Susie never really acted sick or looked ill, so the family followed the doctor's advice but continued to pray. It took four months until finally the tests showed that the blood was normal again.

APPLICATION: Prayers have power. Continue to pray for others either by yourself or as part of a group.

Use What You Have, Now

In the doing does there come the knowledge, the understanding for the next step. Today, now, is the accepted time! Use that in hand.   Based on Edgar Cayce reading 262-25

Don had a problem. He was in a wheelchair, attending the annual meeting of an organization, but since there was no ramp to the therapy building, he couldn't get there for his massages and therapeutic treatments.

Don's friend Mike raised this issue at one of the meeting's sessions. Some people wanted to pass on the idea to the appropriate organizational division for implementation. But the ramp was needed *now.*

Although Mike knew nothing about building, he stood up and asked for volunteer labor and for funds to get the materials to build the ramp. When the hat was passed, the collection was over $800. On top of that, one of the men who volunteered was a building contractor.

So Mike and several others spent extra hours that week working on a ramp to the entrance of the therapy building. At the end of the week on the night of the big social, they were just finishing up. People who had contributed money earlier came by in their evening dress clothes wanting to do just a little something more. So he handed them a shovel and let them do some of the finishing touches. Even women in long formal dresses were smoothing out piles of dirt.

The entire experience reinforced in his mind the thought to "Start with what you have and the rest will be given."

APPLICATION: The next time a task looks overwhelming, begin with the first step knowing that the next step will be given you as it is needed.

People Can Surprise You

They that open, He enters in. For as He has said, "Though you wander far away, though you make your bed in hell, I am there. If you call, I will hear—and if you will be my children, I will be your God." Based on Edgar Cayce reading 1404-1

Not being the most popular man in town, he really didn't expect anyone to step aside so he could get a better view. However, Zaccheus, noted tax collector, had made plans for such a possibility. He merely walked a little farther to the giant sycamore tree that hung over the road. Up he climbed and waited.

As Jesus approached, Zaccheus leaned out on the branch to get a good look. However, when he thought his eyes had caught the Master's, he pulled back, trying to hide in the branches. But he didn't move quick enough.

A few seconds later Jesus stopped right below him and called out, "Zaccheus, come down. I'm going to your house to eat."

While they ate, the crowd stood outside and talked. They wondered why Jesus would eat at the home of a hated tax collector. Didn't He know how much Zaccheus had misused his position and cheated people?

When Zaccheus stood up after dinner, they heard words they never expected to hear. "I am giving half my wealth to the poor. If I have cheated anyone, I will return it twofold."

That night there was rejoicing in Jericho. New life had been given to so many and in such a surprising way.

APPLICATION: Name someone whose actions surprised you in a positive way. Be ready. It could happen again.

Working with Nightmares

In that state of mind when the body loses consciousness in sleep, the soul mind may be impressed by suggestions that will be retroactive in the waking body.

Based on Edgar Cayce reading 5747-1

Have you ever had to help someone overcome a series of nightmares?

Andrea and Jim had just read in the Cayce readings about pre-sleep suggestions being helpful for children. They talked about it and decided to try this idea on their son, Billy, to help him handle a series of nightmares he was having.

Each night as Billy fell asleep, Jim or Andrea would sit with him and quietly whisper suggestions to him. They never used the term "nightmare" because the subconscious mind would pick it up and perhaps produce one. Instead, they mentioned Billy's dreaming about fairies and angels or sleeping peacefully and waking up excited for a new day.

At other times they would speak to some insecurities that might be provoking the bad dreams. They would make statements such as, "Mom and Dad love you" or "We will be here for you."

Their efforts had two positive results. The frequency of the nightmares diminished, and Billy's strong fear of them disappeared.

APPLICATION: Try a pre-sleep suggestion on your child or on yourself to overcome a fear, insecurity or anxiety.

The Daily Presence of God

Whoever expects nothing shall not be disappointed, but whoever expects much—if living to use what is in hand day by day—shall receive full to running over.

Based on Edgar Cayce reading 557-3

One of the guiding principles of Jerry's life is his belief that God is available to him every moment of every day.

When the company for which he had worked for many years merged with another, Jerry was forced into "early re-tirement." Immediately he began planning and eventually opened up a new business. He asked God every day to show him what was needed to make his business operate successfully. He found that he was getting answers to his prayers.

The best time for him to pray, he learned, was on the way to work. Instead of listening to the car radio, he began to look at the day, pray about the problems, ask for guidance, and give thanks for discovering what he needed to do that day. Then he would let go and open himself to what would happen.

He discovered that prayer led him to be more receptive to people and to surprising experiences which he might otherwise have overlooked. He has now learned to be open at every moment, to be led by God to use any unexpected opportunity.

APPLICATION: While on your way to work or before begin-ning work around the house, pray for God to be present. Then look for the unexpected as a sign of God's presence.

Risking with God

This, then, should be the ideal of this body, "In God will I put my trust, so as to open the way that I may have a better insight as to what God would have me do, day by day."

Based on Edgar Cayce reading 3871-1

William's accident had left him partially paralyzed. He didn't know what to do. Before the accident he had thought about changing jobs, but now he didn't know if he would ever work again.

Two years after the accident, he had recovered enough to serve on the Board of Directors of an organization. During his term on the Board, he was asked twice to take positions in that business. Both times he said no because it didn't feel right and because he didn't know if he were strong enough for a full-time job. However, he told God that if he were asked a third time, he would accept.

He didn't think that that would be likely, but a few months later he was asked to take a newly created position in the company. He didn't say yes at first. Most aspects of the job felt right, but he did have doubts about some of his qualifications. He also had to think about finances. He was receiving a comfortable disability payment that would leave him financially secure for the rest of his life. He would have to give that up to take this job. What would happen if he found out he couldn't keep up the pace of full-time work?

He finally accepted, knowing there was a significant risk but believing God was calling him and would watch out for him. Several years later he was still working full time.

APPLICATION: The next time you take a risk repeat the prayer, "In God will I put my trust." Then go ahead.

All God Does

*Count your hardships, your troubles, even your disappoint-
ments as stepping-stones to know God's way better.*
Based on Edgar Cayce reading 262-83

On his journey a Jewish rabbi took with him his donkey, his
reading lamp, and a rooster as a gift for a friend.

One night he could not find a room at the village inn so
he decided to sleep in the woods. As he headed toward the
woods, he whispered, "All that God does, God does well."

Before going to sleep, he lit his lamp to study the Holy
Books. Suddenly a gust of wind blew out the lamp, knocked
it over, and broke it against a stone. As he lay down to sleep
he commented, "All that God does, God does well."

During the night wild animals killed his rooster and
thieves stole his donkey. When he woke up and saw the loss,
he proclaimed again, "All that God does, God does well."

He returned to the village where he had stopped the
night before only to discover that enemy soldiers had in-
vaded during the night and killed most of the inhabitants.
Then the soldiers had traveled through the woods near
where he had slept. If his lamp had not broken, he would
have been seen. If his rooster had not been killed, it would
have crowed and alerted the enemy. If his donkey had not
been stolen, it would have brayed and he would have been
found.

As he walked home, he said again, "All that God does,
God does well."

APPLICATION: Look at a series of disappointments in your
past. See if you can now view them as stepping-stones to
understanding God's broader plan for your life.

A Nurturing People

This individual should be in close touch with the teachings of the church—not as of a dogmatic influence, but for its beauty, its truth, its basic forces.   Based on Edgar Cayce reading 1990-3

Edgar Cayce books were always lying around the house when Paul was growing up. He remembers those books being on the coffee table and on the bookshelves. He could ask questions about their contents or read them anytime without being forced to do so by his parents.

However, Paul struggled constantly with the tension he felt between what he read and what he was hearing in church. He remembered questioning his parents about this. His dad's response was to point to the parts of the readings that talked about the church being relevant to many people at this time in history. So his family continued to attend.

Today Paul realizes the Cayce readings are talking about the way that the church nurtures people. Over the centuries people have invested so much positive force in the church that it carries this kind of energy. So at those times when he attends and is not getting much out of the sermon he is hearing, he concentrates on the fellowship of the people around him. He reflects on the spirit of love he has received from these people and puts himself fully into the singing which has a rejuvenating effect on him.

This is the positive value Paul has found in the church.

APPLICATION: Find a group of people who give you this kind of positive nurturing energy and fellowship.

Strength from Within

Know that if God be with you, what does it matter if all others are against you. For peace and harmony will reign within you. Based on Edgar Cayce reading 3581-1

Carolyn was in graduate school studying hospital administration, but not knowing exactly how this course of studies would fit in with her career plans. She did not want a traditional role as a hospital administrator, but her inner voice had told her this was the right program for her.

As she sought guidance from her professors, she told them of her interest in preventive medicine and holistic health. They said she was in the wrong field. Hospitals would not buy into her ideas. They recommended the social work field. Still her inner voice said she should stay.

Along the way Carolyn tried to integrate her interest in holistic health into the traditional curriculum. She looked for a professor who would assist her in a research project in this field. Many said no and tried to get her to focus on another program.

However, she persisted and found a professor who would help. Her research project was printed in a respected national journal and won an award. Interestingly enough, the article focused on hospitals entering the health promotion/wellness field, which many of them are now doing.

Carolyn had followed her inner voice all along and, even in the struggle, felt a certain internal harmony from being in tune with a higher power.

APPLICATION: Are you hesitating to follow your inner voice because others are giving you conflicting advice? Listen carefully to that voice and take steps to follow its guidance.

Who Has Changed?

Little by little, line upon line—this is the manner, this is the growth.
Based on Edgar Cayce reading 416-10

The incident that occurred at her metaphysical group today had reinforced Jackie's belief that spiritual growth is a process of slow, subtle changes. In fact, many times people aren't aware anything is happening until one day they have a sudden insight or a new outlook on life.

Jackie had always felt a real harmony with the members of her group. They discussed issues openly; they could question each other and respond to each other in loving, challenging ways; and they exhibited a lot of patience with people like Emily. Emily, who had been attending for about a year, had an abrasive manner that kept her from mixing harmoniously with the group. Nevertheless, she continued to attend even though confiding to Jackie that the group was a cold and distant one.

However, today Emily had participated in the group with a new sensitivity, openness, and enthusiasm. The group had responded favorably, and the discussion had been exceptional. Afterward, Emily commented to Jackie and another member that the group had finally developed a real sense of harmony and acceptance.

Jackie and the other member watched as Emily left. Then they turned to each other and smiled. Jackie whispered softly, "I wonder who's changed."

APPLICATION: Growth takes time. If you feel you haven't changed as fast as you had hoped, be patient and give yourself time. Apply the same principle to a friend.

Pregnant Dreams

In this condition there are more often closer communions in sleep or rest from outside forces—of more dreams, more visions as are termed spiritual.

Based on Edgar Cayce reading 136-50

Rita never dreamed about her dad after his death until years later when she was trying to decide on a career change, talking with her husband about moving, and just learning she was pregnant with their fourth child—all at the same time. Then her dreams were not ordinary dreams to reassure her of life after death. Her dreams were philosophical discussions.

In one dream her dad said dreams were as real as the real physical body and important learnings could occur in them. In another dream she remembers asking about reincarnation. Her father said it was true and went on to tell her more which she could not remember after she awoke.

The months before the birth of her fourth child were important transition months in Rita's life. Perhaps that is why she had these dreams then. Regardless of the reason, many of her questions about life were answered in profound ways.

APPLICATION: Dreams during important transition moments in life can be very significant. Make a special effort to remember dreams at these times in your life.

It's Time to Rely on Each Other

For the greater satisfaction of the individuals, there should be sought those relationships in which each can supply what is needed in the other's experience.

Based on Edgar Cayce reading 528-16

It was Roberta's wedding day, and she didn't want it to start out this way. Last night she had laid her crystal by her coat, and now it wasn't there. She really wanted that stone today. She had bought it just before she and Jim had begun dating and was convinced it had helped bring them together.

She got down on her knees to look around on the floor, but she couldn't see it. Her dad came in the room and asked what she was doing. When she told him, he began to look as well. Still no crystal showed up.

Finally she went upstairs to dress. When she met Jim in the hall, he could tell she was upset. After she told him about the missing crystal, he went to look while she dressed.

As Roberta put on her gown, her inner voice spoke to her. It said, "Today is the day you begin to rely on your husband." She wasn't quite sure what that meant.

However, a few seconds later, Jim came back upstairs and handed her the crystal. He had found it by her coat exactly where she said she had left it the night before.

As Roberta looked at the crystal in her hand, she realized that this wedding was the beginning of a new part of her life. She and Jim would be relying on and meeting each other's needs as a married couple after today. Slowly she put the crystal in her jewelry box and turned to take Jim's arm.

APPLICATION: Think of a close relationship you have in your life. Do something for that other person that the individual couldn't do alone.

The Results of Prayer

Keeping the mental image constantly before the mind builds that in the experience of others in such a way and manner as to bring about circumstances, conditions that clarify much that worries or troubles.   Based on Edgar Cayce reading 257-43

The phone call had devastated her. Teresa's daughter-in-law had called to say that her year-old son Gerry had just been diagnosed as having cerebral palsy. Teresa knew what that meant. Gerry would never ride a bike and would have trouble with muscle motor skills all his life. She could not accept that.

Immediately she called her prayer group. Then she began to remove the thought of her grandson's diagnosis from her mind. She worked to picture him healthy, and she and her friends prayed daily for his renewed health.

A month later her son called with news of the latest checkup by a different doctor, who was confused and said that the tests seemed inconclusive. The doctor told them to come back in a month for more tests. Her son concluded by saying he felt in his heart that Gerry didn't have cerebral palsy. Teresa told him to hold that thought and keep picturing his son as a healthy child. She and her prayer group kept praying as well.

The next month the news was glorious. The tests showed no sign of any disease. In fact Gerry even had above-average intelligence. This second doctor couldn't understand how the first doctor could possibly have made such a diagnosis.

APPLICATION: Prayer does change things. The next time you want something to change in your life, try prayer as a tool.

Natural Selection

Opportunities exist for each soul to give expression to those activities in which the soul may gain knowledge of what is constructive in that soul's own experience.

Based on Edgar Cayce reading 1603-2

Today a woman named Marilyn had visited Barbara's prayer group and everyone had welcomed her. She had participated in the discussion and prayers. Barbara had even stayed an extra half hour to get better acquainted. She liked Marilyn, but something didn't feel right. In spite of all these signs, Barbara didn't feel Marilyn would be attending their group sessions for long.

As it happened, after three visits Marilyn stopped coming.

For the past ten years Barbara had experienced this pattern with this particular prayer group. She sensed that she had spent significant lives in Egypt and as an Essene with many of the members of this group. With other members she wasn't sure what the connection was, but she felt they belonged together. But Barbara sensed with some visitors that they had a different calling in life. They would probably never feel as if they belonged to this group. Within a few weeks, those individuals would stop coming.

Somehow with this group there was a process going on that went beyond surface words and behaviors. People were always made to feel welcome, but people always knew quickly if they belonged with this group or not. No one ever had to tell them. It was a natural part of the life of this group.

APPLICATION: People are called to different services. If you feel you do not belong to a group you are currently involved with, find a group to which you do feel you belong.

Judging in a Helpful Way

Hold to those things in which, in dealing with others, you may see only the pure, the good! For until you are able to see within the life and activities of those you have come to hate, something you would worship in your Creator, you haven't begun to think straight.   Based on Edgar Cayce reading 1776-1

Allen's psychic reading from Edgar Cayce forced him to look at himself and his attitude toward others. He was told that he had a tendency to condemn others and himself without cause. As Allen read the reading over and over, he began to feel that what was stated was accurate.

The reading spoke about two significant past lives. In one lifetime his behavior aroused the hatred of the community in which he lived. Thus he had become an outcast and still carried a condemning attitude toward himself and others from that experience. In another in Roman times, as a judge, he had sentenced others harshly and unmercifully.

The reading said Allen could transform this condemning nature if he chose to do so and turn it into a discerning ability to help others. He could use his gift to see other people's abilities and show them how they could use their gifts to fit into a larger picture, to harmonize their lives with others around them.

The choice belonged to Allen.

APPLICATION: Be alert for how you can evaluate other people's abilities positively so you can help them use their abilities in a cooperative and productive way.

Making It Through

The abilities are here to accomplish whatever the soul would choose to set its mind to, so long as the soul trusts not in the might of self but in God's power.

Based on Edgar Cayce reading 3183-1

When Linda and her husband discovered that his cancer had spread to his lungs, they knew it was just a matter of time. After years of fighting and hoping, they felt drained. Linda felt as if she had lost her purpose in life.

One night she had a dream. She was in a tunnel with a light at one end. She thought at first she was dead. She wanted to get to that light. However, as she tried to get there, she heard voices on both sides of her.

One set of voices said, "She can't make it. She's given up."

Another set of voices said, "Yes, she can make it. She just needs some encouragement."

Finally she said out loud in her dream, "I want to get to the light."

After saying these words, she experienced a comforting peace, security, and assurance. She felt, "I can make it through this."

At that moment her dream ended. However, the experience gave her the courage to move forward and to find new purpose and new direction in life after the death of her husband.

APPLICATION: The next time you need encouragement to get through a difficult event in life, look within for that part of you that can give you the encouragement and power to go on.

What's in a Name?

For a life truly lived is indeed a shining life in any community.
                              Based on Edgar Cayce reading 342-1

Virginia had always believed that people should be judged on their own merits. However, she realized this was easier to say than to experience when she married into a well-known family in her community.

Suddenly she found herself with a famous last name and an ego to go with it. She was surprised that some doors did not open to her as she thought they would. She was surprised that some glory didn't automatically accompany her and even more surprised to find out she was angry and hurt by that. She had to struggle for several months with conflicting feelings about not getting some special recognition.

Eventually she found herself back at the belief she had before her marriage: that people should not be automatically judged by a name, either positively or negatively.

Now she has begun to be known for who she is as a person and for her commitments and accomplishments. She is grateful that her name didn't earn her this recognition but that people recognize her for what she has become as a person.

APPLICATION: Do something today that shows others you are living your life and building your own reputation.

Letting Go of Worry

Q. How may the body leave off the mental worries?
A. Fill the mind with something else.

Based on Edgar Cayce reading 294-91

Frances could feel herself starting to worry about her husband's airplane trip. However, this time she wasn't going to let that worry, that fear get to her.

Worry had always been a problem in Frances' life. She had an active imagination. When she let it go, it could quickly build up the worst scenario and then the worry would begin that it might happen. This would make her so upset she couldn't do anything except sit and worry more.

However, she had learned something from one of the Edgar Cayce readings. To one person prone to worrying, the reading had said, "Repeat to yourself, 'Everything is all right now.'"

Her mind was starting to do that. Her husband was flying on a business trip. There had been two plane crashes in the last month. She was feeling the anxiety that her husband's plane might be next. So she began to repeat to herself, "Everything is all right now. Everything is all right now."

For the next four days whenever her anxiety would threaten to get the best of her, she would begin repeating this phrase. This helped her accomplish what she wanted to do and kept her more relaxed than she had ever been before when her husband was out of town.

APPLICATION: When worrying threatens to control your mind and immobilize you, try using this phrase, "Everything is all right now." Observe what happens.

The Healing Power in Nature

There is within the grasp of humanity an antidote for every poison, for every ill in the individual experience if there will but be applied nature, natural sources.

Based on Edgar Cayce reading 2396-2

How can you tap the healing power that is found in nature? Using castor oil, one of nature's own products, is one way.

Evelyn knew her six-year-old son, Jeffrey, had a high tolerance for pain. Sometimes this frustrated her because he would not let pain be a warning signal to him.

One day her young daughter told Evelyn that Jeff's foot was swollen. She went to see it and noticed that it was red and there was a black spot on his heel. When she poked at the spot, out came a black sticker along with blood and pus from an infection. Jeff had stepped on the sticker, but had been walking on that foot for several days.

She applied castor oil on the opening, put a bandage with castor oil on it, and put several socks over his foot so his teacher would keep him in during recess that day.

At work one of her nursing colleagues heard about her story and told her about someone who had died of blood poisoning from such an infection. Red lines going up his leg would indicate that condition. Evelyn wanted to rush to Jeffrey's school and bring him in for a shot. But her boss, a doctor, told her that if she had put castor oil on his foot she had nothing to worry about.

That night there were no red lines on his legs and the swelling was almost gone. The next day his heel was back to normal.

APPLICATION: Find a resource to teach you about the healing power in nature and how you can use it.

Life Is a Stage

So live each day that some portion may be added to your inner, your soul, self. So may you gain strength, knowledge, and virtue in such measures that life with its experiences becomes more and more worthwhile, with more joy.

Based on Edgar Cayce reading 1745-1

Carl was discouraged and dissatisfied with his job and his life. He wanted guidance, so he obtained a psychic reading from Edgar Cayce.

His reading mentioned two previous lives where he had been either an actor or involved in some way in dramatic expression as a speaker. It also said he could have been a great actor in this life, but he had made other choices. That was why he was feeling out of place in his work.

Carl was told he could still fulfill a part of his original purpose by changing his attitude toward his work and toward other people. He was to begin to think of all life as a stage upon which to act. Wherever he was, he could act as a channel of service so all who met him would feel better because they had known him.

He was also told to apply for a supervisor's position at work so he could be a more prominent example to others and thus add something to their lives as well as to his own life. This action would lead him to feeling he was not only using his talents but also fulfilling the purpose for which he had entered the earth at this time.

APPLICATION: Act in some way that you make use of one of your talents and thus feel that you are fulfilling your purpose in life.

Saying Good-bye

Let there be that satisfaction, that knowledge within self that you are doing the right thing yourself.
Based on Edgar Cayce reading 1183-3

The friendship had been enjoyable. However, for the past few months Sandy had known that the relationship was too intense. She needed more freedom but, more important, she didn't feel the relationship was growing any deeper. She had to do something, but she wanted to be sensitive to Gary's feelings as well.

Her work with the Edgar Cayce readings had taught her two lessons. One, she had to be sensitive to people's feelings. Two, she had to feel right about a situation she was in or she had to do something to change it.

She finally had a good talk with Gary. He seemed to handle the breakup well and appreciated her openness and honesty.

Over the next few weeks Sandy was surprised at how well she was reacting. She remembered the last time a similar breakup had occurred. She had felt at loose ends for weeks. She hadn't known what to do with herself.

She realized she had broken a pattern because she had taken responsibility for changing a situation with which she was uncomfortable.

APPLICATION: Think of a situation in your life with which you are uncomfortable. Take a step to change that situation.

Very Different Approaches

*Do not question as to what others will say or do, but find in
yourself how and why God has given you the opportunity to
be a witness for God in the earth.*

Based on Edgar Cayce reading 3359-1

Harold and Joanne joined a spiritual growth organization at
the same time. They read the material and attended the discussion groups regularly. They had similar beliefs about the
material. However, they realized that they are exact oppo-
sites when it comes to telling others about what they have
discovered.

Joanne says she is the quiet type who will wait until
someone comes up to ask her a question before giving a
reply. Then she will give information that speaks to the
question and will tell the person where to find other information if the individual is interested.

Harold takes his career as international businessman
into this interest as well. Joanne says he will talk to stumps,
trees, or people. If anything will listen, he will start talking
about how this group and this material has changed his life.
She is amazed because he gets away with it. Because of his
personality, people are receptive to his approach even if
they end up disagreeing with everything he says.

This seems to highlight for her what she has learned
about people being different and having different ways of
serving and working in the universe.

APPLICATION: If your way of talking about what is important to you is different from another person's approach,
don't worry about it. People on a spiritual journey find the
way that is best for them and for the people they will meet.

There's More Than Money

It is not sufficient to merely live that you may outwardly appear as a successful individual—not too bad nor too good— but to be one who, irrespective of others, chooses the better place.   Based on Edgar Cayce reading 2080-1

Tammy can't even imagine what her life would be like now if she hadn't changed her career three years ago. However, at the time she was making that decision, her future didn't look as if it were going to be this bright.

Three years ago she had a good job as an airline flight attendant. The benefits were great. The salary was great. She loved the traveling. Her husband was even supportive of her remaining with this job for a while if that's what she wanted.

Then Tammy had begun meditating regularly and taking seriously some of the spiritual philosophy of the metaphysical books she was reading. She was beginning to feel an inner call from God to change her career even though at the moment she didn't know what her new career would be.

Her parents and friends couldn't believe she was even thinking about quitting. How could she give up the money, the benefits and everything else?

After several agonizing months, she decided to quit.

The first two years were not easy. She didn't really settle on a new career. Even what she was doing now could not be called a career, but her life had purpose and direction. She is happy now to let the future unfold as it will.

APPLICATION: Following an inner call to change doesn't always mean everything will fall into place quickly. Choose a part of your life you want to change and enjoy the transition time.

Dead Bones Walk

You, too, often doubt. Yet He is surely with you. If you will believe that He is, you may experience.

Based on Edgar Cayce reading 5749-6

Desolation lay all around him. All Ezekial could see before him was a valley of dry, parched earth covered with bones bleached white from the heat of the sun. Any sign of life had deserted this area years ago.

While Ezekial viewed this pit of death, he heard God ask, "Will these bones live again?"

Ezekial thought to himself, "How silly. Of course not."

But before he could utter a response, he heard a rustling noise coming from the valley. He looked and saw a few bones stirring. Then he saw more bones moving as they came together to form skeletons. Finally he saw these bony frames take on flesh, and soon the entire valley was filled with people walking around rejoicing in life again.

At that point Ezekial woke up from his vision. Could he really believe what he had seen? Did he dare tell a discouraged people what he thought this vision meant? His people, Israel, had been in exile from their homeland for many years. Living in exile was like living in death. Was God about to bring them back to life? Was God about to lead them home again?

Whatever form the new life would take, Ezekial was convinced that God was about to lead the people to it. The dry bones had lived again. So would the people of Israel.

APPLICATION: Bring to mind a part of you that is dead. Do something to show you believe that God can help you bring that part to life again.

Bending the Rules

These impressions represent experiences in emblematical ways to be heeded, especially when such are gathered as to bring the feeling of experiencing a vision.

Based on Edgar Cayce reading 538-25

For several weeks the ache had been so persistent that Connie decided to get a special massage. She called a woman who had training in a unique kind of massage-healing technique and made an appointment.

While she was on the massage table, she repeatedly experienced the feeling that the woman was not working on the right spot, even though she was massaging her shoulder and upper back. Then an image flashed through her mind.

Connie saw herself in a classroom. The teacher was standing up in front of the class with a ruler in her hand. As she shook it at the students, it bent over in the middle.

She told the masseuse about this image and interpreted it to mean that the rules should be bent. Then she asked the therapist if there were any rules she was following.

The masseuse said that with this technique she was not supposed to massage below the waist.

Connie said it was all right to do that.

As soon as the masseuse began working on the upper thigh, Connie could feel energy flowing in a new way. Within a few days the ache in the shoulder was gone.

APPLICATION: The next time you get an intuitive thought or mental picture about how to handle a situation, write it down and act on it where possible.

The Heart Attack

When life is made consistent with the ideals, we will find health, greater relationships, greater help of every character may be experienced in the body, in the mind of the soul.

Based on Edgar Cayce reading 3503-1

Walt wasn't sure why he had suffered a heart attack at this particular time. Maybe it was just the result of his stressful life style. Maybe there was some truth to the idea that his heart really wasn't in his job anymore. Regardless, God was using it to set him on a new path in life.

Two years earlier he had been asked to serve on the Board of Directors of a metaphysical organization. He had said no because he was too busy with his two companies. Then the next year the president of that organization asked him to become an officer of the business. He wanted to accept, but his wife didn't want to relocate. They talked about the businesses he had and finally agreed to sell them gradually over the next year or so.

Two months after that decision had been made, he had had his heart attack. As he was recovering, his wife now insisted that he sell the businesses immediately and move. The job with the metaphysical organization would be much less strenuous and less time consuming. He did, and they moved.

He knew within a few weeks that this new job was right for him, and his wife loved their new home. In addition, he had no further heart problems. The right decision had been made.

APPLICATION: Choose something you are doing for which you no longer have any enthusiasm. Take a step to discontinue doing it or find a way to get your heart into it.

Erupting Volcanoes

Love divine is love manifested by those in their activities who are guided by love divine. These bring happiness and joy, not mere gratification of the material things. But differentiate—put the proper value upon the proper phases of one's experience.   Based on Edgar Cayce reading 262-111

A month before her trip Cindy dreamed that she was in Italy and a volcano was about to erupt. Trapped in her hotel room, she couldn't find a way out.

Now that she was touring in Italy, she knew exactly what that dream meant. She was with a guy who was as rich as she was and politically powerful as well. He also loved to spend money on her, and she loved it.

While visiting Florence and Venice, Cindy had flashes of past-life memories. She felt she had been rich and powerful in these cities and had used those tools selfishly. She could sense the tension in her now between wanting to use money and power in that same way and wanting to have other desires and feelings motivate and guide her life.

During her trip she meditated daily. In cathedrals she stopped to pray that she could overcome these selfish desires and be able to put money in its proper place in her life.

At the end of the trip she had a similar dream. The volcano was about to erupt, but she wasn't afraid. She walked up to it and saw the lava run smoothly down its sides in rainbow colors. Her meditation and prayer had been beneficial and internally she had won her battle.

When they returned home, she and her boyfriend broke up. She had met that karma in herself and made choices for a more positive use of her money and power.

APPLICATION: Look at how you use money and power in your life. Do something to use these tools in wise ways.

Helping in the Right Way

Study to show yourself approved unto God, rightly emphasizing what is necessary in the experience of each soul, each individual.   Based on Edgar Cayce reading 2786-1

One follower of Rabbi David was very rich and enjoyed doing good deeds. Abruptly his fortune changed—he lost all his money and found himself in debt. Upon telling Rabbi David about his state of affairs, he was told to go to the rabbi's brother-in-law, Rabbi Jacob, and tell him his story.

Rabbi Jacob heard his story and said, "Today I will take the bath of immersion in your name and credit its benefit to you." When Rabbi David heard this answer, he sent the follower back to Rabbi Jacob, saying, "The bath of immersion will not pay creditors."

Rabbi Jacob pondered this response and said, "Very well, today I will dedicate the merit of the prayer phylacteries to you." When Rabbi David heard this, he responded, "Prayer phylacteries will not rid one of tormentors."

Again the man returned to Rabbi Jacob and repeated these words. Rabbi Jacob said, "Very well. All the prayers I say today will be dedicated to you." Rabbi David's response was, "All this will not pay a single debt."

Upon hearing this reply, Rabbi Jacob returned with the man to Rabbi David's house. When he faced his brother-in-law, he asked, "What is it you want of me?"

Rabbi David said, "I want the two of us to go around and collect money from our people because that is the kind of help our friend needs." And that is what they did.

APPLICATION: The next time you help someone, give that person the kind of help that is needed.

Let God Choose

God's ways are not past finding out to those who attune themselves to that inner consciousness which is the birthright of each soul.   Based on Edgar Cayce reading 2402-2

This year Lorraine's metaphysical discussion group was not going to elect officers. They decided to meditate and rely on each person to receive in meditation a suggestion for which office position to hold. Lorraine was sure she would receive the message to be secretary, but she blocked that thought from her mind as the meditation started.

Strangely enough, the words that came clearly to her were "healing prayer." The only problem was her group didn't have any office called healing prayer. She was confused, as was the group when she told them.

Within a week she was called to take a friend to visit a metaphysical organization. They were browsing through the building when one of the hostesses said the healing prayer group was meeting and would welcome any visitors. Lorraine was startled and couldn't pass up this opportunity to see what might be going on.

By the end of the hour Lorraine felt as if she had come home. She continued her contact with this group and took some of their ideas back to her own discussion group. Through a strange set of circumstances she had become the healing prayer officer.

APPLICATION: If an internal voice tells you to do something that you don't understand at the moment, stay open so the future can bring you understanding.

What Did She Learn?

Do not count any condition lost. Rather make each the step-ping-stone to higher things.

Based on Edgar Cayce reading 900-44

Susan's friend Joyce had felt nothing but frustration with her current boyfriend for the past three months. Susan didn't know why Joyce stayed with him, but she sensed something was about to happen.

Finally Joyce came to talk, and Susan got the entire picture. Joyce spoke about Jim leaving town a lot and always assuming she would be there for him when he got back. She talked about nights alone waiting for him to call even when he was in town. Yesterday evening she had told Jim not to call anymore.

Now Joyce felt as if she had wasted the last eight months of her life. She was angry and also blamed herself for waiting so long to break off the relationship.

Susan tried to tell Joyce that if she could look at what she learned, she might have a better feeling about the last eight months. For example, if she had a pattern of hanging on to relationships or seeing something that really wasn't there, she could observe where that pattern had led her and not repeat it again. If Joyce learned that much from this experience, she certainly had not wasted those months in her life.

Joyce wasn't quite ready to believe that yet, but she did agree to think about it.

APPLICATION: The next time you feel you have wasted time on a relationship or a situation, look at what you have learned about yourself and affirm that learning.

Attracting the Right Help

That which is sure, peaceful, harmonious can only be founded on the spiritual ideal.

Based on Edgar Cayce reading 1931-4

Adele had been hired to be the administrator of a new nursing home. Impressed by the facility's ideal, "to be of service to people," Adele knew she must hold this in her mind.

As she searched for a quality administrative staff, she recalled the ideal, meditated for guidance, and sent out a prayer that the correct people would be sent to her.

The hiring process was filled with struggles. Adele's intuition said that Cathy would be excellent as director of nursing. At the last minute, though, Cathy wanted to withdraw to take another job. Instead of debating with her, Adele silently affirmed the ideal and told herself that whatever Cathy chose to do would work out for the best. Then, speaking to Cathy, she affirmed Cathy's capability to do the job and promised her support. Cathy decided to accept the job.

While conducting interviews for another staff position, Adele intuitively felt Mike should be hired. The other staff who were helping with the interviewing did not feel he was the strongest candidate. Adele, checking her intuition through meditation, felt her guidance was correct and hired him. It was apparent from his first day at work that he believed in the ideals of the nursing home and was committed to being a team member to make it a success.

APPLICATION: The next time you need someone to work with you on a project, choose an ideal, hold it in your mind, and affirm that you will attract someone with ideals similar to yours.

Where God Dwells on Earth

To express love in your activities to your neighbor is the greater service that a soul may give in this mundane sphere.
Based on Edgar Cayce reading 499-2

There once lived two brothers who shared equally the produce and profit of the farm their father had left them. One brother was happily married with two children; the other brother was still single. The single brother reasoned to himself, "I live by myself while my brother must support a family. I have no need of all the grain in my barn." So in the middle of the night he took a bag of grain from his barn and put it in his brother's barn.

Meanwhile the married brother reasoned, "I have a wife and children to look after me. My brother has no one to care for his future." So at night he would take a bag of grain from his barn and put it in his brother's barn.

Both were puzzled as to why for many years their grain supply did not diminish.

One night, as chance would have it, both left their barns at the same time and in the dark bumped into each other in the middle of the field. At first they were startled, but soon they realized what had been happening. They dropped their grain sacks and embraced.

God, looking down, thought, "On this spot I will build My Temple, for where people meet in love, there My Presence shall dwell."

APPLICATION: Do a loving act for a neighbor today.

A Deep Internal Breath

*Know that the kingdom is within—that it is within yourself
and the temple of your own soul that you may meet God.*
Based on Edgar Cayce reading 1497-2

This day at the office had been a frustrating one for Rick.
First, two people who had promised to have reports ready
did not have them done. Some of their reasons were valid,
but those missing reports had prevented him from moving
ahead on a project he had set aside this day to do.

Next, a business deal he had been working on for three
months fell through. A company had changed its mind and
refused his proposal. Neither Rick nor anyone else in his
office knew yet what had made the firm back out at the last
minute. After being treated that way, he had been tempted
for a few minutes to pull out of another project he and this
same company were discussing. However, he resisted that
temptation because he wanted some time before making
that decision.

Rick needed some space alone. He needed to find that
place within where he could detach a bit and rid himself of
some of the anger and frustration he was feeling so he could
think more clearly. He needed to take a deep internal breath
and come back refreshed.

More and more Rick was glad he had begun meditating
three years ago. After days like today he needed that space
in his inner life where he could go for calming renewal.

APPLICATION: When people disappoint and frustrate you,
find time to turn to that inner space in your life so you can
be renewed and gain a clearer perspective on what to do.

Grief and Reincarnation

Death is separation and thus have people dreaded it; yet it is but the birth into opportunities that will bring joy and harmony into your experience.

Based on Edgar Cayce reading 1776-1

Debbie believed in reincarnation so she knew that her grandfather at some level was still alive. However, her belief did not prevent her feeling grief and loss at his death because her relationship to him would not be the same again.

The special relationship she had enjoyed with her grandfather was important to her. Until she had graduated from high school, she and her grandparents had lived within a few blocks of each other all their lives. Even in recent years going back home had meant going to see them as well as her parents.

Even though Debbie knew that she would see her grandfather after death and that they would probably spend other lifetimes together, it would not be the same. They would not have the same grandfather/granddaughter relationship. The whole family would never live together in their home town as they had this time.

Feeling this loss helped Debbie affirm something—belief in reincarnation did not eliminate feelings of grief over the death of loved ones. That was good because it meant these relationships had been meaningful. However, her belief in reincarnation also helped her affirm that opportunities for life still existed for her grandfather. So, accompanying her sense of loss was also a deep feeling of hope and peace.

APPLICATION: The next time a close friend or loved one dies, affirm your sense of loss, however you feel it, but affirm that person's continuing life as well.

Showing People Up

*Learn to use every influence within the soul's understanding
so that less and less of self-glory, more and more of the glory of
God may be manifest in the experience of self in relationship
to others.*   Based on Edgar Cayce reading 264-50

It was the first day of nursing school. Sally was finally moving toward her goal of working in a clinic that specialized in holistic health care. This seemed like the perfect job for her to live out her ideal of service.

When first semester grades came out, she was upset because she had missed an A in one class by one point. However, she couldn't tell anyone how angry she was that this would probably keep her from being valedictorian—a goal she had set.

During semester break she came down with infectious hepatitis. The prognosis was six weeks for a recovery—and she had only one more week before classes resumed. Unless she could get well by then, she would have to quit the program. She asked her prayer group to pray for her, then went to see her doctor, who told her to use castor oil packs, eat only fresh fruits and vegetables, and come back in a week.

The night before her next appointment she realized what had led to her illness. She had let her ego get in the way of her ideal. That's why she had gotten angry over the grade. Burying her anger had made her susceptible to disease. Having admitted this to herself, she suddenly relaxed and felt the prayers of her group.

The next day the doctor was surprised. She was no longer infectious and could go back to school on Monday.

APPLICATION: The next time you get sick, look at your life and try to discover why you are getting ill at this time.

It Was Tempting

*The power comes in letting the self, the personality of the self,
become less and less in its desires, letting God's desire be the
ruling force.*   Based on Egar Cayce reading 696-3

The first one was difficult. "Give the people bread," the voice
had said. "The people are hungry."

Jesus knew the people were hungry. He knew many of
them went to bed with empty stomachs. But He also knew
that the people had another kind of hunger. They had a
hunger that could not be filled with food or with material
things. They had a hungering for words of life from God. So
He said, "People need more than bread to live."

The second one was even more appealing than the first.
"Throw Yourself off the temple and let God catch You."

What a way to make an entrance! What a way to show
whose side God was on! What a self-exalting, egocentric dis-
play of arrogance! Pride could overtake one in the sneakiest
disguises sometimes. His was a servant role. So He said,
"Don't tempt God like that."

The third would be expedient. "You can have it all if you
fall down to worship me."

How nice it would be to have this great enemy out of the
way! But His mission was to defeat this one and not exalt
him. He would gain nothing if He gained the world. So He
said, "Worship God and God alone."

How tempting it had been. But now that it was over, the
work of love was about to begin.

APPLICATION: Name an area of your life where you are
tempted to take the easy way to your goal. Stop and think
about your reason for wanting to reach that goal.

Symbolic Pain

Fear is as the fruit of indecision respecting what is lived and what is held as the ideal. Fear is the beginning of faltering. Faltering makes for disease throughout the body.

Based on Edgar Cayce reading 538-33

Here she was lying in bed again. Her chronic back pain had struck without apparent cause. For many years Anne had suffered from these pains which forced her into complete inactivity for several days. She had never figured out why.

This time, however, she had been reading a book on physical ailments and talking with a friend. She had read that the sciatic nerve causing her pain was frequently related to a fear of moving forward. With the help of her friend, she looked at the history of her back pain and discovered three times in her life when the pain had been this intense.

The first occurred during her husband's illness, which was eventually fatal. For a while she had lost her purpose for living and didn't want to make any effort to move on with her life.

The second time came when she could not decide which graduate school to attend. For several weeks she had put off making a decision and avoided moving forward.

The third time came right before her recent move. She had thought for a long time about whether or not to relocate from a familiar place to a new state.

All three of these instances involved a fear of moving forward and of taking a chance. Now she began to ask herself where she was not moving forward in her life and why.

APPLICATION: The next time you have a major ache or pain , see if you can determine the symbolic meaning of the pain and what it might be saying about your life.

The Invitation

It is free will, the choice that an entity makes regarding its ideal that governs whether the application of self is toward soul development or only the gratifying of material gains.
Based on Edgar Cayce reading 1470-1

Tess did not want to join any spiritual or religious organization that claimed it had the truth and all she had to do was memorize its beliefs. She did not want a group that claimed that its rules and regulations were God's absolute words for how to lead one's life. These did not allow for free will, for her right to think and choose for herself.

One night she was invited to an evening discussion. During the evening she found out that the metaphysical organization sponsoring this group believed there was truth in all religions and that no religion had all the truth. It maintained that people could learn something from each.

Even though it was her first time attending, she was invited to speak and share her opinion. When she asked questions, she was encouraged in her searching. As she continued to attend, she discovered that it did not present a system with numerous rules and regulations; instead, she found a few truths about loving God and neighbor. But more important to her, she found an emphasis on her using her free will to apply whatever else she might find of value in the material.

Because she felt invited to use her free will responsibly, she has continued to work with this group for many years.

APPLICATION: Look at your relationship to God and others. Are these based upon free will and response-ability or rules and regulations? Make adjustments if you wish.

Psychic Powers and Daily Life

The psychic lies latent within yourself. First find deep within that purpose, that ideal to which you would attain.

Based on Edgar Cayce reading 2533-1

People often asked Jim how they could develop psychic powers. In some cases Jim liked to ask in return, "Why do you want to be psychic?" He wasn't trying to lay a guilt trip on people or make them feel as if they were being selfish by desiring this, but he was asking people to clarify their motives.

Jim knew that motives and ideals gave people clues as to where to look in their lives for their psychic powers to awaken. If their motive was a desire to help children, for example, then they should examine those relationships for their own emerging intuition and inner promptings.

If the desire was to make better business decisions, they should look in that part of their lives. As they prepared themselves to make a decision, they should put the rational mind aside for few moments and listen to what the inner voice was trying to tell them. Then they could use their rational mind to reflect on the answer which came from within.

Over and over Jim would say that if people knew the motive for developing psychic abilities, they would know where to look in their lives for such experiences to begin to occur.

APPLICATION: Name an area of your life where you want to increase your psychic abilities. Become aware of the intuitions that come to you in those areas of your life.

The Quiet Influence

Know that as you open the way—sow the seed in activity and in word—you are to leave the rest with God. God gives the increase. Based on Edgar Cayce reading 2602-3

When he was young and before he became a famous Jewish rabbi, Isaac would at night take off his traditional, orthodox clothes, put on regular clothes, and join in the amusements of the other young men his own age—singing and dancing with them. They enjoyed his company, and his casual comments guided the behavior of the entire group; yet he never gave them orders. When Isaac left town to study with another rabbi, the young men gave up their nights of amusement because without him they found no pleasure in them.

After several years one of Isaac's boyhood friends was visiting in another city when he heard people talk of a great Rabbi Isaac. It did not seem possible that this rabbi could be the companion of his youth, but he was curious. He went to the rabbi and instantly recognized him.

His first thought was, "My, he certainly is good at deceiving the world."

But when he looked into the eyes of Rabbi Isaac, he understood the meaning of his memories and how he and his friends had been guided in their youth without their knowing it. He remembered how their celebrations had been uplifted by the influence of a presence they did not grasp.

He bowed his head before the rabbi who was looking at him with kindness and said, "Master, I thank you."

APPLICATION: As you relate to others who do not share your values, do something or say something that will plant seeds of other values for them to consider.

Building with the Mind

Changing of the mental status is ever the builder—mental and physical. That which the mind dwells upon is builded.
Based on Edgar Cayce reading 257-53

Chatter, chatter, chatter—that's all Emily ever did. She constantly chattered about her clothes, her dates, and anything else in her life. It seemed as if she never kept quiet. The rest of the riders in Marian's carpool seldom got a chance to say anything.

Marian had been doing some reading about spiritual growth and decided to try one of the principles with Emily—the idea of positive thinking.

The next day it was Marian's turn to drive when Emily began to chatter away. Marian tried to ignore the irritation she was feeling and concentrate on all the good qualities she liked in Emily. She thought about Emily's creativity, sense of humor, and intelligence. She was trying to "magnify the virtues and minimize the faults."

After a few minutes Emily suddenly stopped chattering. She paused a few seconds, then began to tell Marian—out loud—all the positive qualities she liked in Marian! This shocked and astounded everyone in the car.

The relationship took a turn for the better as Emily and Marian began to share what they liked about each other.

APPLICATION: The next time you meet someone whose faults you notice immediately, stop and magnify that person's virtues.

The Fun Jesus

Did you find the Master worked continually or did He take time to play? and time to relax? He is a good example in everyone's life. Based on Edgar Cayce reading 528-13

Andrew loved to talk about Jesus. People used to sit and listen to his stories as often as possible because the picture of Jesus he painted was not like the one most of them had received in church as they were growing up nor was it like the one some of them got from reading the Bible on their own.

The Jesus that Andrew knew was not the serious, somber individual people imagined Him to be. Andrew's Jesus was one who was sought by people because He was fun to be with. He was the kind of guy people liked to have at parties. He had a sense of humor, was entertaining, and enjoyed a good laugh like everyone else. The Edgar Cayce readings tell us Jesus joked at the Last Supper and on the way to the Garden of Gethsemane. The portrait Andrew painted of Jesus fit this image exactly.

Many people found a much closer relationship to Jesus after listening to Andrew's stories. Jesus became much more real, much more approachable, and much more of a friend.

APPLICATION: Formulate in your mind an image of Jesus that makes Him real, approachable, and a friend.

Moving Beyond Defensiveness

A criticism, if sincerely given, is often more effective or helpful than too much praise when not wholly justified.

Based on Edgar Cayce reading 3054-4

Because Joan had performed so well in a previous class, Mark agreed to supervise an independent study course for her. However, he was disappointed in the quality of her work on this project and gave her a lower grade than she was used to receiving. When her parents saw this grade, they called the school. Since they were influential people, the president of the university got involved.

As the situation unfolded and Mark was asked to write a complete report on the matter, he was both angry and concerned about his position. He was aware that he was getting very defensive. Before he could write a fair report, he knew he had to get his ego out of the way in order to be clear about what he should say.

A series of meditations helped him reach a point of acceptance. He knew he had to control his emotions and be honest and objective—even if it cost him his job. He sat down and wrote an explanation of the grade. After reading it, the college president and the parents understood the situation and there was no further problem.

APPLICATION: The next time you feel extremely defensive in a situation, take time to move beyond the emotions for a while so you can respond in a constructive way.

The Spirit of the Work

Blame not that upon others of which self is the cause.
Based on Edgar Cayce reading 4162-3

Karen had become very sensitive to an issue that kept happening at work. She was being overlooked and ignored.

When the agenda for the Board of Directors was posted, she discovered her presentation had been "forgotten." Her name had to be typed in at the last minute. A few days later in a discussion with some of her colleagues everyone was offering suggestions on a project. For quite a while no one asked her opinion and every time she tried to speak someone else would begin speaking and drown her out. Finally someone said in a peculiar way that maybe Karen might have something to say.

She thought about this and knew she wouldn't accomplish anything by blaming someone else. She had to look at herself to see if she were doing something to provoke this.

The Edgar Cayce readings told her that people had to bring the right spirit to an organization. She realized she was carrying a negative attitude about some recent business decisions. She didn't want to forget them and move on.

Karen is not sure she has found the answer but has resolved to change her attitude about the organization.

APPLICATION: The next time you feel you are being ignored or unfairly treated, ask yourself what you may be doing to cause this. Do one thing to change your attitude or behavior.

The Joyful Spiritual Life

Keep in accord that there may be the greater love shown day by day, not in long-faced nor somber manner but rather in the joy of living, for those who lend to the Lord should be the happiest of individuals. Based on Edgar Cayce reading 1742-4

Mary can remember the first time she saw Richard. He was known for delivering inspiring spiritual messages, and he was scheduled to speak in her home town. She went to the meeting not knowing what he looked like. However, based upon what she had heard about his strong spirituality, she tried to pick him out by looking for a man who, to her, looked spiritual. She finally decided it was this distinguished, rather sober-faced individual seated near her.

When Richard was introduced, the man she had selected did not move. Instead, up jumped a round-faced, rosy-cheeked man who began by cracking a few jokes and telling some funny stories. He was so happy and jovial that Mary decided she wanted whatever he had.

She had always thought spiritual people were very serious and somber, but Richard was so radiant and happy. She learned then that spirituality is meant to shine through a person in a glowing and happy way.

APPLICATION: Do one thing to show people that your spiritual growth is a joyous experience.

The Dark Side of Competition

*We will work together for the good that is in the experience of
each. Get that—together!*

Based on Edgar Cayce reading 1158-14

Marilyn and Betty worked in the same office for years and
became close friends because they both tried to apply similar principles like cooperation, positive imaging, and seeing
a spark of God in all people. Even after Betty got a new job,
they still saw each other. One day Marilyn asked Betty how
she liked her new job after three months.

Betty talked first about some of the training programs
she had been attending. She had to smile a bit because she
could see that these programs were introducing many of the
same ideas the two of them had worked on, only the instruc-
tors were using different terminology. They were talking
about positive thinking and mind power.

The one aspect of her work she didn't like was the competitiveness she found. She didn't like the way people
climbed over other people to get promotions. She didn't like
the back-stabbing and other behind-the-scenes maneuvers
that people pulled to make another person look bad and
themselves look good. This type of behavior made the workers less cooperative and less friendly.

In spite of this competitive atmosphere, Betty hung on to
her ideal of cooperating with others. She noticed that after a
while people treated her differently, and she did begin to see
some changes in the behavior of her colleagues.

APPLICATION: Do something to help someone else accomplish a goal while at the same time helping yourself accomplish your goal.

Resisting Temptation

When these confusions arise, there may be an entering into the holy of holies within you where the Lord may meet you and be your guide. But let your desire, your will ever be, "Others may do as they may, but for me and my house, my body, we will serve the living God."

Based on Edgar Cayce reading 657-3

Anna was struggling to get to know herself. She was becoming more and more conscious that parts of her wrestled with other parts. One night she was aware of a desire pattern in herself that wanted to pull her out of balance, that beckoned her to thoughts and actions that were contrary to her ideals. She decided to sit down and read the biography she had started. She would focus all her attention on the life story of this woman she admired.

Several times before, Anna had used this technique to overcome temptation. In moments of struggle she would remind herself of her ideal and choose to do one small thing that would lead her in the direction of that ideal instead of in the direction of the temptation. She didn't look for big changes in those moments. She didn't look for the old patterns to disappear overnight. But she discovered that if she did consciously choose some action in the direction of her ideal, gradually the old patterns lost their power and their demand diminished.

APPLICATION: Pick a thought or behavior you want to change. The next time the old pattern wants to surface, choose to move in the direction of your ideal.

The Queen's Decision

For your body is the temple of the living God. There God promises to meet you often. Harken to that voice within that may direct you in your choices of this or that experience, of this or that relationship. Based on Edgar Cayce reading 528-14

What was she supposed to do? It was a bad law. It was an unjust law. Even though Esther was a queen, she was not allowed to approach the king to protest unless he summoned her. If she did and the king refused to see her, it would mean her death.

But she thought about her uncle and her people. The law had deliberately been phrased to discriminate against the Jewish people in Persia. They could not possibly obey that law without denying their faith. Many of them would choose to die rather than do that. She was sure the king was unaware of how that law would be enforced.

Now she had to choose and choose quickly. Tomorrow the killings would start unless someone—unless she—did something. She was the only one who could get the king's attention quickly enough to prevent the death of innocent people. After several difficult hours of prayer, she got dressed. She put her trust and hope in God. She put on her royal tiara and walked directly to the king's throne room. Even though they knew who she was, she saw the guards draw their swords in case the king refused to see her.

The king looked up. He was surprised to see her standing there and realized the risk she was taking. He held out his sceptor to greet her, and Esther and her people were saved.

APPLICATION: The next time you have to take a risk, take some time in prayer and meditation to find God's guidance and strength for the situation.

Beginning the Day

As the soul seeks for that which is food for the body, so are the words of truth sought that make for growth for the soul.

Based on Edgar Cayce reading 254-68

Have you discovered how to begin the day so that you can face the world refreshed and invigorated?

Every morning Carolyn goes through the same ritual. This is her way of preparing for the day by balancing out the needs of her body, mind, and soul.

When she gets up, she does a few stretching exercises. She reaches up toward the ceiling, relaxes, then repeats the series. She follows this exercise by reading the Bible or some of her favorite affirmations from the Edgar Cayce readings. This helps her to attune her spirit to an uplifting thought for the day. Finally she thinks about the coming day and the positive, constructive attitude she wants to carry with her throughout.

In the evening Carolyn reflects on the day and on how well she has lived up to her ideal. If she feels a need to, she will also spend time reading some inspirational book or article.

She has discovered that daily feeding her soul and mind as well as her body makes her life more attuned to her ideals.

APPLICATION: Do something that is food for your soul.

Self-Responsibility

First analyze yourself. Know that the world, the people, the environment are what you yourself make of them.

Based on Edgar Cayce reading 1367-1

Steven finally realized that trying to lay the blame on others can have unpleasant consequences. In addition he learned about adopting an attitude of being responsible for himself.

Several years ago Steven was experiencing states of depression. He would suddenly go into black moods for days and not know why. During one of these moods he realized that he had blamed his wife for something insignificant that had happened to him. He was embarrassed by this thought and that helped him wake up to what he was doing.

He realized that he had been refusing to accept responsibility for himself and for his own actions. He was constantly trying to find someone else on whom to lay the blame. When he finally accepted the blame for what was happening in his life, his depression left and he has not been bothered by these episodes again.

That experience taught Steven a lot about accepting the credit or the blame for his own life and how important it is to have this attitude of self-responsibility.

APPLICATION: The next time you want to blame someone else for what is happening in your life, accept the responsibility yourself and do something to change the situation.

NOVEMBER 4

Experience Is a Necessary Teacher

*Not that there should be regrets, nor condemnation of any—
neither of self nor the excusing of self. But rather use that
which is before you that there may be the greater vision of the
purpose for which each and every soul enters earth.*

Based on Edgar Cayce reading 1302-2

Alice couldn't figure out what had gone wrong. When she
had adopted Jeff as a young boy, it was a dream come true.
For the first several years of their life together everything had
gone well. Then when Jeff became a teenager, he began to
have some problems. He couldn't stay out of trouble.

It was then that Alice began to doubt the wisdom of the
adoption. She blamed her inadequacy as a parent for Jeff's
problems. She believed she had made a terrible mistake.

Her friends finally helped her through all the self-guilt by
talking about reincarnation and soul lessons. They told her
that in spite of what other people did, there are some experiences people have to go through. She could be much more
supportive of Jeff if she could get rid of the self-blame and
see this situation as a series of lessons he needed to learn.

At first this idea sounded callous and uncaring, but eventually she could see the truth in this approach. The relief she
felt as she let go of the guilt was immediately noticeable.
She became more relaxed. She could be more objective and
thus able to give better advice and support.

What seemed like a very callous belief at first turned out
to be a life-saving concept that allowed her to live her life
and be better able to reach out to her son.

APPLICATION: There are some lessons in life that souls
have to learn by experience. Name someone you know who
is learning a lesson through experience. Support that individual while he or she is learning.

The Two Brothers

Put into active, prayerful, working service what you know to do day by day. Your daily acts, words, speech will bring the realization of the ideal being manifest in you as well as in others.   Based on Edgar Cyce reading 262-12

The two brothers were almost as different in their likes and habits as two people could possibly be. Jim was the philosophical type, always coming up with new ideas for expanding the family business and visualizing where it could reach next. Alfred was more concerned about practical matters, interested in seeing that the business had a sound organizational structure that could respond to the needs of the future.

Dealing with people came naturally to Jim. He could approach them easily and make them feel wanted and needed. He recruited good workers. Alfred worked behind the scenes, checking on personnel issues such as annual reviews for the people his brother brought in. On moving day it was Alfred's very practical approach that got everyone involved. His well-organized plan got the entire job done in one day.

The two brothers were so different. Yet it was their differences that gave them the necessary balance that allowed them to accomplish so much when they worked together.

APPLICATION: Name someone you work with that is very different from you. Affirm how you both bring some talent or skill that brings a balance to what you do together.

The Power of the Imagination

Visualize and you will make it and can use it to the advantage and the help of others.

Based on Edgar Cayce reading 5103-1

Betty's novel was going well—slow but consistent. She did not plan to make writing a career, but she was enjoying using her writing talents in this venture. More important, she was learning about the power of her imagination and just how real some thoughts can become.

For Betty writing was not a physical process or the use of a skill she had learned in college. Writing was letting her imagination work and then putting on paper the ideas that came through. An idea could come to mind as she was running, washing dishes, or doing something totally unconnected with writing. She would allow the idea to develop for a few minutes, then later would record on paper what her imagination had produced.

She also let her characters live in her imagination and got acquainted with them; she learned how they felt and how they would react to various situations. Then when she wrote, she didn't have to struggle so much to decide how the characters would respond to an event; she knew because they had a life of their own that she understood.

Writing had reinforced what she had read in the Edgar Cayce readings: thoughts are real and the imagination creates a form of reality.

APPLICATION: The next time your imagination wants to run free for a while, let it. Then write down what happened and read it once or twice to see what you might learn from the thoughts that were created.

The Artist Emerges

For with God's peace there comes contentment, no matter what may be the vicissitudes of life. There can come—with that peace—that contentment of heart and mind that God is in the holy temple and all is well with those who have made Christ the ideal. Based on Edgar Cayce reading 451-2

In 1967 following surgery on her hand that left it crippled, Marian read *There Is a River*. She was intrigued and began to read more Cayce books. Inspired by this material, she began to meditate. Then one day in the middle of a meditation experience she had the urge to pick up the pen and paper lying next to her and write. She discovered that she could write with the hand that at other times she could not use, even to sign her name. Hope for healing was revived.

After this meditation inspiration, she began painting to exercise her hand. The early days were painful, but she continued her efforts. She was also applying castor oil, peanut oil, and other remedies. However, Marian believes that clearing her mind of doubt and maintaining a strong desire to work with God were the real miracle workers.

During her slow healing process, she had moments of frustration and anger about her crippled condition. However, she also watched a talent emerge that would have remained buried if she had not been forced to work with God to overcome her condition.

Twenty years ago Marian was sick in body and mind. Today she no longer has time to sit and think about who she used to be because she is too busy living in the present and making it count. She has learned one important lesson—whenever she must carry a cross, God carries her.

APPLICATION: The next time you face a difficulty in life, open up to God's love and let God go along with you.

Two Dreams Come True

Make known the desires to others, to those associations and connections that may be had. Then wait on God.

Based on Edgar Cayce reading 243-15

When Peter and Marian decided to move, Peter was adamant about selling his real estate business first. He didn't want to move all the way across the country and have someone else run his business. He figured it would take him several months to find a good buyer, but he offered it first to Joan, his best agent. Joan was surprised. She hadn't suspected that he wanted to move.

Peter also told some friends about his desire to sell his business and move. He asked them to start passing the word around. In addition, during their evening meditations, he and his wife prayed for the right buyer to come along.

A week later Peter was astounded when Joan walked in with a check to buy the agency. Joan had been discussing this new opportunity at a friend's party. Some people she had never met before encouraged her to buy the business. However, Joan had said she didn't have the money.

Two days after the party she had received in the mail from the people she had just met a check for the full amount. A note was attached saying, "Good luck!"

Instead of his search lasting for months, this series of events enabled Peter to sell his business in a week. Two weeks later he and his wife were finalizing their moving plans.

APPLICATION: Be alert for changes in other people's lives that open up opportunities for you as well. Look for God to help both you and the other people realize your dreams.

Finding Your Spot in Life

Does the life's work lead to those conditions that make for antagonisms to God's will as understood by self? Then change so that the work may be in accord with what you have set as an ideal service to God.

Based on Edgar Cayce reading 853-2

Marian's headaches were occurring almost every day. The doctor didn't find anything physically wrong with her so he asked her some questions about her life. This made her think. She really didn't like her job anymore, but she didn't find it stressful either. At least, she didn't realize she did.

She saw a notice for a job with another business and mentioned it to a friend at work. The friend encouraged her to apply for it if she thought she would enjoy it. Marian considered it for several days, but still could not make a decision.

Several weeks earlier she had scheduled a psychic reading with Edgar Cayce about another issue. When the time for the reading came, she also took the opportunity to ask about the job. The reading strongly encouraged her to apply. It said she would get the job and work there the rest of her life.

Although she thought that statement was a little too strong, she decided to apply for the job. There was a lot of competition, but she got it. Her headaches disappeared the first week of working at her new job, and she knew within weeks that she had found her place in life. She retired from that firm thirty years later.

APPLICATION: It's important to find a "place in life." Examine your life to see if you have found that place or are working toward that goal.

A Reason for Friendships

Nothing happens by accident, but that the glory of God may be manifested in the doings and the relationships of each individual as one to another.

Based on Edgar Cayce reading 1432-1

Linda was working in a bookstore the first day she met Cindy. Cindy had come in the store to look around. When Linda offered to help, Cindy asked her what books she should read. While Linda wanted to help Cindy choose for herself, Cindy kept insisting that Linda knew what she should read. Finally Linda recommended three titles.

Cindy came back two weeks later and repeated the request for recommended books. This happened over a period of months and a friendship began to develop out of these encounters. When Cindy and her husband moved, they continued to maintain contact with Linda and her husband.

About a year after their move, Cindy was in an accident that left her in a coma. Linda and her husband went to visit.

Most doctors gave up any hope of rehabilitating Cindy's mind. However, with the encouragement of Linda and her husband, Cindy was sent to a specific clinic. Slowly, with this special treatment, she began to make progress.

Linda and her husband continued to see Cindy and support her and her husband. Over the past two years, they have been amazed at the progress she has made.

When Linda looks back at those strange encounters in the bookstore that turned into a deep friendship, she knows that the universe brings people together for a reason.

APPLICATION: Think about one of your friendships that began in a rather unusual way. Give one reason why you think the friendship started.

Look Through God's Eyes

For you know, you understand, that all stand as one before God. There is no one above another.

Based on Edgar Cayce reading 1662-1

One midnight a rabbi was studying the mystic teachings when he heard a noise at the window. A peasant, who had been drinking too much, was knocking and asking to be let in and to be given a bed for the night. For a few seconds the rabbi was angry, and he thought to himself: "Can this drunk really be so insolent and rude as to be asking this? What business does he have in this house?"

Then he heard other words in his heart. "Does he not have some business in God's world? If God can get along with him, do I have the right to reject him?"

He opened the door and prepared a bed for the man.

APPLICATION: Think about all people being one in God's eyes. Today help someone you have not helped because of his or her looks or because you considered that person to be in a different class of people.

It Was in the Air

*Put in the hearts of your children when they sit at mealtime
or when they rise to play, those tenets of the living God that
will be in their thoughts by night and by day.*

Based on Edgar Cayce reading 2118- 1

Norma and her husband began working with the Edgar
Cayce readings before their son was born. As David grew up,
he would be at the table when they discussed the latest
pamphlets and brochures they were receiving. Much of their
view of life they tried to pass on was based on these readings, even if they never used the Cayce name.

David never seemed to show much interest, so they
didn't force anything.

Now that David is older and married and his father has
died, he comes to have lunch with his mother frequently.
They talk about many things, including his childhood
memories. He says now that he never really knew any philosophy other than the one his parents talked about at the
dinner table.

The most important concept he remembers is the idea of
cause and effect. As he has lived his life, this idea has made
him stop and think many times before he did something. It
also helped him phrase his thoughts and statements in positive rather than in negative ways when he had the choice.

He may not have shown much interest when he was
younger, but he admits he absorbed ideas that helped him
in later years.

APPLICATION: Think back on what you learned from your
parents and how you learned it. Think about how you can
pass on to others the ideas that are important to you.

Two Bees

A beautiful symbol. For it would create that necessary for the understanding of self and self's relationships to the world about self and the associations with the Creative Forces or God. Based on Edgar Cayce reading 1747-3

Tom wasn't really laughing at the group, but the group thought he was. During a week-long conference they had been working for three days on the dream of one group member and still didn't understand it. Tom had joined the group, listened to it once, and begun laughing.

After a few seconds he stopped and told the group that everyone in the room knew the answer. If they would listen *closely* while he himself repeated the dream narrative, they would understand, too.

The woman had dreamed that she felt something in her hand. When she opened her hand, there were two bumble bees in it. She had *two bees* in her hand.

People began smiling as Tom emphasized the *two bees*.

Of course, it was a clue to the beginning of Hamlet's famous speech, "To be or not to be."

The woman in the group admitted she did have a big decision to make and she had been thinking about it for several weeks. It involved taking a job near home and continuing to live at home or taking a job in the city nearby and getting an apartment.

The dream was impressing upon her that this was not just a vocational decision. This was a decision about living a full life—the person whom she was to be.

APPLICATION: Dreams can be filled with puns or plays on words. Tell your dreams out loud to someone and listen to the words you use to describe your dream images.

I'm Going to Marry Whom?

Do not allow yourself to become so material-minded that judgments are measured only by the yardstick of material accomplishments. Based on Edgar Cayce reading 3436-2

When Patty first met her future husband, Jack, she thought he was married. Even when she found out later that he was single, she didn't give him much thought until her date with Frank.

She thought Frank represented everything she wanted in a man—a law degree, an intelligent way of speaking, lots of money. On their date they stopped in a specialty jewelry store to look around. Patty was attracted to one particular crystal and bought it.

During supper she held it in one hand while she ate with the other. As the dinner progressed, she began to have second thoughts about Frank. He sounded so intellectual that she couldn't sense any feeling in what he was saying. When she went to the restroom, she set the crystal down by the mirror to redo her lipstick. When she picked up her crystal again, she heard her inner voice say, "You are going to marry Jack." She was stunned and thought to herself, "I'm going to marry whom?" The voice repeated Jack's name.

She walked out of the restroom, had Frank take her home, and immediately called Jack to talk. She couldn't tell him what she had experienced, but they talked for over an hour. The next time she saw Jack he treated her very differently, and they were married in a few months.

APPLICATION: Your inner voice can give guidance about which people to avoid and which people with whom to build relationships. The next time it speaks, listen to it.

Letting Go of Fear

*Keep the faith, the faith in your God to use you as a blessing,
as a channel of understanding to others.*

Based on Edgar Cayce reading 816-3

While working with children at an art museum, Amy came in one day unprepared for class and planned to ad-lib a bit. But upon her arrival she discovered that today people were going to videotape her program for promotional purposes and that one of her major financial supporters was present to observe.

She said a quick prayer, affirming to herself, "Possibilities will open. I will be a channel to do what is right for the children."

As she relaxed, her inner voice told her to go to her supply room. She was attracted to the yellow construction paper and began to cut it up into triangles, not knowing at all what she was going to do with those pieces of paper. When the children arrived, she gave each child a different-shaped paper to hold. Then they went to the gallery and stopped at the painting Amy's assistant had chosen for that day. To her utter amazement this painting had yellow triangles of all sizes in it. The children then began to match their paper triangles with the ones in the painting. They talked about colors and shapes and how these go together in a painting.

Amy relearned from this experience how to handle anxiety: She needed to go into an open space within, get her ego out of the way, and let the Creative Forces come through.

APPLICATION: The next time you face an anxious situation pray before you begin, set your ego aside, and affirm that you are a channel for God's work.

It's Not How Much That Counts

The giving with hope of reward or pay is in direct opposition to the law of love.   Based on Edgar Cayce reading 3744-4

Jesus was standing in the temple in Jerusalem talking with His disciples. Ever observant, He noticed two people approach the box in which people dropped their offerings to God.

One well-dressed man walked up to this box and cleared his throat loudly. Then he pulled out his purse and, holding it about a foot above the box, dropped the gold coins into it. From that height they made a lot of noise when they hit the other coins in the box. The man looked up, smiled at all those who were now looking at him, and walked away.

Jesus could only shake His head sadly.

A widow dressed in ragged clothes quietly approached the offering box. She quickly reached out her hand, dropped in two small copper coins, and scurried away.

Jesus could barely keep back the tears. Speaking to His disciples He said, "The first man in spite of all the gold he put in gave nothing. His efforts were for his pride. The woman's two small coins were given to God as a gift from the heart. They are the real treasure in God's eyes."

APPLICATION: The next time you get ready to give to someone or some charitable organization, think about how you can make it a gift from the heart.

Making the Blood Flow

Cultivate the ability to see the ridiculous and to retain the ability to laugh.   Based on Edgar Cayce reading 2984-1

Doris was getting a physical exam at a special clinic she had visited before. All the nurses and staff knew her and loved her and wanted everything to go well.

When it came time to draw blood for tests, problems developed. The nurses found veins to stick the needle into, but no blood would come out. They tried for almost a half hour and got nothing.

Doris admitted that she had had this problem before. She simply didn't bleed easily. Nevertheless, that didn't eliminate the pain everyone knew she was feeling by being stuck so often.

Finally one nurse who knew Doris well came in and said something that made her laugh. As soon as she started laughing, the blood flowed. They had no trouble getting the amount they needed without having to stick her again.

Later on, she remarked that she had a good sense of humor and that laughing seemed to make the energy flow in her. However, she had never known before how laughter really did make her blood flow.

APPLICATION: Laughter can help relieve tension and blocked energy. The next time you feel "blocked" up, find something to make you laugh.

Ideally the Same

Choose one who is in accord with some of the activities you desire to make as ideals.   Based on Edgar Cayce reading 520-3

Gary and Audrey had dreamed for years of setting up a holistic living center. In it they planned to have a counselor for people to speak with, books to read, and presentations.

When a friend of theirs expressed interest in the project and offered financial backing for a while, they agreed to work with him. They found a building and moved in. They began publicity and received positive comments from some of their first customers.

However, they also ran into obstacles. They experienced how traditional approaches to living and health care are deeply ingrained in the minds of many people. Many refused to read their publicity or consider trying anything new. They also began to have disputes with their friend about how to operate the center. As they discussed these issues, they realized their ideals and their friend's ideals were far apart in some crucial areas. One day their friend announced he was pulling out. Since they didn't have the money, they had to close the center.

As they reflected on this experience, they realized the importance of ideals. They could have overcome the resistance of the public but not the differences with their friend. The next time they begin another center, they are going to make sure their partners have the same ideals as they do.

APPLICATION: The next time you begin a venture with someone, discuss ideals with that person and see if these agree with yours.

You Get What You Need

For man and woman are given the opportunity to be one with God. Hence they are given attributes through which the soul may become conscious or aware of God's presence already with or withdrawing from the soul's activities—dependent upon how the soul uses the opportunities.

Based on Edgar Cayce reading 945-1

Mary and Anne were having another one of their conversations. Anne was close to finishing her book of short stories for children. Having kept a dream log for about a year, she was telling Mary how her dreams over the past few weeks had given her ideas for her stories. The day after each dream, she would sit at her typewriter and in a few hours have another story written. Mary envied Anne a little for her ability to write so easily and bring a beautiful message to each story.

Anne, on the other hand, envied Mary. Since Mary had begun meditating about a year ago, she had developed a unique ability to tune in to people at times.

It was not unusual anymore for Anne to see Mary head for the telephone and pick it up before it rang. Anne was also used to Mary having feelings that something was going to happen to someone. Within a few days something would happen. Or if Mary had warned someone, an event might narrowly be avoided if the person took precautions.

On occasion they would share their envies. However, they always concluded that each was developing gifts and skills that were meant to be used. Each of them had a particular gift that for some reason was best for her own growth. That was the gift each should be thankful for and should use.

APPLICATION: Choose one gift or skill that is furthering your spiritual growth. Use this gift in your unique, creative way.

The Value of Trying

For the try, *the effort, the energy expended in the proper direction is all that is required of* you. *God gives the increase.*

Based on Edgar Cayce reading 601-11

The Olympic games offer people the opportunity to achieve athletic excellence. Unfortunately, in the glitter of gold, silver, and bronze, we often fail to remember the numerous athletes who participate but do not win medals. In the Calgary games in 1988, one of these persons was Dan Jansen.

Dan's sister had died of leukemia the morning of his event. Nevertheless, he went to his speed-skating race because his family wanted him to and because he had a chance for the gold medal. He wanted to win not only for his sister but also for himself. The normal pressure of competition was heightened by the emotions of his family's experience. What a story a victory under those conditions would have made! Unfortunately, he fell.

The glory of "bringing home the gold" did not come to Dan. Neither will headline-making victories come to most of us in our lives. But, in the eyes of God it is the try that is important. Too often we let the thought of not having a chance to win or to achieve a big success keep us from trying.

Too often we let disappointing results lead us to feel as if our efforts are meaningless. At these moments in life, this thought encourages us: trying will always have value even if our efforts never result in victory.

APPLICATION: Try something without thought of success but simply for the value of trying.

The Next Step

We meet few people by chance, but all are opportunities in one experience or another.

Based on Edgar Cayce reading 3246-1

Marsha looked closely at the people in her discussion group. It seemed that her group had a higher than usual proportion of members who were dealing with addiction or had close relatives or friends dealing with it. This insight was reinforced at the next meeting.

On that night Tom attended for the first time. During the dream-sharing session he related one of his dreams. As the group listened, Marsha received the strong impression that Tom's son had some kind of addiction problem even though the dream didn't specifically state this.

Later that evening, Tom confessed that his son was an alcoholic who could not yet admit his drinking problem. Because of the work Marsha did, she was able to give Tom some advice on what his next steps should be in working with his son and with himself.

Seeing that yet another person dealing with an addiction problem had come into her life made Marsha realize that, if people are truly seeking help, they will be attracted to others who can help them find the next growth step in their lives.

APPLICATION: Look at the people in your life. Take the oportunity to learn from the ones whom you believe can offer you your next growth step.

The Way to Wisdom

Would you have wisdom without preparation? Would you have happiness without being able to comprehend, to understand? If this is so, you have not learned your lesson of wisdom. Based on Edgar Cayce reading 262-107

Why was everything happening to her all at once—a bad business deal, her son's accident, the burglary of their house while they were gone, and an argument with her best friend just when she needed someone to talk to? Sarah couldn't figure it out. She examined her feelings and discovered that these experiences didn't really feel like karmic ones. She didn't feel she deserved them because of some past-life deeds, but she was confused because she couldn't explain them.

As she read this passage about wisdom from the Edgar Cayce readings, she began to realize that just before these troublesome events had happened she had been praying for wisdom. When she re-examined the events of the past few months, she felt the pain again, but she also saw how she had learned from them.

Sarah had asked for wisdom and purification. Her soul realized she needed to experience these in order for her to learn more about compassion, in order for her to gain the wisdom and purification for which she had prayed.

This experience helped Sarah see that everything that happened to her was not karmic debt. Some experiences came so she could continue her learning process.

APPLICATION: Look again at an experience you thought was a karmic debt you had to repay. Tell yourself what you learned from that experience and see it in a new light.

Dreams for Teens

The mind of a developing soul gathers in dreams compari-
sons of conditions through which the soul has already passed
or those conditions which are shaping future development.
Based on Edgar Cayce reading 487-5

Dream discussion had become a regular part of the Robbins'
breakfast ritual for the past five years. Every morning Bill
and Martha would question their boys about their dreams
and what they thought the symbols were trying to reveal to
them. Because of these frequent morning talks, they had all
learned a lot about how to derive insights from dreams.

The great benefit came during their sons' adolescent
years when many important decisions were debated. Instead of these situations becoming a parent-son clash, they
turned into a process involving dreams as a third point of
view. Bill and Martha found comfortable roles as question-
ers on the themes and patterns in their sons' dreams. By
merely asking thoughtful questions they were able to avoid
assuming authoritarian positions that would surely have
stimulated rebellion. The boys ultimately made their own
decisions using their dreams as guidance plus their parents'
efforts to bring out all possible shades of meaning. Following this process, they discovered that dreams never led to a
choice which was harmful in the long run.

Life seemed so much more meaningful and pleasant in
their family than in the families of some of their friends,
embattled as they were with their teenagers' lives.

APPLICATION: Begin taking time each day to talk about
dreams that you or your family members had the night before.

The Loud Voice of Our Actions

What you are speaks so loud, others seldom hear what you say.　　　　　　　Based on Edgar Cayce reading 3292-1

A man once came to a famous rabbi. He was concerned about his sons. "How can I make my sons devote themselves to the Torah?" he asked.

The rabbi answered, "If you want them to devote themselves to the Torah, you yourself must spend time studying the Torah. They will do as you do. Otherwise they will not spend time over the Torah but will tell their sons to do so. And on it will go. For if you forget to study, your sons will forget and only urge their sons to study. Their sons will forget the Torah and tell their sons they should know the Torah. Thus no one will really know the Torah."

APPLICATION: Are you telling someone to do something but then acting differently yourself? Take one step to change this behavior.

Understanding Others

If you will meditate the more upon what He gave—love and forgiveness, faith and hope may overcome spites, fears, distrust—you may open yourself to the opportunities that constantly lie before you in your activities in the present.

Based on Edgar Cayce reading 1599-1

As a child, Donald struggled against feeling like a victim. Whenever anybody criticized him, he knew it was all his fault and accepted the blame for what was happening.

His parents tried to explain to him that he didn't have to accept what others said. However, instead of teaching him to tease back or get even, they encouraged him to see the stresses and weaknesses in others that caused their behavior. He could then understand their behavior and be able to release the anger he might be feeling toward them. This would also keep him from blaming himself or the other person.

The big test came when someone stole Donald's bike. At first he was really angry. He wanted to find the kid and punch him out. But he tried to follow his parents' teachings. He tried to understand why someone might steal his bike. Maybe that child really needed one. Maybe that child couldn't afford one and thought he had to have one.

After he calmed down, he tried to find out who had taken his bike. He couldn't. However, his parents' teachings helped him to let go of his anger. He finally reached a point where he didn't blame himself or anyone else and was able to focus his energy on other things in his life.

APPLICATION: The next time someone speaks unjustly about you or treats you unfairly, take time to try to understand why that person did this. See if this helps you handle your anger.

Commitment to a Companion

Gentleness, kindness, patience, long-suffering—these bring their fruits into the hearts and souls of others.

Based on Edgar Cayce reading 1531-1

When Carol's teenage brother began having severe emotional problems and had to be hospitalized, the whole family looked for ways to help. Since Carol and her husband had become interested in the Edgar Cayce health readings, they talked to their friends who had worked with these ideas. One man recommended what had worked for others he knew.

Some people had gathered ideas from the readings and put together a program called "a companion project" to help people like her brother. This called for a variety of treatments to supplement counseling. One element of the program called for someone no more than a seven years' age difference from the patient to commit himself or herself to spending a lot of time with the patient. It also called for time spent in nature, diet and health recommendations, and massages.

Carol volunteered to be the companion to her brother. She visited him regularly in the hospital. When he was released, she let him come to her home frequently. She took walks with him, talked with him, gave him massages, and helped him stick to a healthful diet.

He had three or four relapses during the next two years, but after that he got a job, got married, and lived a complete life.

APPLICATION: Go out of your way to do one thing for someone who needs help.

Let the Individual Decide

As to what your attitude should be in conversation and in your dealings with all: it isn't the attempt to force the issue with anyone. God has given each soul a free will. Each must come to the acknowledging of needs first.

Based on Edgar Cayce reading 257-244

When Betty discovered the Edgar Cayce readings, she was excited. The insights she found in that material helped her change her life and overcome some limitations she had been living with for years.

Betty had a next-door neighbor whom she knew could benefit from these ideas as well. At first when she started sharing, the neighbor was interested. However, as Betty became more pushy with her new-found ideas, the neighbor's response cooled—as did their friendship.

She learned from this experience what she later found in the Cayce readings: to tell people her story. She was to be an example to others and offer invitations to others to study with her. But she was not supposed to compel or try to tell others what to do. She was to wait for them to decide if they wanted to join her on this journey.

APPLICATION: Recall something you are excited about and want to tell others what you have discovered. Share it with others in a way that invites them to join with you without being pushy.

Living the Example

Be joyous in the service God would make of you—even in trials—as one that would be a bright and morning star to your neighbor.   Based on Edgar Cayce reading 640-1

Mike believed that everything that happens to us has a purpose. Therefore, how we handle a situation is important. He found this idea tested in an unexpected way.

One evening he was involved in an accident that left his legs partially paralyzed. In the rehabilitation center, it was unclear for a while exactly how much use of his legs he would regain. Because of his work with the Edgar Cayce readings, he decided that this was an opportunity for growth and he didn't dare mishandle it. So he began to laugh and joke with the nurses and doctors. He could still have fun.

Billy, a 13-year-old boy, helped Mike as much as Mike helped him. Billy had lost both his parents in an auto accident that had severed his spinal cord, leaving him paralyzed from the waist down. The two liked to play jokes on each other.

On one occasion Mike had tricked Billy earlier in the day. That evening when Mike got back to his room and tried to turn on the TV, his hand slipped off the controls. Billy had put butter on all the controls on the set.

Some days later the doctor, having observed his behavior, remarked, "Mike, you are a very important example for others." Without really being aware of it, in the midst of his trials, he had been helping people by living joyfully.

APPLICATION: Even when life seems overwhelming, do one thing that will show you are "a bright star" to someone else.

Your Natural Talents

Each soul has a job to do but you alone may find and do that job.   Based on Edgar Cayce reading 2823-1

Alice planned to study the Edgar Cayce readings for just a few days during her vacation. However, once she started, she discovered she couldn't quit. The references to a variety of historical eras intrigued her, and the new insights into these times expanded her understanding of history.

This study became more than a historical study when she discovered that she could apply some of the insights from those stories. For example, vocational guidance was a major emphasis in the Cayce readings on Egypt. People were helped to examine their gifts and talents and pursue occupations that used those talents.

This led Alice to examine her own interests and talents. She began to use her music and dance interests in new ways. In doing so she found a new fulfillment in her life.

As she talks to people now, she encourages them to do the same. She encourages people to examine their natural talents, strengths, and abilities and to find ways to use those abilities to find a richer experience in life.

APPLICATION: Take one step to develop a talent or interest you are not using in a fulfilling way.

Success and Intuition

Success will follow the efforts of the soul if the soul will answer to the intuitive forces from within.

Based on Edgar Cayce reading 240-2

Richard has come to rely more and more on his intuition when making business decisions. For him intuition means not only listening to his internal gut feelings but also being in touch with what is happening in other people or in his surroundings. This might be a look in someone's eye, a certain inflection in the voice which sounds a little out of the ordinary, or some other subtle clue. The following episode demonstrates the importance of using this approach.

Reading through a number of invitations asking him to lecture, he did not feel right about any of them. However, he did go to speak with his assistants to get their thoughts. One of his assistants had seen the invitations and encouraged him to consider one of them. She really didn't have a good reason, but the unusual tone in her voice as she talked told him intuitively that she was right. He accepted that one.

When he arrived for the lecture, he had deep regrets. The place felt wrong. The group of people felt wrong. He was wishing he had followed his first rational thought and said no. However, during the evening he made contact with one talented individual and they developed a relationship that has had a major impact on part of his business.

Even though he is still working on trusting this kind of intuition, he has had some very positive results.

APPLICATION: Be alert to subtle clues around you to which your intuition may call you to respond.

December 1

Curing Bad Habits

Q. What is the best method to be used in curing children of injurious habits formed?
A. In using that of suggestion to the subconscious or soul mind of the body as it goes to sleep.

Based on Edgar Cayce reading 5747-1

John and Susan used pre-sleep suggestions on their children for various difficulties. These suggestions have been particularly effective in helping their four-year-old son with some behavior patterns. If they noticed during the day that he had problems sharing, for example, they would sit with him as he was going to sleep. After saying prayers with him, they would then say quietly to him, "It's fun to share" or "You enjoy having people share with you and you share with them."

If their children had been fighting more than usual, John would sit with one of them as the child was going to sleep, and his wife with the other one. They would talk about how much fun it is to get along together and to be helpful and understanding of one another. Or they would mention the specific issue that had caused the fight and describe it in a new, more constructive way.

Pre-sleep suggestions have helped correct several kinds of behavior problems in their children.

APPLICATION: Try a pre-sleep suggestion on your child or yourself as a way to cure a habit or correct a behavior problem.

Your Creative Potential

*It is God's way that you be ever creative. This, too, must be
more often directed by the consciousness within.*

Based on Edgar Cayce reading 4071-1

Matthew was convinced that what he was reading had
something to do with him, but he wasn't quite sure what.
He was intrigued by the idea of a creative spiritual potential
that existed in every one. For several months he wondered
how this idea applied to him and his art work. He finally
decided he was not being as creative as he could be.

He went back to square one with his style of art. He began experimenting with design, color, and subject matter.
He took risks in abandoning his established style and in
sharing his new approach with his friends. He found he had
to ignore many comments and not be self-conscious about
the criticisms he was receiving. He did what he had to do.

This led him to new stages of growth at times, but he
never felt as if he could put all the pieces together into a new
style. It took twelve years of struggle, but he finally found
himself in a summer art class that helped him pull together
all his ideas and years of experimenting.

The time spent working with his talent and the belief in
his own creative potential finally led him to his unique artis-
tic style.

APPLICATION: Name an area of your life which has creative
potential. Do something to express the creativity you have
within you.

A Laugh a Day

Don't forget the recipe of making three people laugh every day! Based on Edgar Cayce reading 798-1

A man camping in the woods fell asleep in a cave. He awoke refreshed. But when he got back to town, he discovered it was the year 2,020 and not 1990. He ran to the nearest pay phone and immediately called his stockbroker. Expressing surprise at hearing this man's voice again, the stockbroker informed him that his stocks were now worth eight million dollars.

"I'm rich," the man shouted, only to be interrupted by the telephone operator who said, "Your three minutes are up. Deposit one million dollars, please."

A middle-aged mother was bursting with pride as she talked to her friend.

"Do you know about my son?" she asked her neighbor.

"No, what is he doing now?"

"He's going to a psychiatrist. Twice a week he goes."

"Is that good?" her neighbor asked. "Of course, it's good," came the reply. "Fifty dollars an hour he pays. Fifty dollars! And all he talks about is me."

APPLICATION: Tell these stories or one of your favorite funny stories to someone.

The Guidance of Your Intuition

Depend more upon the intuitive forces from within and not harken so much to that of outside influences.

Based on Edgar Cayce reading 239-1

Mona's daughter was scheduled to have a specific ear treatment, but a dream had warned Mona about it. So, at the last minute, she told the doctor to try it on her first. When he administered the treatment to her, she felt as if her ear exploded. The doctor insisted that everything was all right, but she did not let him give the treatment to her daughter.

After a few days of pain Mona entered the hospital emergency room. The doctors there said everything was fine, but in reality her eardrum had been punctured. She did not feel well for the next eight days, but kept trying to have faith in the doctors. Meanwhile, a massive ear infection was building up. When she finally went to another emergency room, the intern immediately put her on medication.

Two days later facial paralysis developed. She was readmitted and scheduled for surgery. However, every time she thought about surgery from the assigned doctor, she saw a big black "X" on her face. She refused the operation. Finally a surgeon she had known returned from vacation, and she agreed to let him operate on her. It was successful.

Though Mona did lose the hearing in her right ear, no damage was done to her face. Reflecting on this series of events, she realized that during this time she started to listen to her inner voice, which she had formerly blocked out.

APPLICATION: When people encourage and advise you to act one way, listen to your inner voice and what it is trying to tell you.

Preparing the Way

As you would be the channel to hasten that glorious day of the coming of the Lord, then do with a might what your hands find to do in order to make for the greater manifestations of the love of God in the earth.

Based on Edgar Cayce reading 262-58

One day a famous Jewish rabbi was discussing the promise of the coming Messiah with his disciples. One of them, recounting the many years of Jewish suffering and waiting, asked with great insistence, "Why doesn't the Messiah come?"

The rabbi replied, "It is written: 'Why didn't the son of Jesse come yesterday or today? Why doesn't he come?' And the answer was: 'Because today we are no different than we were yesterday.'"

APPLICATION: Do one act today that shows you are a more loving person than you were yesterday.

Nurturing Imagination

Let your imagination run wild and you will find you can make just as interesting a life experience as you want to make.   Based on Edgar Cayce reading 5251-1

How can imagination in children be nurtured?

David and Diane decided when they got married some years ago that they would not have a television set in their home. Diane admits now that there are some times when the children demand her time because they don't have TV as an outlet. However, she has learned that taking a few minutes to read a book with them or watch them color is all they really want. She can then return to her work, and they will continue coloring or find something else to do. She has also watched their imagination blossom.

One day when she took her children with her to her exercise class, Diane's mother was concerned about how they might behave while the class was in session. But the children looked in Mom's purse for a few seconds, found some tissues she uses to clean her glasses, and then spent thirty minutes playing with these tissues in a variety of ways.

When boredom does set in, instead of panicking, she tells the kids that she knows they are bored and offers ideas. Within a few minutes they have found something to do, and many times it has nothing to do with her suggestions.

She believes that children can find imaginative ways to entertain and educate themselves if given the opportunity. Not having TV in the home is the way she and her husband have chosen to give their children that opportunity.

APPLICATION: Do something that requires you to use your imagination more.

The Doctor and the Castor Oil Pack

Then in the mental attitudes there should be the attitude not only of hopefulness but of daily practical application.
Based on Edgar Cayce reading 1844-3

Janet had used some of the Edgar Cayce remedies for minor aches and pains, but she had never tried them on anything like this before. An annual checkup had just discovered some tumors in her abdomen. The doctor had scheduled her for surgery the next day, and now she was at home thinking about it.

It was close to Christmas, and she didn't want to be recovering from surgery during that time. Also she had heard favorable reports about castor oil. She decided to try it.

She called the hospital to cancel the surgery and went the next day to a leading gynecologist who agreed to monitor her condition while she followed her treatments. If any sudden change were noticed, he would tell her immediately.

She had regular appointments while using the castor oil packs. After three months her gynecologist looked puzzled because there appeared to be some improvement. He told her to continue what she was doing. After six months he was amazed at the improvement. In about a year the tumors were almost gone, and by the end of two years the doctor couldn't find a sign that she had ever had any.

Janet is convinced that the castor oil packs and the confidence she maintained by remaining under a doctor's supervision were the primary factors in her cure.

APPLICATION: If you want to change something in your life, a mental attitude desiring change is often not enough. Try taking a practical step in the direction of the change.

The Message of Symbols

Symbols, whether from the vibrations of numbers, of metals, of stones, are to become influences to make you in attunement with the Creative Forces—use them to attune yourself.
Based on Edgar Cayce reading 707-2

Howard detested mandala drawing. As an art student, he admired several styles of art and thought of himself as open to many ideas, but he considered this an easy way out. All one had to do was draw one quadrant of a canvas and then repeat it in the other three quadrants. The other concept he did not appreciate was the idea of symbolism. To him it was silly.

Then Howard began to read about Carl Jung, Edgar Cayce, and others who wrote about dreams and the importance of symbols in dreams. He was awakened to the spiritual value of symbolism and the power that symbols could convey if used in a conscious, positive way. He changed his mind completely about this approach to art.

He also began to notice how symbols played an important role in his life outside of his art work. He started to attune himself more to the symbolic messages from his unconscious and found his life enriched because of his new awareness.

APPLICATION: Look about you for the next several days. Find some symbols and think about what their meaning is for you.

The Larger Purpose in Life

Be patient. In patience you become aware of your soul and its relationship to God. Based on Edgar Cayce reading 1857-2

As Linda was making final preparations for a series of lectures on Egypt based on the Edgar Cayce readings, she had a dream. In the dream the real meaning of the period of Egyptian history that was covered in the readings became clear to her: to prepare the way for the coming of the Christ. Of course, individuals had had meaningful experiences of growth and development, but the primary focus was on an event that would not occur for thousands of years.

This dream taught Linda the value of patience and waiting. She also learned how to view her life. There were times when she felt she was doing something that she needed to be doing, but she was not sure *why* she was doing it. She knew she was growing, using a talent, or completing a task. However, she felt there was more that she could not understand at the moment. She knew she needed to wait for that larger purpose to unfold.

The Egyptian readings helped her to see that she might not fully understand the contribution she was making in this lifetime. However, she knew that her life was contributing to a larger goal as she made an effort to attune her ideals to it. She might not see the final results in this lifetime, but she had faith that they would come at the right time.

APPLICATION: The next time you find yourself wondering why you are doing what you are doing, affirm that there is a larger purpose unfolding and that your life fits into that larger purpose.

Why God Feels Distant to Us

The experiences in the earth are the opportunities for the soul to prepare, to meet the conditions necessary that it may be one with God. Based on Edgar Cayce reading 2786-1

A disciple once asked a great Jewish rabbi, "Why do people who rely on God sometimes feel that God is distant and remote?"

The rabbi answered, "When parents teach a young child to walk, the parents begin by kneeling in front of the child and holding the child so he or she will not fall. Then the parents slowly back away, still holding out their arms and urging the child to come toward them. The moment the child gets close, the parents back up a little more and encourage the child to take a few more steps before holding the child again. The parents keep backing up more and more each day so that the child may learn to walk."

APPLICATION: Look at your life experiences today as God's lessons for teaching you how "to walk," how to become fully human, and thereby how to become fully at one with God.

Trusting the Source

They that trust in themselves alone are not wise! Rather know who is the author of your wisdom. Who is the keeper of your hopes? In whom have you believed?

Based on Edgar Cayce reading 1599-1

Do you have times when fears and uncertainties fill you with indecision?

Janet had wanted to move to a certain area of the country for many years. However, she had resisted making that move because of doubt and fear. She wondered if she would be able to get work there. She wanted everything all laid out for her before she moved—a job, a house—all details planned out carefully.

When she finally got her master's degree, she received job offers from all around the country except from that one area. She asked herself what was happening and realized she was building her life around having things convenient and being in control instead of trusting in God. She realized this lack of trust was leading to her fear and indecision. She finally decided to make the move, trusting that God would provide.

Once Janet made that decision, she quickly found a house there. She moved into it and within two months had a job that was a major advancement for her in her career.

When she placed her trust in the proper source, her doubts, fears, and problems were resolved.

APPLICATION: Name an area of your life where fear and doubt are preventing you from acting. Place your trust in God and take a step forward.

The Phone Call

If there is kept the ideal in God as the guide, often in the soul's experience opportunities come that become as stepping-stones to the way that leads to life in God.

Based on Edgar Cayce reading 540-3

Barbara was frustrated. She had undergone a series of surgeries. Every time she was ready to go back to work, she would need more surgery. Her prayers seeking God's way for her life seemed to go unanswered.

Thinking a new job might help her attitude, she scheduled an interview with a family counseling agency. Then a few days later she called to cancel the interview. But as soon as she hung up the phone, her inner voice began to remind her of her lifelong desire to help families in crisis.

Barbara's response was, "Then let the interviewer call me." She knew this was unlikely and went out for a walk.

She returned as the phone was ringing. It was the interviewer asking her to come and look at the place even if she still decided not to apply. Barbara agreed to do this.

When she arrived, she recognized the building at once. As a little girl, she used to walk by this building, which even at that time was a crisis center for families, and think about working there. Over the years the organization had changed its name so she did not recognize the new name nor the address. She interviewed for the job and got it.

Later on when she learned that she never could have kept up with the demands of her old job after her surgeries, she realized some higher power had led her to this new one.

APPLICATION: Look at an unusual series of events in your past. Look for the higher power working through them to lead you to new life.

The Higher Power Within

Of yourself, you may do little. Take the Lord in partnership with you! Based on Edgar Cayce reading 815-3

Andrew's son, Bob, was so afraid of standing up in front of people to speak that he absolutely refused to do it. Even though Bob was an intelligent young man, Andrew knew he would miss out on a lot of opportunities in life if he couldn't overcome this fear. He also knew that the Edgar Cayce readings frequently spoke about each person having a higher power within to turn to for courage and strength. He began to talk to his son about this and even gave him portions of the Cayce material that discussed relying on a higher power.

As Bob read and pondered this information, he realized that the basis of his fear was his relying on his own strength, which was not sufficient. He began to look to this power that was greater than his own ego and draw on the courage that he was finding.

Now whenever Bob has to do something that causes him to feel afraid, he meditates and prays and struggles to move beyond his ego and into attunement with this higher power. As a result of his efforts, he feels more relaxed around people and more confident when called upon to speak because he knows he can turn to this higher power for strength and support.

APPLICATION: The next time you don't feel strong enough to do something, look for your partnership with the higher power within.

Ideals Are Difficult to Live By

Then knowing your ideal, practice it. Don't have an ideal and then not practice it in your daily activities.

Based on Edgar Cayce reading 5256-1

Ideals can be very important, especially during the time of a person's greatest test.

Diane's divorce was painful. During the course of the process, she came to realize that she couldn't change anyone else, just herself. She would be her own biggest problem if she weren't careful. She knew she would have to work daily with her emotions and her attitudes and keep them clear in order to come through this.

Many times she reminded herself moment by moment that her ideals were love and forgiveness. She tried to be non-judgmental, non-condemning, and struggled with anger, worry, and jealousy.

Looking to God as the source of her strength, she found she could deal with her feelings of abandonment and help her children deal with their feelings of being deserted. It was not easy. It required patience, but in the long run she was a healthier person because she kept her ideals in front of her and did not give in to more destructive emotions and attitudes.

APPLICATION: When you are tempted today to do something not in keeping with your ideals, stop for a moment and choose an action that would be in accord with your ideals.

The Announcement

Keep the faith—the faith in your God to use you as a blessing, as a channel of understanding to others.

Based on Edgar Cayce reading 816-3

Sitting in the garden during the early morning was something Mary enjoyed doing. The air had a freshness and newness to it. The birds sang joyfully as they greeted the dawn. Quiet and serenity ruled before the hurried activities of the day took over.

As Mary sat down in her favorite spot, a light suddenly appeared before her. A voice came from the light, "Hail, favored one of God."

It was a holy fear that filled Mary as she stared into the light.

"You have pleased God. Therefore, you shall have a child. He will be a special child, the hope that Israel has been waiting for."

Questions filled her mind. She spoke. The voice answered. Then she didn't feel the fear anymore but only the holiness of the moment, and she opened herself to it.

"Here I am, God's servant. Let me be used for God's plan on earth."

As Mary trusted and opened herself completely, the power of the Divine entered her and filled her, and newness for herself and for the world came forth.

APPLICATION: Choose one area of your life and open it to God so God's work can be done there.

Giving and Receiving

Universal love is that there be unity of purpose among the parts of groups or individuals in their presenting themselves to be of aid to others in finding themselves.

Based on Edgar Cayce reading 262-2

It sounded risky to Wendy. One of the members of a tour group going with her to China had just suggested that the group bring Bibles along with them to give away to the Chinese. They had been told that they were not allowed to do such a thing. However, after some discussion, the group decided that they would work together and carry ten Bibles with them.

During the trip the members had the opportunity to visit several Christian churches in China. The hymns were familiar, they exchanged greetings with the people, and all experienced a loving and meaningful worship even though they could not always understand what was being said.

They had learned from people who worked with the churches in China not to make a big presentation when distributing their Bibles, but to do it quietly. So after worship, Wendy and two others placed the Bibles on the seats and silently left. They encountered no problems and felt they had given a meaningful gift to those who had so warmly welcomed them.

APPLICATION: Make plans with a group you are involved with to meet a need in your immediate community or somewhere outside your local area. This may be as simple as praying for the leader of another country or supporting an organization working for world peace.

God's Channel

Keep the faith—the faith in God to use you as a blessing, as a channel of understanding to others.

Based on Edgar Cayce reading 816-3

Shortly after her husband died, a business firm asked Audrey to work for them. But she didn't have office experience and told them so. They said that what they needed was her experience in working with small groups and she would be given a secretary to assist her. So she accepted.

For many years Audrey traveled around the country making personal contacts with people and small groups. She shared with them what was important to her, what gave meaning to her life, what helped her through difficult times. For her this included a belief in reincarnation and that people are to take responsibility for themselves. She also talked about the Bible and how she turns to it for faith and inspiration. People thanked her for the words of hope and encouragement she offered.

At the time Audrey wasn't really sure how others were hearing her words or what was her impact. However, years later people came up to her and told her how important maybe one little phrase she had spoken had been to them. Most of the time she couldn't even remember having said it or even having seen that particular person. But she believed that God had taken the seed that was hers to give and nurtured it for growth in that person.

APPLICATION: Act today knowing that God can use all your positive actions and increase the results.

Learning by Example

Then, let your life be a pattern that your children may take as the light along the road. Based on Edgar Cayce reading 3292-1

Jack remembers how, as a child, he was taught concepts from the Edgar Cayce readings—in particular, how he learned to meditate.

He can still picture his parents meditating. He remembers asking them questions and hearing their answers. But more important, he remembers his dad taking some time off and spending it with him in meditation. He had several experiences with his dad that convinced him of the value of meditation.

With their children Jack and his wife use the same approach, teaching by example and answering questions when asked. Their boys see them meditating and ask questions. They notice that the food their mother puts on the table is different from the food they eat at school or at their friends' homes. Even though some of their friends think that they eat strange food at times, their family doesn't change their diet just because of those comments.

For Jack, example—day-to-day example —and answering questions as they arise have been the best ways he has found for teaching his children ideas that are important to him.

APPLICATION: As you go about your life, stop and see if you are living a good example for children to follow.

Overcoming Dry Spells

Meditation is emptying self of all that hinders the Creative Forces from rising along the natural channels of the physical body.   Based on Edgar Cayce reading 281-13

Do you have times when you hit dry spells with your meditation and it feels like nothing is happening?

Vic had hit another dry spell with his meditation and was ready to quit. For almost two weeks now nothing seemed to be happening, and he felt totally out of touch with his inner soul.

Then he paused and considered the purpose of meditation. Meditation is a way to attune oneself to God. God is love. Love is giving. So Vic asked himself how he could prepare his mind for an attitude of giving.

When he examined this, he discovered he had been preoccupied with getting. He wanted to see the white light in every meditation. He wanted to get a tingling sensation in his spine. He wanted the experience of floating. So he had become quite judgmental about his lack of experiences and preoccupied with receiving these wonderful sensations.

He knew he had to give up expectations and all criteria for judging. He had to stop giving meditation a grade.

When he gave up these things, then he could give himself back over to God and begin to remove what had blocked his attunement to God.

APPLICATION: If you are having trouble meditating, give up all expectations and judgments. Just open yourself to God.

The Return

Thus does one comprehend that it is in God that one lives and moves and has one's being and that we, as individuals, may be co-workers with the Creative Forces or God.

Based on Edgar Cayce reading 2399-1

At first the adventure was great fun. He took his share of the family estate and went off on his own. He could live the life he wanted to live. No one standing over his shoulder watching his every move. And so he lived. Wine, dance, and lots of friends. Yes, he had lots of friends until his money ran out. And so did his friends.

Now working in the pig pen, life wasn't fun anymore. Something was missing. It wasn't just the money or the good times either. Inside he felt a deep emptiness that he had never felt before. He knew money could not fill it. He knew fancy clothing could not fill it. So he decided to go home.

He would not go home and ask for wealth again. He would go home to find his father. He sensed now that being around his father so he could talk to him, learn from him, and just be with him was what he needed. Being around his father as a servant would be enough as long as he could be home.

The young man rose and headed home. Headed home to work for and with his father because he knew now where life was.

APPLICATION: Spend some time each day affirming who the source of your life is.

The Perfect House

If ideas are in keeping with the ideals, follow them.
Based on Edgar Cayce reading 1739-6

Joyce had been house-hunting for three months. She and her three young teenagers had looked at large homes and middle-sized ones, at property in the city and in the country. Nothing was working out, and they were all frustrated.

One day she confessed to her friend, Karen, that she felt a bit guilty but had decided not to look at any more houses with fewer than four bedrooms. She knew her family could get by with two of the boys sharing a room, but she was not going to do that.

Karen asked her how she had come to this decision.

Joyce explained how she had talked again with her children about what they wanted. She realized in the discussion that they each had different personalities and different ideas about how to fix up their rooms. They were also at an age where each needed space to be alone.

So Karen encouraged Joyce not to feel guilty but to phrase this decision as a positive ideal of what she wanted for the good of her family.

Joyce saw the benefit of this. Her ideal became: to find a place where each member of the family could have space to grow and express his or her unique individuality.

Two weeks later she found the perfect four-bedroom home.

APPLICATION: The next time you are looking for something that is important to you, create an ideal that tells you in positive terms why you want this.

Reaching Out in Understanding

Live and be the experience in the hearts of those who are seeking to find their way. Be the experience to someone to light their lives. Based on Edgar Cayce reading 281-25

At work Don was always swearing at people. He was constantly having difficulties with his co-workers and was branded as a troublemaker.

Don's supervisor, Bob, knew he needed help. He decided to reach out and extend a friendly hand. Each morning Bob took time specifically to greet Don. For several weeks all he got in return was a string of angry grunts, but he kept trying. Finally after a few months Bob was surprised to hear a somewhat pleasant "Good morning" in return. After that breakthrough the friendship between the two men grew.

Bob next tried to show Don how his attitude was affecting his relationship to his co-workers.

One day when the two were alone, Bob suggested that Don try seeing the other person's viewpoint and not take comments so personally. Don agreed to try this.

An opportunity quickly presented itself. A few days later Don was about to respond angrily to a co-worker because he felt he was being attacked unjustly. However, instead of reacting out of habit, Don paused and tried to understand his co-worker's viewpoint. It was difficult at first, but with Bob's encouragement this new approach became easier. Don's attitude toward people and toward the world improved, and he became a happier, more productive worker.

APPLICATION: Choose someone you work with or know who is having difficulty relating to people. Do something to spread your light to that person.

Waiting with Certainty

The soul should realize that the Creative Forces or God is aware of it and of the soul's needs—that the soul may be one with God.　　　Based on Edgar Cayce reading 2786-1

Virginia had lived several years facing a number of financial situations, and she was wondering how much longer she would have to wait. Items around the house needed to be fixed. The carpet was worn in several spots, and some kitchen appliances needed replacing. She believed that God would care for her, and she would get what she needed. So she had told God her needs and now she was waiting.

However, God's time schedule appeared to be moving very slowly, so she began to look at herself and wonder why. Finally she realized that she was concentrating every day on just waiting. She had to let go. So she let go—not in any Pollyannish way but with a certainty that things would happen. Her friends called her impractical, but she felt she was now in the correct frame of mind for God to work.

Still these items did not come overnight. Virginia had to be patient. She had to fight times when she got anxious. She had to live not hating the old, but living with the old for as long as necessary.

Finally it did happen. A series of events allowed her to get a new carpet at cost and pay for the kitchen appliances in cash.

The experiences did reaffirm for her the idea of not being anxious. God knows our needs and will respond.

APPLICATION: Stop several times in the near future and say, "God is aware of me and my needs." Be aware of what you feel when you do this.

Accepting the Challenge

As to the abilities of the soul in the present and that to which it may attain—this is limited only to the desires of the soul and its faith in the one force or God.

Based on Edgar Cayce reading 1681-1

Jack was completely surprised. He had been asked if he would consent to being nominated for president of the next annual gathering. So he requested some time to think about it. He knew he could plan and organize well enough to do the job, but he did not feel comfortable as a public speaker. After some thought he decided to refuse the nomination.

However, later that evening he was reading a book about Moses, who had complained to God about being called to return to Egypt to help free the Hebrew slaves. One of his excuses was that he was not a good enough speaker to confront the pharaoh. God promised to send Moses' brother Aaron as a spokesperson with him. Jack figured this was a message to him. He changed his mind and decided he would accept the nomination.

Through a strange set of circumstances the person who was supposed to oversee the election had to leave on an emergency. A substitute was put in charge, and even though the election was democratic, it did not follow the procedures exactly. As a result, Jack was elected president, and a man who was a public speaker was elected vice-president.

The election produced the balance that was needed.

APPLICATION: The next time you are asked to do something and you doubt your ability, ask yourself if God is calling you. Offer yourself to be a channel through whom God will work by giving you help or a new ability you didn't know you had.

The Kings Came

The Christ will come to dwell in the hearts and lives of all— if you will but let Him, if you will but open your own heart that He may enter and abide with you.

Based on Edgar Cayce reading 5749-6

They did not know each other at all. Their paths had never crossed. They lived many miles from one another and came from different religious traditions. But they were united by one belief. They believed that God had spoken to the world in a special way. They believed that God had sent a special child to the world, and they now journeyed together to see that child.

The appearance of a star unlike any other they had ever seen heralded the birth of this child. This had inspired them to begin their journey. They left their countries. They left the lands of their religious heritage. They left behind their ways of worshiping the Supreme Divine One. They left for a country and a people with a different understanding of the Divinity. But they took with them a belief that the Divine One transcended all of these earthly divisions. They took with them a belief that the Divine looked into the hearts of those who truly sought and led them to their goal.

So it happened that these wise men found and honored the one many called the Christ. They found Him because they opened their hearts to be led in God's universal way and not the divisive way of humanity.

APPLICATION: Gain a broader perspective on an idea or a person you have been biased against by reading about it or by talking to someone.

Courage to Dream

*Whoever brings hope in the awareness of the God conscious-
ness indeed makes miracles in the lives of the hearers.*
Based on Edgar Cayce reading 2812-1

Going to college was all but out of the question. The family
did not have enough money and times were rough. When
Frank got a reading from Edgar Cayce that told him to apply
to a university and to major in engineering, he couldn't really take it too seriously. Even though the reading said he
would get a scholarship, he didn't really see any point in
trying.

It's not that the career choice was wrong. He had a talent
in that area. He enjoyed talking to people about technical,
scientific subjects. He picked up the vocabulary easily. He
even seemed to understand how engineers thought and how
they approached problems. In spite of all this, the dream
seemed too far away to be real.

After several months of considering, he realized that he
had nothing to lose by writing a letter. He wrote to the university and even asked for the type of scholarship suggested
in the reading. He was accepted for it and later was able to
get a part-time job to earn the rest of the money to pay for
his schooling.

Four years later he graduated and worked happily in that
career field for many years.

APPLICATION: Name someone who encouraged you to try
something that you wouldn't have attempted without that
encouragement. Look around and encourage someone in
your life in a similar way.

Helping Others Grow

Then the ideal is, "What may I do or be to others that they may have a greater concept of the purposes of life by being associated with me?" Based on Edgar Cayce reading 2030-1

Working in the bank with Jason, Rose found it impossible not to notice him. Jason was a very competent man but he had trouble getting along with people. He was argumentative and was not considered part of a working team. If co-workers learned how to do some of his job, he perceived them as threats to his position, so he never taught them any activity related to his job. After a while, Rose concluded that his actions were defenses for insecurity and low self-esteem.

Sensing this, she started to apply what she was learning from the Edgar Cayce readings about helping others build self-esteem. Slowly she began to form a relationship with him. She treated him with kindness. Noticing that people frequently criticized some of his work, she tried to build his confidence by complimenting him on what he did well.

Gradually he began to show some improvement. Realizing that it was important for other team members to understand what he was doing, he began to teach Rose part of his job.

After two years his self-esteem had increased so much that he applied for and received a better position in a different bank. He recommended to his boss that Rose take his place and even offered to stay an extra two weeks to show her exactly what she needed to know to do the job.

APPLICATION: Think of someone you know who has low self-esteem. Do one thing to help that person recognize his or her worth.

DECEMBER 28

Take One Step at a Time

Each experience, each day, each thought offers a soul an opportunity for development.

Based on Edgar Cayce reading 1913-1

Mike had only been a college art teacher a few years when he found himself feeling a strange mixture of content and discontent.

After one summer class he knew teaching was not right for him. He applied for a sabbatical to study out west. Before he left on the trip he attended a conference on the east coast. During it, he suddenly felt he had to stay, but he needed an inexpensive room and a job. A few days later, he heard about a couple looking for someone to do babysitting in exchange for a room. Mike volunteered.

Feeling more strongly now that he needed to stay, he turned down the sabbatical and resigned his teaching job. Then he went job hunting in his new location. For a few weeks he found nothing. Then a series of unusual conversations got him a job as a layout designer for a magazine. It was a job he loved.

As Mike reflected on this period of his life, he saw how step by step doors had opened for him. He learned that once people began to cooperate with their purpose for this life, great joys and great challenges would be presented. People would feel as if they were in charge of their lives and at the same time feel as if they were cooperating with a power beyond themselves. It would be a brand-new life.

APPLICATION: Do something to show you are cooperating with a power greater than yourself in order to fulfill your purpose for this life.

He Waited a Long Time

Believe in God's promises, that as you sow, so in the fullness of time and in material experience these things shall come about. Based on Edgar Cayce reading 1968-5

It had been a long time since he had received the promise— so long that some people really wondered now if he would live to see it kept. Simeon was his name. He was waiting to see the Christ. Though others doubted, in his mind there was no doubt. He would live to see the Christ.

As old as he was, he still came to the temple almost daily. And on this day Simeon was distracted from his prayer. He didn't know why, but he suddenly looked up and looked around. Coming into the temple was a strange couple. The man was much older than the girl who carried the infant. The infant, that was the reason for his distraction.

His heart beating with a strange excitement, Simeon walked toward them. When he reached them, he held out his arms. Without hesitation the mother put the infant in his arms. He closed his eyes, pulled the child to him, and found the peace that had eluded him for so long.

Returning the child, he turned and said to all who had gathered curiously around him, "I am ready to die in peace. I have seen God's promised one."

He had waited so long. He knew that those who doubted would not yet be convinced. But he knew. He knew the promise had been fulfilled.

APPLICATION: God's time schedule is frequently longer than ours. Affirm your ability to wait for God.

A Life-Long Process

So live then each day that some portion may add to your inner, your better, your soul self. Thus may you gain strength, knowledge, and virtue in such measures that life with its experiences becomes more and more worthwhile with more joy.
                              Based on Edgar Cayce reading 1745-1

Now in her seventies, Grace looks back on a life of working with the Edgar Cayce readings with a certain perspective. Spiritual growth, she says, is a slow process. There were moments in her life when she felt some setbacks or ran up against some obstacles, but basically she noticed gradual continuous changes. At times it took months and years to realize this, but it was happening.

One area in herself she especially notices is her ability to listen to people. When younger, she used to hear words and not understand why people would tell her she wasn't listening to them. Then she discovered herself listening for the feelings in their words. Later, people began to comment on how well she listened to them.

Finally she began to tune in to meanings behind words, meanings of which they weren't even aware. Most of the time she found it best not to verbalize her intuitive insights. However, she could respond to these insights in different ways and help others. Many times people couldn't figure out how she knew what to do for them.

It was a slow, life-long process, but she stuck with it because she knew these changes meant spiritual growth—for her and perhaps for others.

APPLICATION: The next time you get discouraged about growth in some area, look at how you were five to ten years ago and affirm your growth. Then keep working at it.

Healing the World

Remember, you pursue peace, you embrace peace, you hold to peace. It is not something that descends upon you, save as you have created and do create it in the hearts, in the minds, in the experiences of others.

Based on Edgar Cayce reading 3051-2

The healing meditation day had been the beginning of a new life focus for Karen. Several hundred people had come together to meditate and pray for world peace at the gathering she had helped sponsor. For her this was the culmination of several months of reading and the beginning of action. She had learned while preparing for the event that we do have the potential for healing the earth.

She had read that each person's prayer and meditation for peace is important. She now believed that and wasn't going to let this special meditation day for world healing be the last.

She began to organize regular peace prayer meditations once a week. At first she and perhaps one or two others were the only attendees. Whenever the low attendance discouraged her, she would feel internal affirmation to keep going. She would remember the Biblical affirmation about where two or three are gathered. Whenever she felt like quitting, she would remember the Edgar Cayce readings about persistency and consistency for one's ideals.

By the end of a year a group had begun meeting with her. By the end of the next year the group had more than doubled and others had adopted her practice of praying for peace to heal the world. She was gratified that people were beginning to believe their prayers could make a difference.

AFFIRMATION: Each thought for peace has an impact. In your own way find a time to pray or meditate for peace.

INDEX

Accidents 4/3, 5/22, 7/28, 8/15, 9/4, 11/10, 11/21, 11/28

Anger 1/28, 1/31, 4/19, 5/8, 5/10, 5/18, 5/31, 6/1, 7/11, 8/18, 8/21, 9/7, 9/8, 10/17, 10/19, 10/27, 11/25

Anxiety 2/7, 3/27, 9/18, 10/2, 12/23

Application 1/1, 5/15

Attitude 1/6, 1/12, 1/14, 2/20, 2/22, 3/4, 3/16, 4/9, 5/8, 5/23, 7/22, 7/23, 8/1, 8/16, 9/24, 10/27, 10/28, 11/2, 11/11, 12/14

Balance in life 2/24, 3/15, 3/24, 5/28, 6/15, 7/23, 8/11, 8/26, 9/12, 11/2, 11/5

Be yourself 2/9, 9/9, 10/1

Bible stories 1/8, 1/20, 2/2, 2/4, 2/23, 3/5, 3/25, 4/6, 4/24, 5/5, 5/17, 6/2, 6/14, 6/30, 7/5, 7/17, 8/4, 8/16, 9/5, 9/17, 10/8, 10/20, 11/1, 11/16, 12/15, 12/25, 12/29

Business (see *Work*)

Challenge 2/4, 2/9, 3/28, 4/11, 6/13, 9/11, 12/24

Changing self 1/9, 2/15, 4/11, 5/6, 8/18, 9/24, 10/7, 10/28, 10/31, 12/1

Child rearing 3/1, 3/18,
4/16, 6/3, 7/4, 8/10, 9/6, 11/12, 11/23, 11/24, 11/25, 12/1, 12/6, 12/18

Choices (see *Will*)

Christ
in people 1/9, 2/6, 8/9
presence of 2/5, 7/31, 12/25

Church 2/2, 9/22

Communication 6/24, 7/10 8/3, 8/9, 8/10, 8/23, 8/24, 12/30

Community 1/25, 7/2, 7/14, 8/22, 9/22, 9/28, 10/22

Compassion 1/22, 8/8, 11/22

Cooperation 1/25, 3/19, 7/26, 7/27, 10/30, 11/5

Courage 2/4, 2/5, 3/27, 4/3, 4/13, 12/13

Creativity 4/30, 11/6, 12/2, 12/6

Crucifixion 3/2, 3/29

Death 3/22, 4/13, 4/25, 4/27, 5/17, 7/18, 9/30, 10/8, 10/18

Decision making 1/13, 1/28, 2/17, 3/19, 3/30, 4/4, 4/7, 4/18, 4/23, 6/21, 7/20, 8/28, 11/23

Diet 6/25, 7/23, 8/11

Disappointment 2/10, 2/27, 9/21, 10/17

Discouragement 1/17, 2/5, 2/14, 3/25, 4/17, 6/23

Divorce 4/1, 4/3, 8/7, 12/14
Doubt 1/8
Do what you can 2/28, 3/6
Dream 1/16, 2/13, 2/16, 2/19, 2/24, 3/1, 4/2, 4/4, 4/14, 4/23, 4/27, 5/3, 6/30, 7/6, 8/7, 8/14, 8/21, 8/25, 9/25, 9/30, 10/11, 11/13, 11/19, 11/23, 12/4, 12/9

Emptying self 1/21, 2/8, 3/17, 3/21, 4/22, 6/20, 8/14, 8/23, 10/27, 11/15
Exercise 6/15, 7/23, 8/11, 11/2

Failure 2/8, 2/14, 2/26, 6/23, 11/20
Faith 1/8, 3/5, 7/18, 7/20, 9/3, 9/16, 9/20, 9/21, 11/15, 12/9, 12/11, 12/15, 12/24, 12/29
Fear 2/12, 3/5, 3/13, 3/27, 4/7, 5/16, 8/16, 9/18, 10/21, 11/15, 12/11, 12/13
Forgiveness 1/26, 2/14, 2/23, 3/22, 4/6, 5/31, 6/1, 8/16, 8/30, 9/5, 12/20
Free will (see *Will*)
Fruits of the spirit 1/1, 11/26

Gifts (see *Talents*)
Giving 1/10, 1/12, 6/22, 8/1, 11/16
God 3/25, 5/5, 8/17, 9/9, 10/16
   guidance of 8/5, 12/12, 12/25
   in everything 1/18, 2/15, 4/20, 8/8, 9/29
   relationship to 1/11, 2/11, 2/18, 3/5, 3/18, 3/21, 3/27, 4/12, 4/24, 5/9, 5/21, 6/12, 6/13, 6/14, 6/17, 6/30, 7/5, 7/9, 8/17, 8/29, 8/31, 9/1, 9/19, 9/23, 9/30, 11/7, 12/10, 12/11, 12/14, 12/15, 12/20
Gratitude 1/12
Growth
   (see *Spiritual growth*)
Guilt 3/13, 4/6, 9/7, 11/4

Hatred 1/23
Healing 1/23, 2/16, 3/11, 3/24, 5/22, 7/8, 7/31, 9/4, 9/13, 9/15, 9/27, 10/3, 10/9, 12/7, 12/31
Health 3/12, 5/24, 5/28, 5/30, 6/25, 8/6
Heaven 4/2
Hell 4/2, 8/31
Helping others 5/13, 6/18, 7/13, 7/21, 9/13, 9/16, 10/12, 10/16, 10/24, 11/11, 11/21, 11/26, 11/28, 12/16, 12/22, 12/26, 12/27, 12/30
Higher Self 1/27, 5/2, 8/10, 9/12
Home 2/20
Honesty 4/19, 6/29
Hope 3/23, 3/25, 10/8, 12/26
Humor 1/4, 2/7, 5/20, 7/12, 10/26, 10/29, 11/17, 11/28, 12/3

Ideals 1/3, 1/30, 2/8, 2/26, 3/8, 3/10, 3/14, 3/15, 4/8, 4/26, 5/10, 5/26, 6/3, 6/7, 6/26, 7/4, 7/5, 7/20, 7/23, 8/22, 8/27, 9/10, 10/10, 10/15, 10/19, 10/23, 10/31, 11/2, 11/7, 11/18, 12/14, 12/21, 12/31

Illness 2/12, 2/25, 3/12, 3/16, 3/24, 4/8, 4/14, 4/25, 5/22 , 5/28, 7/22, 9/8, 9/27, 9/30, 10/10, 10/19, 10/21, 11/3, 11/7, 11/9, 11/26, 12/12

Imagination 1/29, 11/6, 12/6

Inner power 1/30, 2/11, 6/6, 9/15, 9/30, 12/13

Inner voice (see also *Intuition*) 2/12, 4/18, 7/1, 9/2, 9/23, 10/7, 10/13, 10/23, 11/1, 11/14, 11/15, 12/12

Intuition 1/13, 4/18, 6/2, 7/1, 7/19, 7/24, 7/29, 9/12, 10/9, 10/15, 10/23, 11/30, 12/4, 12/30

Jesus 1/8, 1/17, 4/6, 4/17 , 10/26
    as pattern 3/2, 6/20, 7/13
Joy 10/29
Judging 2/26, 3/9, 5/17, 6/2, 6/4, 8/4, 9/5, 9/9, 9/29, 10/1, 10/15, 11/14 11/25

Karma 1/22, 1/24, 4/7, 5/8, 11/22

Letting go 1/5, 1/20, 7/17, 8/30, 11/4, 11/25, 12/19 , 12/23

Like attracts like 2/23, 5/31, 9/14

Limitations 6/13, 12/24

Love 1/20, 2/14, 2/18, 3/7, 3/18, 4/6, 4/10, 4/15, 4/16, 4/29, 5/12, 5/21, 5/23, 5/31, 6/18, 7/21, 8/8, 9/8, 10/16, 11/11, 12/5

Loving indifference 1/9

Magnify the virtues 10/25
Marriage 5/12, 5/18, 7/4, 9/10, 9/26

Meditation 1/10, 1/13, 1/23, 2/11, 3/7, 3/14, 3/30, 4/4, 4/5, 4/18, 5/11, 5/29, 6/3, 7/10, 7/23, 7/31, 8/11, 9/12, 10/7, 10/11, 10/13, 10/15, 10/17, 10/27, 11/1, 11/7, 11/8, 12/13, 12/18, 12/19, 12/31

Meeting self 1/24, 3/4, 4/15, 7/30, 10/28

Meet people where they are 2/2, 3/20

Mistakes 6/4, 7/12
Music 6/16

Names 2/19, 6/27

Oneness 3/31, 4/20, 5/23, 6/21, 8/2, 8/13, 8/26, 12/25

Opportunities, use of 1/18, 1/24, 3/4, 3/26, 4/2, 5/27,

6/9, 6/28, 6/29, 7/29, 8/3, 8/20, 8/31, 9/1, 9/11, 9/14, 10/6, 11/7, 11/19, 11/21, 11/28, 12/10, 12/28

Patience 1/5, 2/24, 2/27, 3/20, 3/28, 4/22, 5/14, 5/19, 5/22, 7/7, 7/29, 8/21, 9/2, 11/7, 12/2, 12/9, 12/14, 12/23, 12/29

Peace 5/4, 7/2, 7/15, 9/8, 9/23, 11/7, 12/31

Prayer 1/7, 1/10, 2/5, 2/12, 2/25, 3/14, 4/5, 5/1, 5/9, 5/21, 6/1, 6/19, 7/2, 7/23, 7/31, 8/18, 9/12, 9/15, 9/19, 9/27, 10/11, 10/15, 11/1, 12/13, 12/31

Pre-sleep suggestions 6/16, 9/18, 12/1

Pride 3/2, 3/21, 4/15

Problems, learning from 1/24, 3/12, 5/28, 6/28, 8/5, 9/21, 10/10, 10/14, 11/4, 11/22, 12/4

Problem solving 1/19, 2/15, 3/4, 6/4

Psychic abilities 1/15, 5/29, 6/7, 7/16, 7/24, 10/23

Reality 1/2

Reincarnation 1/22, 1/24, 1/29, 2/3, 2/21, 4/5, 4/7, 4/10, 5/16, 5/24, 7/3, 7/15, 7/19, 7/22, 7/30, 8/4, 8/6, 10/18, 11/4

Relationships 4/19, 4/29, 5/6, 5/12, 5/14, 5/31, 6/27, 7/17, 7/30, 8/7, 8/29, 9/26,

10/5, 10/14, 10/18, 11/10, 11/14, 11/18, 11/26

Religion 2/2, 3/31, 7/14, 9/22

Renewal 8/26

Resentment 1/23, 3/16, 7/22, 8/30

Responsibility 1/11, 5/8, 6/10, 8/7, 8/15, 8/31, 10/5, 11/3, 11/12

Retirement 2/13, 3/3, 6/5, 9/19

Revelation (Book of) 6/8

Risking 6/14, 7/29, 8/22, 9/2, 9/20, 10/7, 11/1, 12/16, 12/28

Self (see *Higher Self*)

Self-confidence 2/21, 12/27

Selflessness 1/14, 2/5, 2/8, 2/25, 4/9, 4/22, 8/24

Service 1/11, 3/26, 4/21, 4/26, 5/26, 6/26, 8/3, 8/27, 10/4, 10/19

Soul growth
(see *Spiritual growth*)
purpose 1/11, 1/30, 2/1, 2/3, 2/4, 2/9, 2/19, 5/7, 8/19, 9/11, 12/9, 12/28

Spiritual growth 1/11, 1/25, 1/27, 2/11, 2/13, 2/22, 2/24, 3/6, 3/14, 4/29, 5/6, 5/19, 5/27, 6/8, 6/14, 6/28, 8/13, 8/15, 9/2, 9/24, 10/11, 10/29, 11/4, 11/19, 11/21, 12/8, 12/10, 12/30
in life 1/18, 4/28, 7/25

Strength 2/5, 4/12, 7/22, 9/3, 11/1, 12/13

Stress 1/4, 5/1, 5/2, 7/12, 8/11

Success 1/14, 1/19, 3/10, 11/20, 11/30

Suffering 1/22, 4/28, 8/5, 8/15

Suicide 3/22

Symbols 6/8, 11/13, 12/8

Talents 2/6, 4/17, 5/13, 6/5, 7/9, 9/11, 10/4, 11/5, 11/19, 11/29, 12/2

Teaching 1/4, 1/7, 2/8, 3/23, 4/12, 4/30, 5/10, 10/27, 11/15, 11/24, 12/18

Telling your story 3/20, 3/23, 6/11, 10/6, 11/27, 12/17

Temptation 3/4, 10/20, 10/31

Tension (see *Stress*)

Timing 1/5, 3/20, 5/19, 7/28, 12/29

Trying 6/23, 11/20, 12/17

Turning around 3/21, 4/6, 5/25, 9/17

Uniqueness 2/15, 2/28, 7/25, 10/6

Universal laws 1/20, 2/23, 3/18, 3/26, 5/21, 5/23, 5/31, 6/10

Use each day 6/29, 7/15, 8/20, 9/11, 10/4, 11/5

Use what you have in hand 2/28, 5/13, 9/16, 12/17

Will 2/17, 2/18, 7/26, 8/19, 9/6, 9/29, 10/22, 10/31

Winning 1/19

Wisdom 4/25, 11/22

Work 1/4, 1/6, 1/9, 1/13, 1/14, 1/18, 1/19, 1/31, 2/7, 2/8, 2/10, 2/20, 2/27, 3/10, 3/19, 3/26, 4/4, 4/9, 4/21, 4/22, 4/23, 4/26, 5/1, 5/20, 6/1, 6/4, 6/17, 6/23, 6/29, 7/12, 7/26, 7/27, 8/3, 8/11, 8/20, 8/27, 9/19, 10/15, 10/17, 10/30, 11/5, 11/9, 11/18, 11/30

Worry (see *Anxiety*)

THE WORK OF EDGAR CAYCE TODAY

More information from the Edgar Cayce readings is available to you on hundreds of topics, from astrology and arthritis to universal laws and world affairs, because Cayce established an organization, the Association for Research and Enlightenment (A.R.E.), to preserve his readings and make the information available to everyone.

Today over seventy-five thousand members of the A.R.E. receive a bimonthly magazine, *Venture Inward,* containing articles on dream interpretation, past lives, health and diet, psychic archaeology, and psi research, book reviews, and interviews with leaders in the metaphysical field. Members also receive extracts of medical and nonmedical readings and may do their own research in all of the over fourteen thousand readings that Edgar Cayce gave during his lifetime.

To receive more information about the association, which continues to research as well as make available information on subjects in the Edgar Cayce readings, please write A.R.E., Dept. M13, P.O. Box 595, Virginia Beach, VA 23451, or call (804) 428-3588. The A.R.E. will be happy to send you a packet of materials describing its current activities.